Coastal Plants from Cape Cod to Cape Canaveral

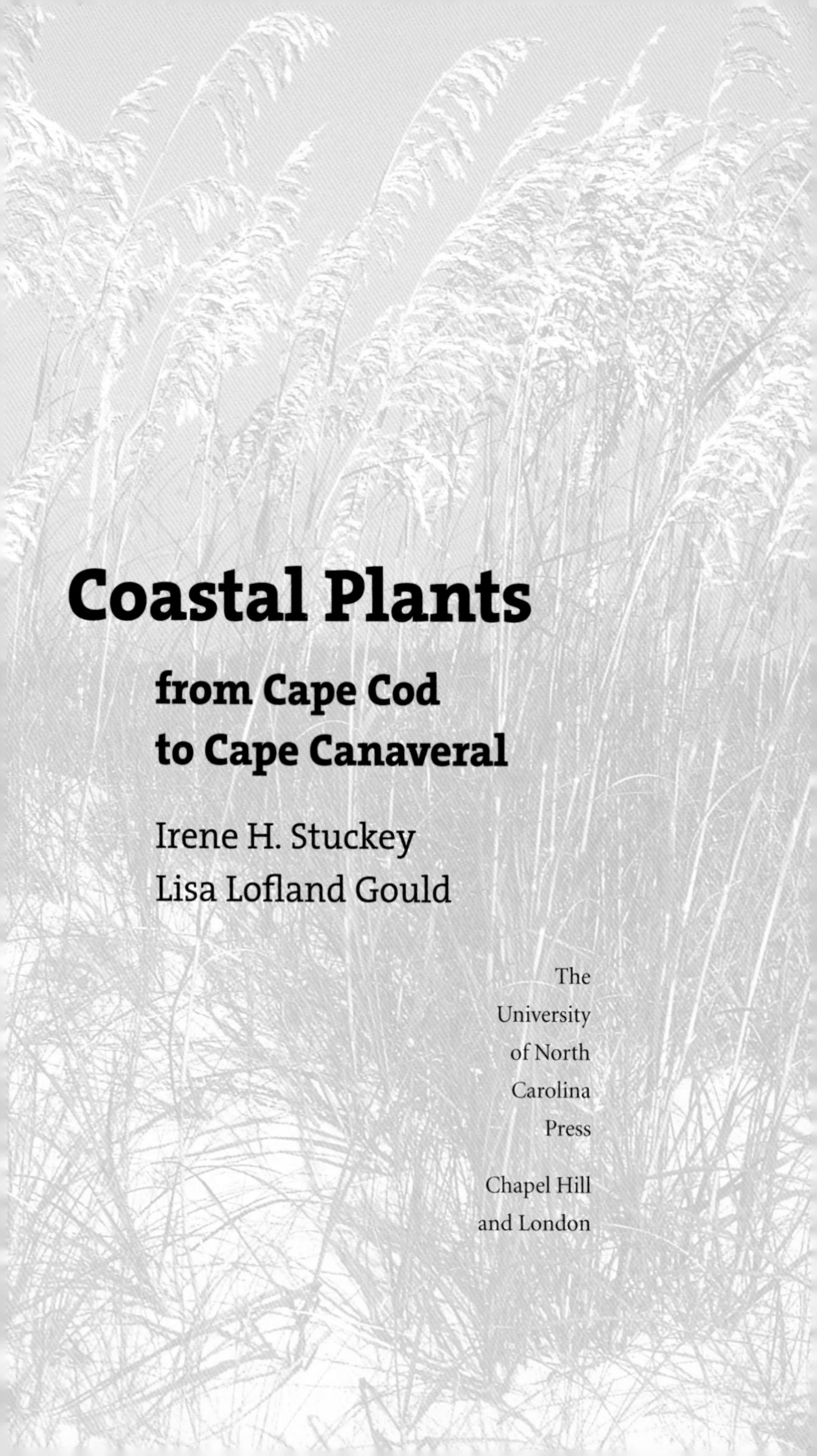

Coastal Plants

from Cape Cod to Cape Canaveral

Irene H. Stuckey
Lisa Lofland Gould

The University of North Carolina Press
Chapel Hill and London

Manufactured in China
Designed by April Leidig-Higgins
Set in Minion by Keystone Typesetting, Inc.

The paper in this book meets the guidelines for permanence and durability of the Committee on Production Guidelines for Book Longevity of the Council on Library Resources.

Library of Congress Cataloging-in-Publication Data
Stuckey, Irene H. (Irene Hawkins), 1911–
Coastal plants from Cape Cod to Cape Canaveral / Irene H. Stuckey and Lisa Lofland Gould.
p. cm.
ISBN 0-8078-2582-4 (cloth : alk. paper)
ISBN 0-8078-4894-8 (pbk. : alk. paper)
1. Coastal plants—Atlantic Coast (U.S.)—Identification. 2. Coastal plants—Atlantic Coast (U.S.)—Pictorial works. I. Gould, Lisa Lofland. II. Title.
QK122.S78 2001 581.7′51′0974—dc21 00-036508

04 03 02 01 00 5 4 3 2 1

The Graduate School of Oceanography of the University of Rhode Island generously supported the publication of this work.

To Polly Matzinger, 1915–1995

Contents

Acknowledgments ix

Organization of This Book xi

Introduction 1

A Look at Coastal Habitats 4

Field Trips to Coastal Areas 15

Plant Descriptions 23

Selected Coastal Natural Areas 271

Glossary 279

References 285

Index 289

Acknowledgments

This book had its origin in a series of articles (62 in all) entitled "Plants beside the Sea" written by Irene Stuckey from 1975 to 1995 for *Maritimes*, a publication of the Graduate School of Oceanography at the University of Rhode Island. She was encouraged to write the articles by Mary ("Polly") Matzinger, former editor of *Maritimes*, to whom this book is dedicated. The popularity of the articles led to the suggestion that they be published in book form. The resulting book, however, has grown well beyond its original Rhode Island borders; over half of the featured species were not addressed previously.

All of the photographs in the book were taken by Irene Stuckey, with the exception of the following, which were taken by Lisa Gould: marsh fern (*Thelypteris palustris*), pitch pine (*Pinus rigida*), little bluestem (*Schizachyrium scoparium*), Spanish moss (*Tillandsia usneoides*), sea purslane (*Sesuvium portulacastrum*), tread-softly (*Cnidoscolus stimulosus*), black ti-ti (*Cyrilla racemiflora*), red buckeye (*Aesculus pavia*), showy evening-primrose (*Oenothera speciosa*), and beach pennywort (*Hydrocotyle bonariensis*). The map in the introduction was compiled by Roberta Calore.

We are very grateful to the following people for their help with questions of nomenclature, plant ranges, and insect names: Peter Ball of the University of Toronto; Frank Golet, Kerwin Hyland, Keith Killingbeck, and Brian Maynard of the University of Rhode Island; Hannah Gould of the University of California–Riverside; Peter Lockwood of Mason & Associates; Leslie Mehrhoff of the University of Connecticut; Gordon Tucker of Eastern Illinois University; and James Zarucchi and Helen Juede at the Flora of North America Project, Missouri Botanical Garden. Frank Golet and Gordon Tucker also provided many helpful comments on the entire manuscript.

For their support during the preparation of this manuscript, we would like to thank Jackleen de la Harpe, editor of *Maritimes*; Margaret Leinen, former dean of the University of Rhode Island's Graduate School of Oceanography and College of the Environment and Life Sciences; and the Board of Directors of the Rhode Island Natural History Survey. The Graduate School of Oceanography helped make the publication of this book a reality. We also thank the school for permission to use portions of articles that originally appeared in *Maritimes*.

We owe many thanks to Elaine Maisner, our editor at the University of North Carolina Press, for her patience and sound advice.

We are grateful to the members of the Georgia Botanical Society for sharing their knowledge and to the members of the Wild Flower Garden Club of Winston-Salem, North Carolina, for a lifetime of inspiration. Finally, we would like to express our deep appreciation to the Stuckey, Gould, and Lofland families for their encouragement and support throughout the duration of this project.

Organization of This Book

Coastal Plants from Cape Cod to Cape Canaveral features vascular plants—ferns and fern allies, gymnosperms, and angiosperms—that grow in coastal habitats from the northern border of Massachusetts to northern Florida. From Cape Cod south, there are barrier beaches, rocky shores, mudflats, and marshes, as well as freshwater streams, ponds, rivers, bays, and estuaries with widely varying salinity. The plant communities that are most often encountered in this geographic area are described in general terms in "A Look at Coastal Habitats" in the introduction. The species descriptions in the main body of the text feature the associated habitats and habitat requirements of particular species.

The number of species of higher plants that can grow in saline habitats is small in comparison with the number that require fresh water. Books on native plants written for the general public often do not describe the saltwater species since many of them are inconspicuous or lack showy flowers. The fact that some of these species are found in wet areas may also dissuade people from taking a closer look. In this book, we have focused on vascular plants that grow in saline situations such as salt marshes and coastal beaches, but we have also included plants influenced by salt spray and many species found in coastal and coastal plain habitats bordering maritime ecosystems. The species described are among those most frequently encountered along the coast from Massachusetts to northern Florida, but the coverage is not intended to be complete. For example, because most people would be unable to view them, we have not included illustrations or descriptions of submersed aquatic plants; however, several of these species are discussed in "A Look at Coastal Habitats."

It is our hope that this book will expand readers' knowledge of the fascinating plants that grow in coastal ecosystems and encourage them to take a firsthand look at them. See "Selected Coastal Natural Areas" for a list of places to visit.

Taxonomy and Nomenclature

The common names used in this book are those most frequently encountered in regional manuals and field guides. The scientific names for the species and plant families are from *A Synonymized Checklist of the Vascular Flora of the United States, Canada, and Greenland*, second edition, by John Kartesz (1994). This work was chosen because it is the only current reference that lists all of the species discussed in the book.

The plants in the book are arranged by family, with the families listed in the same taxonomic order as they appear in Radford, Ahles, and Bell's *Manual of the Vascular Flora of the Carolinas* (1968). This manual lists the ferns and fern allies first, followed by the monocotyledons, and then the dicotyledons. Within each of these three groups, families are listed in evolutionary order, that is, from the most ancient plants to the most recently evolved, according to the best evidence available at the time the manual was written. Placement of a species within a particular family follows Kartesz (1994).

A photograph is included for each of the featured plant species. Unless otherwise noted, the variety of the plant illustrated is the same as the variety named in the heading.

Each plant is identified by its binomial, which is a two-part scientific name composed of the genus and a second, usually descriptive, word. The binomial is followed by the name(s) of the authority(ies) who gave the species its official name. For example, chairmaker's rush has the scientific name *Scirpus americanus* Pers., in which "Pers." is an abbreviation for Christiaan Hendrik Persoon (1761–1836), the botanist who named the plant. Occasionally two authorities will be listed, with one name in parentheses. For example, little bluestem has the scientific name *Schizachyrium scoparium* (Michx.) Nash; André Michaux (1746–1802) originally named little bluestem *Andropogon scoparius*, and then George Valentine Nash (1864–1921) reassigned this grass to the genus *Schizachyrium*.

Synonyms are given when scientific names in regional manuals and guides differ from the system of nomenclature used by Kartesz (1994). Cobb (1956); Gleason and Cronquist (1991); and Radford, Ahles, and Bell (1968), for example, use the scientific name *Polypodium polypodioides* (L.) Watt for resurrection fern, whereas Kartesz (1994) cites it as *Pleopeltis polypodioides* (L.) Andrews & Windham. By giving synonyms, we hope to make it easier for readers to seek additional information in regional field guides and reference works.

Range

The range within North America is given for each species. Generalized inland ranges are included along with the coastal range to provide an accurate picture of the entire geographic area of each species.

Manuals often disagree on the range of a particular species. We used a variety of sources to attempt to compile complete range information. Gleason and Cronquist's *Manual of Vascular Plants of Northeastern United States and Adjacent Canada*, second edition (1991); Radford, Ahles, and Bell's *Manual of the Vascular Flora of the Carolinas* (1968); Haines and Vining's *Flora of Maine* (1998); and Correll and Johnston's *Manual of the Vascular Plants of Texas* (1979) were among the most useful sources.

Habitat

The habitat given for each species is based on the observations of the authors, as well as regional manuals and guides. See "A Look at Coastal Habitats" for an introduction to the plant communities and habitats most likely to be encountered in the range of this book.

Plant Descriptions

Each plant description was written to enable the reader to distinguish that species from similar plants in the area and to give the reader information about its growth habit and life history. As space allowed, we have included descriptions of close relatives that may be found within the range of this book, paying particular attention to the key characteristics that will help the reader distinguish one species from another. When appropriate, we have also included information about pollination biology and seed dispersal, blooming dates, synonymy, uses of the plant by people and wildlife, the derivation of scientific and common names, and other interesting anatomical and ecological facts. A glossary of botanical and ecological terms follows the plant descriptions and "Selected Coastal Natural Areas."

Coastal Plants from Cape Cod to Cape Canaveral

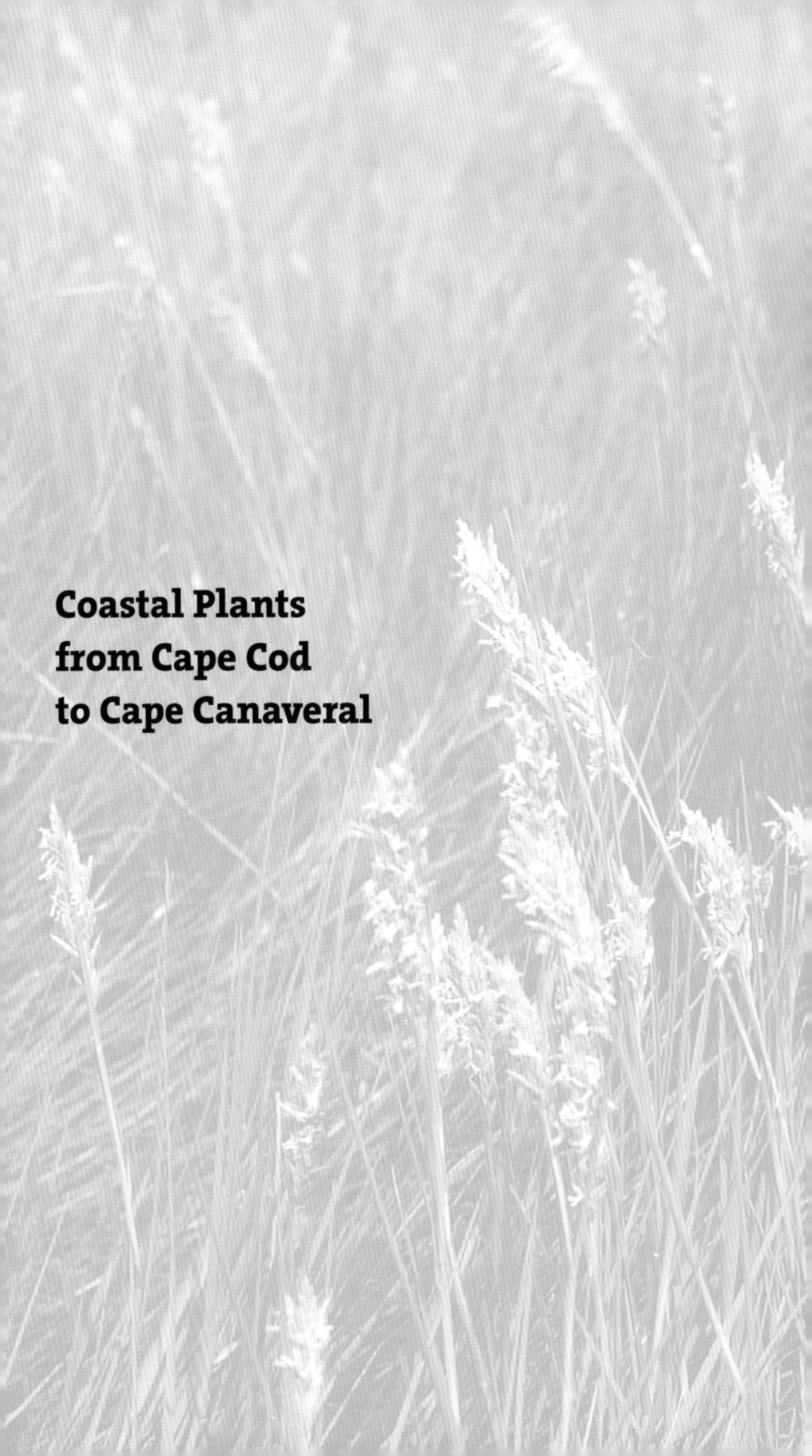

Introduction

Coastal areas have served human beings for thousands of years. The ocean and its edges provide food for people, livestock, and wildlife; embayments furnish safe harbor for commercial and recreational vessels; beaches offer recreation and relaxation; breezes off the ocean provide cooling in the summer; and warm ocean waters moderate the coastal climate through the winter. Coastal habitats are also usually places of great beauty. It is small wonder that nearly two-thirds of the world's human population is located in coastal regions. The coastal zone has also been a convenient place to build highways and railroads, dump garbage, and discharge sewage effluent.

Human use of salt marshes along the eastern coast of the United States has a long history and serves as a good example of how coastal systems have been treated. The European settlers allowed livestock to graze on the marshes, and people have cut marsh grasses for hay up to the present time (see the entry for salt hay grass [*Spartina patens*]). But from colonial times to the mid-twentieth century, as populations grew along the East Coast and fewer people farmed the land, more people considered salt marshes to be wasteland that was merely a breeding ground for mosquitoes. Thousands of acres of marsh were filled, ditched, drained, or used as dumps. Some of the New England states lost as much as 30–50 percent of their original saltmarsh area.

Beginning in the 1930s, duck hunters recognized the importance of marshes—both salt and fresh—in providing waterfowl habitat. Serious interest in saving salt marshes began in Florida after World War II ended and sportsfishermen returned to their favorite activity. They soon realized that the catches of sailfish were declining and sought to determine where the fish lived during its juvenile stages. The fishermen requested help from marine biologists, but it was not until the 1950s that a juvenile sailfish was discovered in a Florida tidal salt marsh. The fish was only slightly longer than 1 inch (2.5 cm), but it had the characteristic sail along the dorsal fin and a long, slender, pointed beak. It was obviously a juvenile sailfish.

With the discovery that salt marshes served as nurseries for fish and shellfish, people began to recognize their value and to conduct research on how salt marshes function. In the early 1960s, Eugene Odum, along with students and colleagues at the University of Georgia, began decades of seminal work in saltmarsh functioning (e.g., Odum and de la Cruz 1967, Teal 1981). During the same period, Massachusetts and Rhode Island passed laws protecting coastal wetlands. Several other New England, Middle Atlantic, and southern states followed suit in the 1970s, at the same time that federal wetland regulations were being developed; now every state along the eastern seaboard has regulations protecting coastal wetlands. Restorative measures were begun in several states in the 1970s and 1980s. Saltmarsh restoration projects are peaking now, along with an understanding of the many functions of salt marshes, although these efforts are progressing more slowly than many people would like.

Interest in saving the salt marshes stimulated interest in the plants that grow in and around them. Higher plants are not particularly tolerant of salt, but some plant families contain a fairly large number of species that can grow and reproduce in varying levels of salinity. These include grasses and sedges and members of the goosefoot and aster families. Other families also contain a few species that can tolerate salinity. Although considerable research has been conducted on the tolerance of plants to salt, scientists have reached no agreement about whether plants that live in saline habitats require salt or whether they simply have developed internal mechanisms that allow them to tolerate it. More research is required to answer this question.

In addition to salt marshes, many different aquatic, wetland, and terrestrial habitats, including beaches, rocky shores, dunes, forests, and freshwater areas, can be found along the Atlantic coast of North America. These habitats are part of a variety of ecosystems. An *ecosystem* is made up of communities of organisms (plants, animals, fungi, etc.) and the physical environment they inhabit. The organisms in an ecosystem interact with one another and with the physical environment to form a functioning unit for the flow of energy and the cycling of materials.

A *habitat* is a location where a particular species is normally found—some scientists call it an organism's "address." Each ecosystem may contain many different habitats in which organisms can live. Saltmarsh ecosystems, for example, include areas that are flushed daily by tides, as well as areas that are inundated only by the highest tides of the month or the year. Different organisms inhabit those different areas—with some overlap—although they are all considered components of the same ecosystem. Some organisms can thrive and reproduce in several different habitats, as long as each habitat provides the appropriate combination of environmental factors. For example, northern bayberry (*Myrica pensylvanica*) may be found growing on coastal dunes, in scrub thickets or woodlands, or along the borders of ponds or salt marshes.

For plants to occupy a certain habitat, light, water, temperature, nutrients, and a substrate on which to grow (such as sand, soil, muck, peat, water, or even another plant) must be within the range of those plants' tolerance. Even a common plant will disappear from a habitat if an essential environmental factor shifts beyond the plant's range of tolerance. Some species of goldenrod, such as gray goldenrod (*Solidago nemoralis*), flourish in full sun but gradually disappear when surrounding trees and shrubs grow large enough to shade the area. Rose pogonia (*Pogonia ophioglossoides*) is another example; this orchid sometimes grows abundantly in freshwater wetlands but will not survive if the wetland soil is drained artificially. In general, common plants tend to be broadly adapted, whereas rare ones survive only where certain narrowly defined environmental conditions exist.

A Look at Coastal Habitats

Beaches and Mudflats

Beaches are sloping habitats composed of loose particles in direct contact with a body of water. They are generally dominated by mineral particles no more than 10 inches (25.4 cm) in diameter and lack significant vegetation cover. In addition to sand, gravel, and cobbles, fragments of mollusk shells or other sea creatures may form a substantial proportion of some beaches (such as the beach at the Cape Hatteras National Seashore in North Carolina).

Most sand beaches on the Atlantic coast are composed primarily of quartz grains. Beautiful sand beaches may be seen in such places as the Cape Cod National Seashore in Massachusetts, Sandy Hook National Recreation Area in New Jersey, Chincoteague National Wildlife Refuge in Virginia, Cumberland Island National Seashore in Georgia, and Canaveral National Seashore in Florida. The shore below the Point Judith Lighthouse in Narragansett, Rhode Island, is a good place to view a cobble beach. Cobble beaches with particles that are flat are sometimes called shingle beaches; such beaches can be found in a few places within the book's range, including the Melville Public Fishing Area in Portsmouth, Rhode Island, and elsewhere along the western shore of Aquidneck Island, Rhode Island.

Coastal shores dominated by stones greater than 10 inches (25.4 cm) in diameter are uncommon south of Cape Cod. These rocky shores are discussed below.

Level areas of sand or mud that are exposed only during low tide are called sandflats or mudflats. Although an amazing variety of animals, such as clams, snails, sandworms, sea urchins, and sand dollars, can thrive in this habitat and many animals, such as waterfowl, shorebirds, and wading birds, feed on them, very few flowering plants are able to survive. Atlantic mudwort (*Limosella australis*) may be found on brackish tidal flats; eelgrass (*Zostera marina*) and shoalgrass (*Halodule wrightii*) also sometimes occur on tidal flats.

Because of wave action and the salinity of seawater, beaches, like tidal flats, are very harsh environments for flowering plants; those that do grow on beaches occur near the highest high tide line. Common saltwort (*Salsola kali*), sea chickweed (*Honckenya peploides*), sea rocket (*Cakile edentula*), and dusty miller (*Artemisia

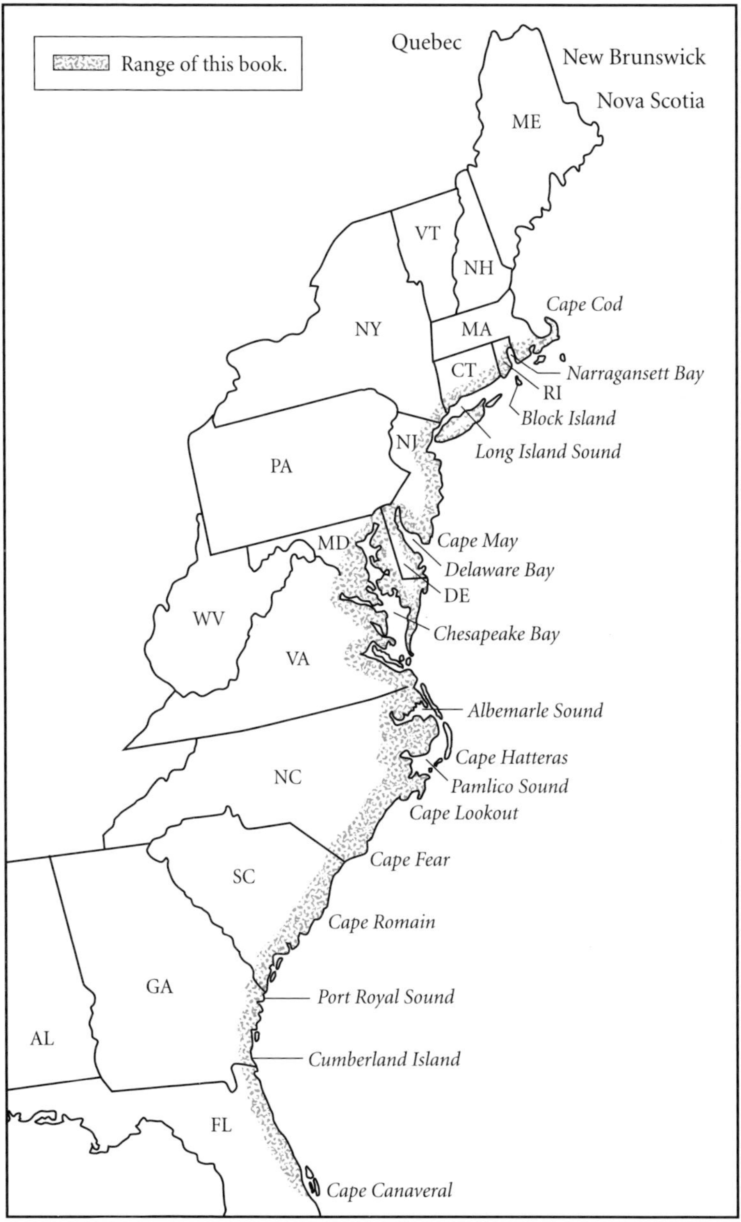
Range of this book.
Quebec
New Brunswick
Nova Scotia
ME
VT
NH
Cape Cod
NY
MA
CT
Narragansett Bay
RI
Block Island
NJ
Long Island Sound
PA
Cape May
MD
Delaware Bay
DE
WV
Chesapeake Bay
VA
Albemarle Sound
Cape Hatteras
NC
Pamlico Sound
Cape Lookout
Cape Fear
SC
Cape Romain
GA
Port Royal Sound
AL
Cumberland Island
FL
Cape Canaveral

stelleriana) are among the plants that can be found growing on beaches from Virginia north; the rare beach amaranth (*Amaranthus pumilus*)—a federally classified threatened species—may also occasionally be found on beaches from South Carolina to Massachusetts. Very few plants grow on open beaches south of Cape Hatteras. Strong winds and high tides cause sand to shift constantly, and the plants most likely to be found there are common saltwort, sea rocket, sea purslane (*Sesuvium* spp.), and silver-leaf croton (*Croton punctatus*).

Since beaches are popular recreation sites, human activities have a strong influence on the survival of beach-dwelling plants and animals. Even moderate foot traffic can destroy the vegetation; off-road vehicles have an even greater impact.

Rocky Shores

Rocky shores are dominated by bedrock outcrops and boulders. They are conspicuous generally only as far south as Rhode Island (Beavertail State Park in Jamestown, Rhode Island, is an excellent place to observe a rocky shore), but smaller outcrops can be found in several places on the Connecticut and New York shores. The lower zones on the rocks are flooded and exposed daily by the tides, whereas the upper zones are flooded less frequently, during unusually high tides or in strong storms.

These shores are a favorite place for fishermen. In most cases, the rocks descend directly into the ocean, but sheltered sites may have tiny gravel beaches and tidal pools. In spite of being frequently washed by sea water, several salt-tolerant land plants have survived by being well rooted in crevices in the lower-lying rocks. They include sea chickweed, a plant that also grows on both cobble and sand beaches; the naturalized scarlet pimpernel (*Anagallis arvensis*); sea lavender (*Limonium carolinianum*) and seaside plantain (*Plantago maritima*), which are also found in salt marshes; and awl-aster (*Aster pilosus*), an inland plant that has a very shortened globular form in this harsh habitat.

Aquatic Beds

Aquatic beds are wetland and deepwater habitats that are dominated by plants that grow on or below the water's surface. Along the rocky coasts of the Northeast, aquatic beds of kelp and rockweed may occur in water as deep as 98 feet (30 m) or in water shallow enough to expose the seaweed during low tide. Many species of algae are also found in estuarine and freshwater habitats. Algae are beyond the scope of this book, but readers who would like more information may find that Villalard-Bohnsack's *Illustrated Key to the Seaweeds of New England* (1995) and Schneider and Searles's *Seaweeds of the Southeastern United States, Cape Hatteras to Cape Canaveral* (1991) are excellent resources.

Several species of flowering plants, known collectively as seagrasses, form aquatic beds in shallow, saline coastal waters. Eelgrass grows from Greenland to Florida and is the dominant seagrass north of the Carolinas. From the Carolinas to the Caribbean, turtlegrass (*Thalassia testudina*) is the primary seagrass; shoalgrass, manatee-grass (*Cymodocea filiformis*), and Englemann's seagrass (*Halophila engelmannii*) are also found in this range. These seagrasses play a major role in stabilizing sediments in shallow coastal waters and are extremely important nursery grounds for many fish and shellfish. Eelgrass is also an important component of the diets of many waterfowl. Water pollution, especially from sewage and agricultural runoff, has had a detrimental effect on seagrass beds all along the East Coast.

Widgeon-grass (*Ruppia maritima*) may also be found in seagrass beds and in permanent pools and tidal creeks within salt marshes, but throughout the range of this book, it occurs more frequently in brackish waters, along with horned pondweed (*Zannichellia palustris*), water-nymph (*Najas* spp.), several species of pondweed (*Potamogeton* spp.), and other aquatic plants. Widgeon-grass, pondweeds, and water-nymph are important sources of food for waterfowl and provide shelter and nursery habitat for fish and shellfish.

Coastal Cliffs

Many interesting species of plants grow at the top of coastal cliffs, some salt tolerant, others not. Plants that grow above the ocean, out of reach of the waves and regular salt spray, are likely to be less salt tolerant, whereas those on the beach at the bottom of a cliff or in rock crevices that are sometimes washed by salt spray must be tolerant of salt in order to survive. Plants rarely grow near the base of cliffs that rise directly from the ocean because the high wave energy prevents them from becoming established. Plants that grow at the top of coastal cliffs include northern bayberry, both golden heather (*Hudsonia ericoides*) and beach heather (*Hudsonia tomentosa*), and several species of goldenrod (*Solidago* spp.) and asters (*Aster* spp.). Block Island, Rhode Island, is home to spectacular coastal cliffs.

Dunes

Dunes are hills of sand that develop above beaches where winds and tides are favorable and an abundant supply of sand is available. Most of the dunes along the Atlantic coast are stabilized by salt-tolerant plants. Some dunes are not stable, such as many dunes along the Outer Banks of North Carolina and some notable dunes on Cape Cod. Even the most stable dunes can be destroyed by a single violent storm.

American beachgrass (*Ammophila breviligulata*) is the primary dune stabilizer along northern coasts (from southern Virginia north), and sea oats (*Uniola paniculata*) and seaside panicum (*Panicum amarum*) stabilize the dunes from North Carolina south. Other plants common to the upper areas of northern beaches and the ocean-facing areas of dunes include purple sand grass (*Triplasis purpurea*), dusty miller, seabeach orach (*Atriplex pentandra*), common saltwort, sea rocket, beach pea (*Lathyrus japonicus*), seaside spurge (*Chamaesyce polygonifolia*), seaside goldenrod (*Solidago sempervirens*), and common cocklebur (*Xanthium strumarium*). On southern dunes, common species include purple sand grass, dune sandbur (*Cenchrus tribuloides*), common saltwort, sea purslane, sea rocket, seaside spurge, silver-leaf croton, beach pennywort (*Hydrocotyle bonariensis*), beach elder (*Iva imbricata*), and common cocklebur.

The backdune and interdune areas feature a fascinating transition from plants that tolerate high levels of salinity and wind action to those with little tolerance. Plants more common to northern (from Virginia north) interdune and backdune areas include pitch pine (*Pinus rigida*), eastern red cedar (*Juniperus virginiana*), hairgrass (*Deschampsia* spp.), both dune sandbur and common sandbur (*Cenchrus longispinus*), switchgrass (*Panicum virgatum*), quaking aspen (*Populus tremuloides*), northern bayberry, black oak (*Quercus velutina*), sand jointweed (*Polygonella articulata*), sassafras (*Sassafras albidum*), shadbush (*Amelanchier canadensis*), beach plum (*Prunus maritima*), wild black cherry (*Prunus serotina*), the introduced salt-spray rose (*Rosa rugosa*), poison ivy (*Toxicodendron radicans*), American holly (*Ilex opaca*), Virginia creeper (*Parthenocissus quinquefolia*), beach pinweed (*Lechea maritima*), beach heather, prickly pear cactus (*Opuntia* spp.), and bearberry (*Arctostaphylos uva-ursi*). Dune swales—low, moist areas between dunes—may also contain rushes (*Juncus* spp.), winterberry (*Ilex verticillata*), red maple (*Acer rubrum*), black gum (*Nyssa sylvatica*), and a variety of ferns.

In the backdune and interdune areas of southern coastal regions (from North Carolina south), in addition to sea oats and seaside panicum, the following species may be found: salt hay grass, bear grass/Spanish bayonet (*Yucca* spp.), perennial glasswort (*Sarcocornia perennis*), sea purslane, wild bean (*Strophostyles* spp.), tread-softly (*Cnidoscolus stimulosus*), silver-leaf croton, cactus (*Opuntia* spp.), beach evening-primrose (*Oenothera drummondii*), seaside evening-primrose (*Oenothera humifusa*), beach pennywort, firewheel (*Gaillardia pulchella*), and grass-leaved golden aster (*Pityopsis graminifolia*). Small saltmarsh pink (*Sabatia stellaris*) grows in the backdune swales, and numerous other species, including southern sweet grass (*Muhlenbergia capillaris*), can be found at increasing distances from the ocean, forming an interesting transition from maritime to nonmaritime habitats.

Tidal Salt Marshes

Tidal salt marshes develop in estuaries where the rate of silt sedimentation equals or exceeds the rate of the rising sea level. In some marshes, water covers the entire marsh for a period of time each day, whereas in others, the bulk of the area may be covered with water only during higher-than-average high tides. The elevation of the marsh substrate determines how often a particular location in the marsh is inundated and for how long.

The frequency and duration of tidal flooding are key factors influencing the distribution of saltmarsh plant species. Many tidal salt marshes have a well-defined upper edge. Salt marshes from Virginia north are often marked by hightide bush (*Iva frutescens*), groundsel tree (*Baccharis halimifolia*), switchgrass (*Panicum virgatum*), or shrubby or forested banks, whereas other northern marshes make a gradual transition into a freshwater marsh. Narrow-leaved cattail (*Typha angustifolia*), common three-square (*Scirpus pungens*), and common reed (*Phragmites australis*) are frequently found in this zone, especially where human disturbance of the soil or discharge of fresh water (decreasing the salinity of the soil) has occurred or where a natural salinity gradient exists. From North Carolina south, cabbage palm (*Sabal palmetto*), saltwort (*Batis maritima*), salt-cedar (*Tamarix* spp.), false willow (*Baccharis angustifolia*), and sea ox-eye (*Borrichia frutescens*) are among the species that may be found on the upper edge of the marsh.

Spartina species are the dominant grasses of East Coast salt marshes. In some areas, notably Georgia and New Jersey, solid stands of smooth cordgrass (*Spartina alterniflora*) and salt hay grass may extend for miles. Other common saltmarsh species include saltgrass (*Distichlis spicata*), needlerush (*Juncus roemerianus*) (from New Jersey south), black rush (*Juncus gerardii*) (from Virginia north), glassworts (*Salicornia* and *Sarcocornia* spp.), sea lavender, and perennial saltmarsh aster (*Aster tenuifolius*). For a detailed description of how saltmarsh ecosystems function, see Bertness's *The Ecology of Atlantic Shorelines* (1999).

Tidal Brackish Marshes

Coastal tidal marshes are often brackish (somewhat salty, with salt levels from 0.5 to 30 parts per thousand; sea water is 35 parts per thousand salt). The vegetation in brackish marshes from New Jersey north includes many saltmarsh species, as well as narrow-leaved cattail, broad-leaved cattail (*Typha latifolia*), seaside arrow-grass (*Triglochin maritimum*), big cordgrass (*Spartina cynosuroides*), freshwater cordgrass (*Spartina pectinata*), bulrushes (such as *Scirpus americanus* and *Scirpus robustus*), orach (*Atriplex* spp.), coast blite (*Chenopodium rubrum*), tall sea blite (*Suaeda linearis*), water hemp (*Amaranthus cannabinus*), saltmarsh sand spurrey (*Spergularia salina*), false indigo (*Amorpha fruticosa*), swamp rose-mallow (*Hibiscus moscheutos*), saltmarsh pink (*Sabatia* spp.), annual saltmarsh aster (*Aster subulatus*), and saltmarsh fleabane (*Pluchea odorata*). In some areas, common reed may form large colonies in brackish marshes; Hackensack Meadows in New Jersey, which can be seen from the New Jersey Turnpike, is a notable example.

Many of the plants found in northern brackish marshes also grow in marshes from New Jersey south, such as narrow- and broad-leaved cattail, big cordgrass, bulrushes (*Scirpus* spp.), tall sea blite, saltmarsh sand spurrey, false indigo, annual saltmarsh aster, and saltmarsh fleabane. Other common components of brackish marshes from Maryland south include southern arrow-grass (*Triglochin striatum*), water millet (*Zizaniopsis miliacea*), saw-grass (*Cladium mariscus*), needlerush, cabbage palm, orach (*Atriplex prostrata*), saltwort (*Batis maritima*), sea purslane, seashore mallow (*Kosteletzkya virginica*), false willow, groundsel tree (*Baccharis glomeruliflora*), and sea ox-eye.

Freshwater Habitats: Swamps, Marshes, Ponds, and Streams

Coastal swamps in the South usually border rivers. A dominant tree in southern coastal swamps (primarily from Delaware south) is bald cypress (*Taxodium distichum*), a rather stark tree characterized by its "knees," woody projections that rise above the surface of the water. Atlantic white cedar (*Chamaecyparis thyoides*), red maple, supplejack (*Berchemia scandens*), tupelo (*Nyssa aquatica*), and ash (*Fraxinus* spp.) are common associates. The Santee Coastal Reserve near McClellanville, South Carolina, contains beautiful examples of southern coastal swamps and maritime forests. The White Oak River, which flows into Bogue Inlet in North Carolina, is also a fine place to view maritime swamp forests and tidal freshwater marshes.

Northern coastal swamps are dominated by Atlantic white cedar, red maple, and black gum, with common winterberry, sweet pepperbush (*Clethra alnifolia*), highbush blueberry (*Vaccinium corymbosum*), and azaleas (*Rhododendron* spp.) among the most common woody understory species. The Marconi Station near South Wellfleet on the Cape Cod National Seashore offers a spectacular example of a northern Atlantic white cedar swamp, with a boardwalk that winds through the forest.

Freshwater marshes are characterized by herbaceous species such as cattail (*Typha* spp.), sweetflag (*Acorus americanus*), arrow arum (*Peltandra virginica*), slender blue flag (*Iris prismatica*), pickerelweed (*Pontederia cordata*), and many species of grasses, sedges, and rushes. A number of plants that grow in this habitat are found from Massachusetts to Florida.

Many plants grow in tidal freshwater marshes and along streamsides, where they must be able to survive the regular ebb and flow of tidal waters. In addition to the species listed above, tidal freshwater habitats include wild rice (*Zizania aquatica*), river bulrush (*Scirpus fluviatilis*), spatterdock (*Nuphar lutea*), seashore mallow, and climbing hempweed (*Mikania scandens*).

Shallow (less than 6 feet deep) coastal freshwater ponds and streams are home to some beautiful flowers, such as golden club (*Orontium aquaticum*), white water-lily (*Nymphaea odorata*), and bladderworts (*Utricularia* spp.). Many of the species that grow in this habitat can be found from Massachusetts to Florida.

Bogs, Fens, and Pocosins

In some wetlands, plant material decays very slowly and accumulates to a depth of at least 16 inches (40 cm); if conditions are right, a peatland may form. Bogs are peatlands that generally have little freshwater input except from a high groundwater table or from rainfall; the soils tend to be very acidic (i.e., pH less than 4.0) and low in oxygen and nutrients. Fens usually have a significant groundwater flow, which helps bring more nutrients to the plants and raises the pH. The mat formed by the vegetation in bogs and fens is sometimes thick enough to walk on but quakes underfoot.

Sphagnum moss (*Sphagnum* spp.) is a major component of the vegetation in bogs and, to a lesser extent, occurs in fens; other species include marsh fern (*Thelypteris palustris*), sedges (*Carex* spp.), cottongrasses (*Eriophorum* spp.), wild calla (*Calla palustris*), sundews (*Drosera* spp.), pitcher-plants (*Sarracenia* spp.), leatherleaf (*Chamaedaphne calyculata*), sweet gale (*Myrica gale*), cranberry (*Vaccinium* spp.), bladderworts, and many species of wild orchids. From New Jersey south, peatlands also commonly include Virginia chain-fern (*Woodwardia virginica*), pond pine (*Pinus serotina*), bamboo vine (*Smilax laurifolia*), red bay (*Persea borbonia*), black ti-ti (*Cyrilla racemiflora*), loblolly bay (*Gordonia lasianthus*), and honeycup (*Zenobia puverulenta*). Because of the narrow range of growth factors in these habitats, many plants found in bogs and fens are rare.

Pocosins are boggy areas of plateaus dominated by evergreen shrubs. They are found from Virginia south, with the greatest concentration in North Carolina. The Algonquians named this type of wetland "pocosin," meaning "swamp on a hill." In addition to the species listed above, in peatlands from New Jersey south, pocosin plants include swamp candleberry (*Myrica heterophylla*), sweet bay (*Magnolia virginiana*), poison sumac (*Toxicodendron vernix*), inkberry (*Ilex glabra*), highbush blueberry, swamp azalea (*Rhododendron viscosum*), and fetterbush (*Lyonia lucida*). Several species of pitcher-plants and orchids may be found in pocosins. The Croatan National Forest in North Carolina contains some fine examples of pocosins.

Coastal Scrub and Thickets

Coastal scrub and thicket vegetation often serves as a transition between maritime beach and grassland habitats and interior forests and wetlands. Coastal scrublands are common in New England. The land was forested when the first settlers arrived, except for cleared places where the Native Americans grew such crops as corn, squash, and beans. With the arrival of the Europeans, the land was cleared quickly and much was intensively cultivated. During the nineteenth and twentieth centuries, as agriculture declined, native trees, shrubs, and vines such as pitch pine, eastern red cedar, catbrier (*Smilax* spp.), northern bayberry, oaks (*Quercus* spp.), sassafras, shadbush, chokeberries (*Aronia* spp.), wild black cherry, poison ivy, Virginia creeper, grapes (*Vitis* spp.), black gum, and both northern and southern arrowwood (*Viburnum dentatum* var. *lucidum* and var. *venosum*) moved in. In the 1860s, after its introduction from Asia, salt-spray rose naturalized and became widely established in coastal areas. In many places, both bayberry and salt-spray rose have reached maturity and are dying. The salt-spray rose is sometimes replaced by bayberry, but in the areas where bayberry is maturing, there are often no other native trees or shrubs to provide seedlings. In such areas, the bayberry is often replaced by invasive introduced plants that are overwhelming the native vegetation. These invaders include multiflora rose (*Rosa multiflora*), Asian bittersweet (*Celastrus orbiculata*), buckthorns (*Rhamnus* spp.), porcelain vine (*Ampelopsis brevipedunculata*), autumn olive (*Elaeagnus umbellata*), privet (*Ligustrum* spp.), and bush honeysuckles (such as *Lonicera morrowii* and *Lonicera* × *bella*). Sachuest Point National

Wildlife Refuge in Middletown, Rhode Island, and Island Beach State Park near Seaside Park, New Jersey, contain excellent examples of northern coastal scrub and thicket habitats.

South of New England, coastal thickets are formed by a variety of trees, shrubs, and vines, including pitch pine, red cedar, saw palmetto (*Serenoa repens*), catbrier, southern bayberry (*Myrica cerifera*) (from southern New Jersey south), northern bayberry (from Virginia north), oaks, red bay, sassafras, laurelcherry (*Prunus caroliniana*), wild black cherry, Hercules' club (*Zanthoxylum clava-herculis*), poison ivy, American holly, yaupon holly (*Ilex vomitoria*), muscadine grape (*Vitis rotundifolia*), devil's walking-stick (*Aralia spinosa*), black gum, and sparkleberry (*Vaccinium arboreum*). In the South, and increasingly in the North, coastal thickets may be overrun with the naturalized invasive Japanese honeysuckle (*Lonicera japonica*). Multiflora rose, autumn olive, and privet are also invading natural communities in the South, along with other escapes from cultivation, including heavenly bamboo (*Nandina domestica*), kudzu (*Pueraria lobata*), chinaberry tree (*Melia azedarach*), Chinese tallow (*Sapium sebiferum*), and princess tree (*Paulownia tomentosa*). Hammocks Beach State Park near Swansboro, North Carolina, and Otter Island in the St. Helena Sound Heritage Preserve in South Carolina are good places to see southern coastal scrub and thicket habitats.

Coastal thickets and scrublands are often bordered by upland forests. These forests vary considerably along the Atlantic coast—from eastern deciduous forests to pinelands—with great diversity in the trees, shrubs, and herbaceous plants present. In some coastal locations, the force of the wind and its salt content have produced dwarfed trees. On Nantucket Island off the Massachusetts coast, red cedar grows on the beaches and dunes. It survives even if half of the plant is buried in sand. On some sea islands off the coast of Georgia, live oak trees (*Quercus virginiana*) are short and rounded as if they had been pruned.

Old Fields, Meadows, and Savannas

Old fields and meadows usually have vegetation that is in transition from cultivated fields or pastures to forest vegetation. Because farming has declined along the eastern seaboard, many pastures and fields have either reverted to forest or been developed for human use. As development has increased, naturally occurring fires have been suppressed; this has aided in the decline of open areas, as well as pine forests and savannas, which are fire dependent. Especially on preserves, open areas need to be managed by mowing or burning at appropriate times. Otherwise, they are likely to be invaded by undesirable introduced species or to revert to forest in a very short time.

The plants found here tend to be species that thrive in full sun. Such sites support some of the most beautiful native grasses, including little bluestem (*Schizachyrium scoparium*) and big bluestem (*Andropogon gerardii*), as well as colorful wildflowers, such as lilies (*Lilium* spp.), orchids (e.g., *Platanthera* spp., *Spiranthes* spp.), fringed gentian (*Gentianopsis crinita*), milkweeds (*Asclepias* spp.), and many members of the aster family. Powerline cuts, especially if they are not treated with herbicides and are not too heavily trafficked by off-road vehicles, often support remnant populations of increasingly rare native meadow plants. Roadsides and roadside ditches sometimes serve a similar purpose, providing regularly mowed, full-sun habitats, from dry to wet, for a large number of plants. Roadsides, however, are also highly disturbed habitats that often function as corridors for weedy and invasive species that thrive in open areas, such as autumn olive, Asian bittersweet, kudzu, showy evening-primrose (*Oenothera speciosa*), and common mullein (*Verbascum thapsus*).

Savannas are open grassy areas with scattered trees and shrubs, occurring from North Carolina south (in parts of New Jersey, mineral-poor fens are sometimes called savannas). Long-leaf pine (*Pinus palustris*) and pond cypress (*Taxodium ascendens*) are two of the primary tree species in savannas, which are also home to a fascinating array of shrubs and herbaceous plants, including white-topped sedge (*Rhynchospora colorata*), saw palmetto, purple flag (*Iris tridentata*), sweet bay, and many orchids and insectivorous plants. The Santee Coastal Preserve in South Carolina is a good place to explore both long-leaf pine and pond cypress savannas.

Field Trips to Coastal Areas

Coastal ecosystems make excellent destinations for field trips, frequently offering the opportunity to view a variety of plant communities within a small area. A well-planned field trip to such an area is a joy, but a poorly planned one can be a disaster. Careful planning is essential to ensure that participants have a good time so they will want to learn more about natural history. Here are some tips for field trip leaders to make the trip more successful.

Pretrip Planning

The leader of a field trip should *know the area* where the trip will take place. You should be familiar with the trails and their condition, the location of interesting plants and animals and other natural features, and the human and ecological history of the area. Participants may also want to know information such as the size of the area and who owns and manages it.

Trip leaders should be familiar enough with the local area to identify places that should *not* be used for field trips. If you decide to visit areas with no trails or roads, explore them thoroughly beforehand to be sure you know exactly where you will lead the group.

Do not take field trips on unstabilized dunes or steep or slippery slopes, and avoid areas with loose stones, such as shingle beaches, or areas with huge boulders. If you will be exploring swamps, bogs, or marshes, do not venture into water more than ankle deep or into muck where someone might get stuck. Sometimes it is advisable for the leader to collect specimens of aquatic plants from a pond or stream if the plants grow too far out and the water is too deep or the bottom too mucky for wading.

Peatlands need special consideration. Some bogs and fens with floating grass mats are safe for a group to walk on, but others are not. Small peatlands should be examined only from the edges since even if they are stable enough to walk on, many peatland species are killed by trampling, and the fragility of the peatland flora should be respected.

Dunes are another habitat that requires special attention. The stems of dune grasses are extremely brittle, and breaking them may kill the plant. Limit the number of people on dune trips, and instruct them to step between the clumps of grass, not on them. Many state parks and national wildlife refuges have boardwalks through sensitive habitats; these are excellent places to use for walks.

If a place is considered dangerous by the local inhabitants, do not lead a field trip there. For example, in New England, even on a calm summer day, some beautiful rocky shores may be inundated by large unexpected waves that could wash people off the rocks.

Determine what number of people can participate safely and comfortably on a walk at a particular site. Fragile habitats such as bogs or areas with very narrow trails can accommodate far fewer people than open spaces such as beaches or dirt roads in preserves. As a general rule, ten to twelve is an ideal number, fifteen is manageable, and twenty is an absolute maximum for one leader. Remember that if people cannot hear the leader or see the specimens, they tend to lose interest. In addition, if too many people try to crowd around a leader, they may trample the plants the leader wants them to see and appreciate. If you find that the number of people who wish to attend exceeds your limit, either split the group up among more than one leader or plan multiple trips on different dates.

Plan the timing of your trip carefully. In general, a walking field trip should take about two hours since it is more tiring to walk slowly than to hike vigorously. For a trip with transportation between stops, about three hours should be sufficient. In estimating the total time for your field trip, do not forget to include the time required for loading and unloading at stops.

You should know how long it takes to traverse the trails at the site and be aware of alternate trails if you find a walk is taking longer than anticipated. Always be prepared to be flexible about the length of the walk to accommodate people who may not have the stamina to complete the entire trip. Remember, the goal of nature walks is enjoyment and appreciation (which hopefully will inspire people to want to protect habitats and species), not a display of physical endurance.

In *tidal habitats*, you should check with the local weather bureau to ascertain the tides to determine the best time for the trip, and on the day itself, make sure that the information is accurate for the site. Know where you can lead a group without being cut off by rising tides.

Know the logistics of the area, such as where to park and the location of the nearest restrooms and telephone in case of emergency. If buses are used, you should find out where they can park and turn around and whether the preserve's roads are wide and smooth enough to accommodate buses; generally, buses should be restricted to paved surfaces or well-maintained gravel roads.

Obtain permission to use the area. Even on public land such as state parks and national wildlife refuges, managers like to know when a group event is planned. Be sure to obtain written permission for a specific date and alternate date and a certain number of people. Bring this written permission with you on the day of the trip. If *hunting* takes place on the property you are visiting, make sure that you are not planning a field trip during hunting season—another reason to obtain permission from property managers.

Determine *specimen-collecting policies* and whether or not pets are allowed. On sites owned by private conservation organizations, such as the Nature Conservancy, collecting is forbidden, and most wildlife refuges ban pets, even if they are on leashes. Clearly state these policies in the material sent to registrants.

Ascertain the *appropriate clothing* for the site to prevent participants from showing up in bathing suits and barefoot or wearing flimsy sandals or stockings and high heels. Long denim or chino pants are best. Discourage participants from wearing white clothing since people with sensitive skin can sunburn through white fabric, especially if it is wet. Long-sleeved shirts with collars provide protection from sunburn and insect bites. Sturdy shoes with nonslip soles should be at least ankle high and worn with socks to protect legs from grasses and shells with sharp edges. For sun and insect protection, a hat with a brim or a cap with a visor is best. If the trip will be taken rain or shine, remind people to bring rain gear if necessary. For cold weather walks, people should wear warm socks, waterproof shoes, gloves, and a warm cap to cover the ears.

A knowledge of dangerous plants and animals is essential. A useful reference is Foster and Caras's *Venomous Animals and Poisonous Plants* (1994). You should be able to identify plants that cause problems on contact, such as the *Toxicodendron* species (poison ivy, poison oak, and poison sumac), and point them out to the group as soon as they are encountered. Remind members that they cannot assume that they are immune to the oil (urushiol) that causes the rash just because they have never had a reaction because body chemistry can change. People should never get cocky in approaching these plants.

In areas where Lyme disease and other tick-borne ailments are common, people should be warned to check themselves carefully for deer ticks within twenty-four hours after the trip. Deer ticks are so tiny that they can be hard to spot on clothing, so participants should wash their clothes after a field trip and dry them in a clothes dryer if possible (the ticks can live through the washing but usually do not survive the dryer). Deer ticks are found most frequently on low vegetation (such as grasses and shrubs along the edges of paths where deer and field mice wander by), so staying on the trails and avoiding the edges is a good idea. Sitting on the ground in areas with a high incidence of tick-borne diseases (such as southern New England) should be discouraged.

Other arthropods to be on the lookout for include chiggers, bees, and yellow jackets. Yellow jackets are the most likely stinging insects to be encountered on walks throughout the range of this book. They build nests in the ground and in decaying logs, so it is always a good idea to keep a wary eye out for holes in the ground, especially in late summer and early fall when the colonies are fully developed. In the South, the naturalized fire ant is a hazard in fields, roadsides, and woodland edges. Although tiny (no more than ¼ inch [7 mm] in length), the fire ant can sting and bite and may cause an allergic reaction. Typical fire ant mounds may be up to 1 foot (30 cm) in height and are easily seen and avoided, but smaller colonies may also be present. The spread of fire ants in the South is yet another reason to urge field trip participants to wear sturdy shoes and socks.

Although people often worry about encountering poisonous snakes on field trips, few venomous snakes live in the North, and even though rattlesnakes, copperheads, coral snakes, and water moccasins may be found farther down the Atlantic coast and into the Deep South, it is unlikely that they will be seen on field trips because most snakes are shy and avoid contact with people. They tend to be fairly inactive at temperatures below 70°F; the higher the temperature above 70°, the more active and quick to strike they become. To avoid snakes on field trips, stay on the trails and do not trample through underbrush and areas where you cannot see where your feet are going. Along the edges of ponds and streams, be careful while examining the branches of shrubs and trees since water moccasins might be curled up there. According to folklore, rattlesnakes are never found in salt water; professional herpetologists, however, have captured large rattlesnakes swimming in the channels between the mainland and offshore islands in the South.

Alligators are another potential hazard in the South but are unlikely to remain near a group of people. Still, they should be respected, and you should keep your distance. Legend has it that they are particularly fond of dog meat—another good reason to leave your dog at home on field trips in southern swamps!

Notification of the trip (e.g., in a newspaper or newsletter) should describe the kind of trip (e.g., saltmarsh walk, fern identification session, winter botany trip), the location, the date and time, and the expected duration. State whether it will be a walking trip or whether transportation will be provided (via vans, buses, or car caravan) between stops to see plants. Indicate how far you will be walking and any special features—such as steep or rocky trails—that might make the trip difficult for people with less physical ability.

Include the cost and whether preregistration is required, and state the policy on cancellations. Be sure to provide a telephone number that people can call to register or get more information. In public notices, it is best *not* to mention the existence of rare plants at a site.

Pretrip information sent to registrants should include the time and date of the trip, a map to the site, parking instructions, the specific place where the trip will begin, and the telephone number of someone who can be reached on the day of the event. Be sure to indicate what will happen if the trip is canceled because of inclement weather or for some other reason.

The instructions should also note whether there will be restrooms at the site and whether participants need to bring any special gear (such as magnifying lenses or field guides) or food. People should be reminded to wear appropriate clothing for the site and to bring sunscreen and insect repellent if necessary. A hiking stick may also be desirable (a lightweight hoe or mop handle makes an excellent hiking stick and is especially useful in rough terrain or mucky areas such as salt marshes and swamps).

As the trip leader, you should carry a first-aid kit, insect repellent, sunscreen, and any field guides you want to show the group. A pair of horticultural clippers is also useful for cutting specimens rather than ripping them off a tree or shrub or pulling them out of the ground; by taking specimens with care, you will serve as a model for respecting other species.

Conducting a Field Trip

Introductions set a pleasant tone for the trip. After introducing yourself, ask the group members to give their names and where they live.

Then tell the group about the area they will be visiting and where they can find more information. This is a good time to make people aware of any available handouts about local conservation organizations or native plant societies (at the end of a trip, people are often tired and less likely to pay attention to such information). The leader may also want to point out useful reference works and, if necessary, explain any ground rules pertinent to the site.

When possible, keep to the trails. Using the trails reinforces the respect you have for the natural area you are exploring and prevents trampling of plants and animals. Most private nature preserves request that visitors stay on the trails. Using the trails may also protect the participants from ticks, poisonous snakes, poison ivy, and other dangerous plants and animals.

If a preserve contains rare or endangered species, do not go near their sites or discuss their location. All too often, revealing the specific location of rare plants ultimately leads to their disappearance. The fewer people who know the sites of rare and endangered species, the better for the organisms.

Make the sun your spotlight. On cloudy days, the light surrounding you and the plants you want to show the group is uniform. On sunny days, however, sunlight can work either for or against you, so learn to use it to your advantage. Be aware of the position of the sun, and make sure that when you are pointing out something to the group or holding up a specimen for display, the sun is shining toward you and not into the eyes of the participants. This simple technique will ensure that the specimen you are showing is illuminated and that the participants are not forced to squint into the sun.

Use your voice to good purpose. It is useless to address the group while walking forward at the head of the line because few, if any, people will be able to hear you. When you want to point out something of interest, stop beside the specimen and let half of the members walk ahead so that you are at the center of the line and can address the entire group. If there are incessant talkers in the group, lower your voice; others will take on the job of telling them to quiet down so everyone can hear (this is an old teachers' trick).

Do not be reluctant to use scientific as well as common names. Although many people are more comfortable with common names, the leader should explain that the meanings of the words used in the binomial help identify the plant. Discuss the origins of scientific names and why they are important. Also point out alternate common names and the fact that some common names are applied to several different plants (such as mayflower).

At the end of the walk, thank the participants, answer any questions they might have, and remind them of literature you have available. Tell them of organizations that lead similar walks in the region, such as the local Audubon Society, the Nature Conservancy, and native plant societies, and welcome them to return to the area in other seasons, if it is open to the public.

Plant Descriptions

Scouring rush,
Equisetum hyemale

Scouring Rush

Equisetum hyemale L. var. *affine* (Engelm.) A. A. Eat.
Horsetail Family, Equisetaceae

RANGE: Circumboreal, as far south as Florida in this book's range; also in California and Central America.
HABITAT: Tidal brackish marshes, moist roadsides, floodplains, banks, and woods.

Scouring rush plants usually look like colonies of slender, erect pipes, from 8 inches (20 cm) to over 7 feet (2 m) tall. Although an occasional single stem may be found and some plants are sparsely branched, the usual habit of growth is as colonies of unbranched plants. The plants spread primarily by black underground stems called rhizomes. The variation in height is mostly geographical, with the more southern and western plants in the book's range being taller than the northeastern ones.

The stems are hollow, with the central open area occupying ⅔–¾ of the space within the walls. The outer surface of the stems is rough to touch, ribbed vertically with 16–50 ridges separated by furrows, with two rows of stomates in each furrow. Stomates are small oval organs specially constructed to allow oxygen to enter the plant and carbon dioxide and other gases to be released. They can be seen without a hand lens, but a lens shows more detail.

The plants are dark green and jointed, shading to cream color toward the upper end of the joint. At each joint is a fringed sheath, usually about ⅜–⅝ inch (10–16 mm) long, with a band of black at the base and another at the upper end.

Some stems taper to a tip at the upper end. Others produce a cone with tapering sides, black fringes, and a black tip. This cone produces spores rather than seeds. The spores are shed when they are ripe, from May to September depending on the geographical region.

Reproduction from spores rather than seeds and the structure of the plants indicate that members of the horsetail family are ancient plants that are associated with the ferns and fern allies; they are known from fossil records to have been in existence for hundreds of millions of years. This group of ancient plants includes not only the ferns and horsetails but also the clubmosses and several other smaller families. However, the fossil record for the horsetails is so limited that we are not sure just what relationship they have to these other ancient plants.

This species of *Equisetum* was given the common name scouring rush because of its high content of silica. Silica is a chemical name for quartz sand, and its presence in the horsetails makes the plants harsh to the touch. In earlier times, scouring rush was used to scrub pots and pans, finish wood, and polish pewter.

This horsetail is certainly not considered an edible plant. Like the consumption of some of the ferns, such as bracken (*Pteridium aquilinum* [L.] Kuhn), horsetail consumption appears to interfere with the metabolism of thiamine, one of the vitamins in the B-complex. Scouring rush has been known to kill horses, and bracken is toxic to both cattle and horses.

In the northern portion of the book's range, field horsetail (*Equisetum arvense* L.) may also be found within sight of salt water, but south of North Carolina, both field horsetail and scouring rush are primarily inland plants.

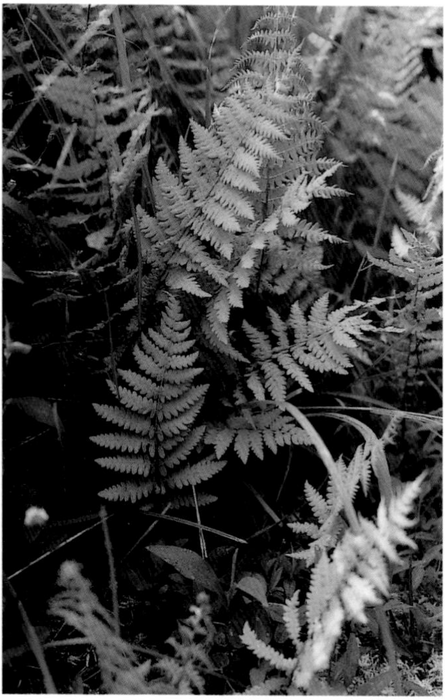

Marsh fern,
Thelypteris palustris

Marsh Fern

Thelypteris palustris Schott var. *pubescens* (Lawson) Fern.
Marsh Fern Family, Thelypteridaceae

RANGE: Newfoundland and Nova Scotia south to Florida and west to Manitoba, Minnesota, North Dakota, Oklahoma, and Texas; also in Bermuda and Cuba.
HABITAT: Upper edges of tidal salt and brackish marshes and edges of tidal freshwater rivers; also in swamps, bogs, marshes, wet meadows, and woodlands.

Marsh fern, also called meadow fern, is one of the most common ferns in eastern North America. A medium-sized fern, it has twisting pale green fronds that add a delicate touch to the marshes and wet meadows where it thrives in the summer. It disappears quickly, however, after the first frost.

Marsh fern grows from slender creeping and branching rootstocks and often forms large colonies in wet soils, although it rarely thrives in standing water. Both the roots and the rootstock are black, as is the base of the stipe (the stalk below the leafy part of the fern). The slender, smooth stipe may be as long as 28 inches (70 cm) and is frequently longer than the blade. The blades are up to 16 inches (40 cm) long and 8 inches (20 cm) wide, with the widest portion near the base of the frond. The fertile fronds (those producing spores) are usually longer than the sterile ones.

The rachis (the midrib) and both surfaces of the frond are covered with fine hairs, especially on younger plants. Each frond has 12–40 pairs of lanceolate sessile (or nearly so) pinnae (leaflets), which are in turn divided into 8–25 blunt, untoothed pairs of pinnules (subleaflets). The longest pinnae can be found from the middle of the frond to just above the lowest pairs of pinnae.

The roundish sori, or fruitdots (where the spores form), develop in tight rows along both sides of the midribs of the pinnules. As they mature, the edges of the pinnules tend to curve over the rows of sori, so that the mature fertile fronds appear darker than the infertile fronds.

Marsh fern is most easily confused with New York fern (*Thelypteris noveboracensis* [L.] Nieuwl.) and Massachusetts fern (*Thelypteris simulata* [Davenport] Nieuwl.). New York fern grows in damp soils and woodlands from Newfoundland south to Georgia and is usually not found in the very wet habitats where marsh fern grows. The pinnae decrease in size both above and below the middle pinnae, so that the frond is strongly tapered at both ends and has a very short stipe. Massachusetts fern is sometimes found in the same wet habitats as marsh fern, especially in acidic swamps and wet woods, from Nova Scotia to Virginia. The frond shape is similar to that of marsh fern, but the stipe has brown scales, and the sori are scattered on the pinnules and do not follow the midrib. The simplest way to tell the two apart, however, is to use a magnifying lens and look at the veins that radiate from the midvein of the pinnules. In marsh fern, these veins are forked on the sterile fronds and unforked on the fertile fronds; in Massachusetts fern, the veins are unforked on both types of fronds.

Some authorities call marsh fern *Dryopteris thelypteris* (L.) Sw.

Resurrection fern, *Pleopeltis polypodioides*

Resurrection Fern

Pleopeltis polypodioides (L.) Andrews & Windham
Polypody Fern Family, Polypodiaceae

RANGE: Virginia south to Florida and west to Illinois, Oklahoma, and Texas; also in Mexico, Central America, and the West Indies.
HABITAT: Limbs and crotches of large trees (such as oaks, magnolias, and elms); also on tree stumps, logs, rocks, fence posts, and buildings.

What a surprise it is to come across a clump of withered gray leaves on a live oak limb on a hot summer day and then to return after a few wet days and find a vigorous stand of small green ferns spreading lacy fronds along the bough, resurrected by the rain! Resurrection fern seems almost miraculous in its sensitivity to moisture and its ability to revive quickly after long dry spells.

Resurrection fern is an evergreen fern that grows on trees and rocks and sometimes even buildings. In areas within the book's range, it is particularly associated with live oak trees (*Quercus virginiana*) and is often entangled in Spanish moss (*Tillandsia usneoides*).

It grows from slender creeping rhizomes that are densely covered with brownish-black scales. The thick, leathery leaves are up to 10 inches (25 cm) long on scale-covered stalks that are usually about one-third the length of the leaves. The leaves are deep green on the upper surface and covered with gray shield-shaped scales on the undersurface. They are cut into 6–20 pairs of narrow, blunt-tipped segments that are not quite opposite one another.

The fruitdots are round and distinctly separate from each other. They develop along the margins on the undersurface of the segments and are embedded so deeply into the undersurface that they form bumps on the upper surface. They are dark brown when mature, from June through October.

The name *Pleopeltis* is from the Greek words *pleos*, meaning "many," and *pelte*, meaning "shield," referring to the shieldlike scales on the stalks and the backs of the fronds. An earlier name for this species was *Polypodium polypodioides* (L.) Watt.

Long-leaf Pine

Pinus palustris P. Mill.
Pine Family, Pinaceae

RANGE: Southeastern Virginia south to Florida and west to southeastern Texas.
HABITAT: Coastal plain (and less frequently inland in piedmont areas), on dry to moist sandy soils.

In a beauty pageant of eastern trees, two pines would vie for first place in the conifer division: the eastern white pine and the long-leaf pine. It would be a close contest, the white pine perhaps excelling for its shapeliness and the long-leaf pine for the music of the wind in its branches, which conjures up visions of pale dusty roads glowing in the moonlight as pines murmur a duet with the chuck-will's-widow.

The long-leaf pine can grow up to 130 feet (40 m) tall, although it is more often 60–70 feet (18–21 m) tall, and it can reach a diameter of 3⅓ feet (1 m). It tends to have a straight trunk and an irregularly shaped crown. No eastern pine has longer needles, from 8 to 18 inches (20–45 cm) and up to 20 inches (50 cm) long on very young specimens. The needles are a deep green, are soft and flexible, and are in bundles of three; typically they droop in close clusters at the ends of the branches.

This tree can produce copious amounts of wind-borne pollen, sometimes so thick it coats the surface of leaves, cars, spiderwebs,

Long-leaf pine, *Pinus palustris*

ponds, and everything in sight with a delicate yellow dust. The pollen is produced at the tips of the twigs on cylindrical brown or purplish-brown male cones that are 1¼–2⅜ inches (3–6 cm) long. The female cones are initially a lovely shade of purple and after pollination develop into elongated woody cones up to 10 inches (25 cm) long and 2⅜ inches (6 cm) wide; the cone scales have a very short, sometimes curved prickle. The cones, which are produced every 3–7 years, tend to open quickly once they are mature and soon drop from the tree.

A seedling long-leaf pine does not immediately develop an above-ground stem but spends its first few years growing a taproot that will help the mature plant withstand drought and fire. At this stage, it looks almost like a clump of deep green grass. Later the stem begins to elongate, but branches may not form for a few more years; during this stage, a thick, fire-resistant bark is forming. Growth may be slow at first, but long-leaf pines can live as long as 300 years.

The long-leaf pine, also known as southern yellow pine, is a very important commercial species in the South, where it is used for lumber, for pulpwood to make paper, and to produce turpentine, tar, and resins.

Eastern white pine (*Pinus strobus* L.) may be found on the coastal plain from Newfoundland south to Delaware (as well as inland to south-central Canada and south to the southern Appalachians).

The tallest of the northeastern conifers, it may reach over 100 feet (30 m) in height and over 6½ feet (2 m) in diameter; old-growth trees are said to have been as much as 230 feet (70 m) tall!

The white pine tends to grow rapidly and straight up, with horizontal branches extending in whorls, like the spokes of a wheel, one whorl added each year. The bark is smooth and gray on young trees, becoming darker, thicker, and more furrowed with age. Its slender, soft needles are in bundles of five, are 3–5 inches (8–13 cm) in length, and have a bluish-green cast. The cylindrical, often curved female cones are up to 8 inches (20 cm) long and 1–2 inches (2.5–5 cm) wide and lack a prickle on the scales of the cones. Heavy crops are produced about every 3–5 years.

The eastern white pine has a long history of valuable commercial use, its wood being light, strong, easy to work with, and not as resinous as that of other pines. Quarrels over who had the rights to take the massive white pines—the ever-building European settlers or the lumber-hungry agents seeking masts for the king's Royal Navy—may have helped hasten the onset of the Revolutionary War. Today the wood is used for framing, cabinet work, wood carving, and pulpwood, among other uses.

Loblolly pine (*Pinus taeda* L.) is also a very valuable commercial species and an important component of southern coastal plain and piedmont ecosystems. This fast-growing tree grows well in old fields and logging sites and may reach 165 feet (50 m) in height and 3⅓ feet (1 m) in diameter. Other tall pines found in the book's range include yellow or short-leaf pine (*Pinus echinata* P. Mill.) and slash pine (*Pinus elliottii* Engelm.). As a group, the pines are extremely important for wildlife. Not only are the seeds and foliage eaten by many species of birds and mammals, but also the trees are home to a host of insects and other invertebrates and provide shelter and nesting sites for scores of animals.

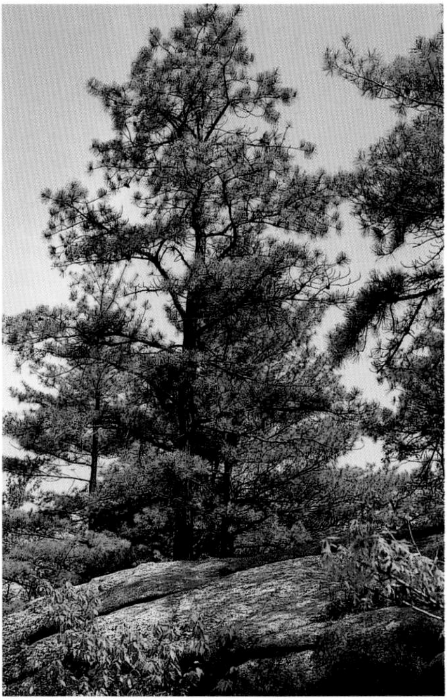

Pitch pine,
Pinus rigida

Pitch Pine

Pinus rigida P. Mill.
Pine Family, Pinaceae

RANGE: Southern Quebec, Ontario, and Maine south to northern Georgia and west to Kentucky, Tennessee, and West Virginia; a coastal plain species from southern New England to New Jersey; inland and mostly in the mountains south of Maryland.
HABITAT: Dry, sandy, or sterile soils, including interdune and backdune areas from Massachusetts to New Jersey.

Pitch pine is the dominant pine on Cape Cod and in the pine barrens of New Jersey and Long Island. The coastal plain pitch pine forests are home to a fascinating group of plants and animals, which somehow manage to survive in the sterile sandy soils that are interlaced with acidic bogs.

Each pitch pine tree has a unique shape, especially in areas influenced by salt-laden winds off the ocean. It is rare to find a pitch pine with a perfectly straight trunk, and the spreading branches, too, are irregular and often crooked. Pitch pines have long taproots and strong lateral roots that anchor them in the sandy or rocky soils where they thrive. Although pitch pines can grow as tall as 100 feet (30 m), they are more typically 40–60 feet (12–18 m) in height or even shorter in frequently burned areas or sites exposed to salt spray. In the pine plains of New Jersey, for example, the pitch pines have a shrubby, dwarf form and may grow no taller than 4 feet (1.2 m).

The stiff, twisted needles of pitch pine appear in bundles of three, are usually 3–6 inches (7.5–15 cm) long, and can often be found growing in clusters directly out of the tree trunk. The dark gray bark is composed of rough, thick plates divided by furrows; the twigs are reddish-brown.

As in all pines, the male and female flowers are separate. The male flowers are clustered at the tips of the twigs in purplish cylindrical cones, often yellow with pollen, less than ¾ inch (2 cm) in length; they release the pollen and then wither away. The female flowers develop into short-stalked, squat woody cones that are often in bunches of two or three and may persist on the tree for several years. These cones may be almost egg-shaped or quite broad at the base; they are usually 1½–3⅛ inches (4–8 cm) long. Each cone scale has a sharp curved prickle at the tip.

Because of their thick bark and long taproots, pitch pines are extremely resistant to damage from fires and can sprout from stumps and roots. The cones are actually dependent on fires to open, and periodic fires also help eliminate competing species that would crowd out pitch pine, which is less tolerant of shade than many other species.

Pitch pine has been used to build houses, boats, floors, and bridges. The wood is very durable, but it has a reputation for being weak, being difficult to work with, and holding nails poorly (a distinct disadvantage for a ship at sea!). The tree was once used to make charcoal, and tar, pitch, and turpentine have been extracted from it; because of its high resin content, it has also been used to make torches.

Other short to medium-sized pines grow on the coastal plain. From extreme southern New Jersey to central and western Florida, pond pine or pocosin pine (*Pinus serotina* Michx.) may be found in bogs, swamps, pocosins, and wet woods. It grows 40–80 feet (12–

25 m) tall and like pitch pine may have an irregular shape, with many short, crooked, tangled branches. Its flexible needles are in bundles of three or four and are 4–10 inches (10–25 cm) long. The short-stalked, often-clustered cones are egg-shaped or rounded, are 1½–3⅛ inches (4–8 cm) long, and have a weak prickle (or none at all) at the tip of each cone scale. Similar to pitch pine cones, the cones of pond pine are dependent on fire, and the trees can sprout from burned-over stumps and roots.

Virginia or scrub pine (*Pinus virginiana* P. Mill.) may also be encountered on the coastal plain from Virginia north to Long Island, although it is more common inland into the piedmont and mountains of the southeastern and south-central states. It prefers dry rocky or sandy soils and is often a pioneer species in old fields and poor soils. It grows 33–66 feet (10–20 m) tall, with flexible, soft, dark green needles up to 3 inches (8 cm) long and typically in bundles of two. The egg-shaped cones of this species have slender, straight prickles and may persist on the tree for many years. It is often used to restore forests on exhausted soils.

Sand pine (*Pinus clausa* [Chapman *ex* Engelm.] Vasey *ex* Sarg.) grows in northern and central Florida and southern Alabama and thrives on nutrient-poor, sandy soils both inland and along the coast. It is a short tree that often takes a bushy form; although it may grow as tall as 80 feet (25 m), it is usually much shorter. The needles are in bundles of two and are 2–3½ inches (5–9 cm) long. The cones are 2–3⅛ inches (5–8 cm) long and may remain on the tree for many years unless the tree burns.

Bald Cypress

Taxodium distichum (L.) L. C. Rich.
Bald Cypress Family, Taxodiaceae

RANGE: Coastal plain from Delaware (and perhaps Long Island) south to southern Florida and west to Texas and Mexico; also up the Mississippi River valley to southern Indiana and Illinois.
HABITAT: Margins of lakes, swamps, and rivers and occasionally in brackish water; grows best in soils of moderate fertility where moisture is abundant and usually permanent.

Bald cypress is a long-lived tree that can be up to 2,000 years old (although 500–600 years is more common), by which time it may

Bald cypress,
Taxodium distichum

reach 130 feet (40 m) in height and 5–13 feet (1.5–4 m) in diameter. It can be recognized easily because it usually grows in standing water, has a distinctive wide, flaring base, and is surrounded by conical pointed structures called knees that grow from the roots of the tree.

The flaring bases and knees provide support for the trees, and both are composed of material with much larger cells than the wood of the trunk. It is believed that these large cells supply extra air to the trees to make up for the oxygen-poor wet soils in which the trees grow, but they may also serve to store carbohydrates.

Young trees have narrow pyramidal crowns, but with age, the crown becomes flatter, rounder, and smaller in proportion to the height of the tree. The bark of bald cypress is thin, and on older trees, ridged.

The leaves are light green, linear, and flat. They are up to ⅝ inch (16 mm) long and lie in a flat plane along a short twig or branchlet, giving the twig a feathery appearance. In the autumn, the whole branchlet is shed, and new ones develop the following spring.

Unlike most trees in this region, bald cypress is monoecious (meaning that the male and female flowers grow in different places on the same tree). The male flowers are 1⁄16-inch (2 mm) structures borne on cones that dangle on branching clusters up to 5½ inches (14 cm) long. The female flowers are globular cones approximately ¾ inch (2 cm) in diameter and are composed of angular scales attached at the center. Both male and female flowers are produced from buds that develop in autumn and mature and are shed during the following summer or fall.

Although very little bald cypress remains for lumbering—due primarily to overlumbering and drainage of the wetlands where the tree grows—it is extremely valuable timber. The lumber is of medium weight, strong, extremely resistant to decay, and of a texture that can be used for almost any type of construction: siding, shingles, and even dugout canoes. The heartwood is especially beautiful, with alternate light and dark brown stripes. It is used for interior finish work and paneling.

Bald cypress makes a fine ornamental tree, especially when planted near wet areas (although it is able to grow in more upland areas). In cultivation, it grows as far north as Boston.

Pond cypress (*Taxodium ascendens* Brongn.), which some authorities treat as a variety of bald cypress, grows from southeastern Virginia south to Florida and west to Louisiana. The mature leaves of pond cypress often droop and are needle-shaped with sharp tips; they press against the stems rather than having the flaring, feathery appearance of bald cypress. The knees of pond cypress tend to be more rounded than those of bald cypress. Pond cypress is less common than bald cypress and grows in scattered locations on the coastal plain in swamps, pocosins, bogs, pond margins, and wet savannas.

The name *Taxodium* means "resembling yew," referring to the fact that the leaves have the appearance of the familiar yew plant used for hedges around many suburban homes.

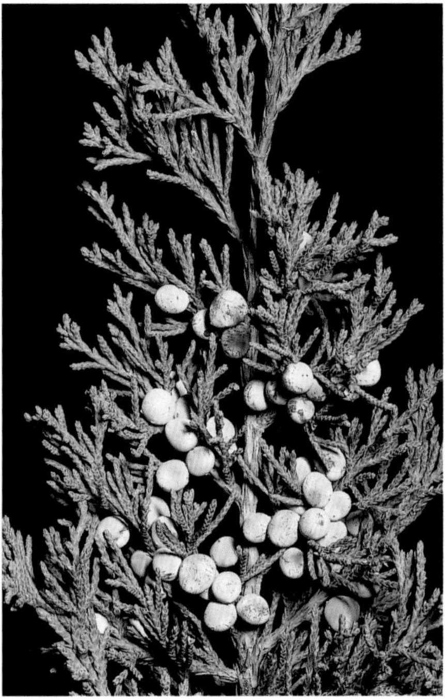

Eastern red cedar,
Juniperus virginiana

Eastern Red Cedar

Juniperus virginiana L. var. *virginiana*
Cypress Family, Cupressaceae

RANGE: Southern Quebec and southern Maine south to northwest Florida and west to North Dakota, Oklahoma, and Texas.
HABITAT: Borders of tidal salt and brackish marshes and in a variety of soils, especially dry, infertile, or calcareous sites such as abandoned fields and pastures.

Eastern red cedar is the most widely distributed conifer that grows to tree size in the United States. It is a medium-sized evergreen tree with yellowish-green to dark green foliage and shredding bright brown bark. Mature plants may be 33–65 feet (10–20 m) in height.

The shape of the tree varies widely in different regions, often taking a pyramidal shape in the South but a more slender columnar form at its northern limits. Some trees in the northern portion of the range may be only one-fifth as wide as they are tall.

The foliage of red cedar has a pleasant fragrance. Juvenile leaves are needlelike and arranged in nonoverlapping, opposite pairs (or sometimes whorls of three) of flat, sharp-pointed leaves that are pale on the upper surface and shiny green underneath. Mature leaves are scalelike and arranged in opposite, tightly overlapping pairs. A single branch may have both needlelike and scalelike leaves.

Red cedar is usually dioecious, with separate male and female trees, but occasionally a tree will have both male and female flowers. The male flowers are in cylindrical cones approximately 1/8 inch (3 mm) long borne in large numbers on the tips of small twigs; the pollen may be shed from January to March. Female cones are small and hardly visible at the tips of small twigs. The fruits are technically cones, but they look more like round berries. They are up to 5/16 inch (8 mm) in diameter and change from pale green to turquoise blue to blue-black with a waxy bloom like a blueberry by the time they are ripe in October or November. These ripe berries have a pleasant aromatic taste and are used in cooking as well as to flavor certain alcoholic beverages, including gin. They are also an important source of food for many birds, such as cedar waxwings, and mammals.

Red cedar lumber is highly prized. It is rusty red and cream-colored in wide irregular stripes and is sought after for use in closets or chests because the aromatic oils and resins in the wood repel insects that damage cloth, especially wool. Cedar trees were once used to make rail fences; then, when the wood became scarce many cedar rail fences were sold to make pencils. Now pencils are made from a variety of other substances, including plastic.

Eastern red cedar is more likely to be found growing in infertile soils inland, but it also grows along the edges of tidal salt and brackish marshes in both the northern and southern portions of its range, where it is often associated with vigorous stands of salt hay grass (*Spartina patens*). Healthy plants can be found in areas that are inundated by salt water at irregular intervals, such as places flooded after storms, but not in areas covered by daily tides.

Southern red cedar (*Juniperus virginiana* L. var. *silicicola* [Small] J. Silba) is similar but tends to be smaller with a more rounded crown. It grows in sandy coastal plain habitats, including dunes and the upper edges of tidal marshes, from North Carolina south to central Florida and west to southeastern Texas. The branches of southern red cedar are often pendulous, sometimes sweeping the ground, and the branchlets tend to be more slender than those of the eastern red cedar. The needles have a yellowish-green cast, unlike the dark green needles of eastern red cedar, and the tree sheds its pollen in January and February.

Narrow-leaved Cattail

Typha angustifolia L.
Cattail Family, Typhaceae

RANGE: Nearly cosmopolitan and throughout this book's range.
HABITAT: Freshwater and brackish marshes.

Narrow-leaved cattail is common in wet to damp areas near salt water and appears to be spreading along inland bodies of water and wetlands. The broad-leaved cattail (*Typha latifolia* L.) has leaves, stems, and "cattails" that are more than twice as wide as those of the narrow-leaved cattail and is more often found in fresh water. Another species with fairly narrow leaves, southern cattail (*Typha domingensis* Pers.), also grows in this book's range. This species is pantropical, reaching as far north along the Atlantic coast as Maryland and Delaware and inland as far west as Nebraska, Utah, and northern California. Like the narrow-leaved cattail, it grows more frequently in alkaline and brackish waters. The three species are known to hybridize.

Cattails are perennial plants with creeping rhizomes. They are monoecious and have structures somewhat similar to those of Jack-in-the-pulpit (*Arisaema triphyllum*) and skunk cabbage (*Symplocarpus foetidus*). The spadix (equivalent to the "Jack" in Jack-in-the-pulpit) is the elongated structure that bears the male and female flowers. The spathe (the "pulpit" in Jack-in-the-pulpit) is reduced to a bract at the base of the male or female flower segment and may be lacking entirely in some species of cattail.

In all cattails, the male flowers are arranged around the upper portion of the flowering stalk. Forming a cylinder below the male flowers are the female flowers, which develop the familiar brown, sausage-shaped structure and then the cottony fruit.

In broad-leaved cattail, usually little to no space separates the lower portion of the male flowers from the upper portion of the dark brown female flowers, and the female segment frequently does

Narrow-leaved cattail,
Typha angustifolia

not have a bract at its base. The flat leaves of this species may grow 3⅓–10 feet (1–3 m) in height and usually are taller than the flowering stalks.

In narrow-leaved cattail, a distance of ⅜–4¾ inches (1–12 cm) may separate the male flowers from the reddish-brown female flower segment. In the southern cattail, at least a slight space usually divides the two types of flowers, and the female flowers are pale brown. Both of these species have convex leaves and a bract at the base of the female flowers. The leaves of narrow-leaved cattail are usually strongly convex and overtop the flowering stalk, whereas the leaves of southern cattail are weakly convex and generally about the same height or a little shorter than the flowering stalk. This species, however, is the tallest of the three and may grow to over 13 feet (4 m) in height.

Cattails are very important to wildlife, offering shelter, breeding sites, food, and materials for nest and den construction for a variety of mammals, birds, reptiles, amphibians, fish, and invertebrates. People have also used these plants for centuries as sources of food, medicine, and fiber.

Seaside Arrow-grass

Triglochin maritimum L.
Arrow-grass Family, Juncaginaceae

RANGE: Circumboreal, as far south as Delaware in this book's range; also in southern South America.
HABITAT: Salt, brackish, and freshwater marshes.

Seaside arrow-grass is a component of the irregularly flooded upper areas of salt and brackish marshes, where it often grows in association with black rush (*Juncus gerardii*), saltgrass (*Distichlis spicata*), and salt hay grass (*Spartina patens*). In New England, seaside arrow-grass is common in marshes with a well-developed peat substrate but is rarely encountered where the substrate is predominantly sand.

Seaside arrow-grass is an inconspicuous rushlike perennial, with erect leaves growing directly from the base of the plant. Although it resembles both true grasses and rushes, it is a member of the arrow-grass family, a small family with only about ten species worldwide. Unlike members of the grass family, which have leaves with flat blades attached to hollow cylindrical sheaths, arrow-grass has fleshy leaves that are flat on top and cylindrical underneath. In cross section, the leaves are shaped like half circles. The flaring sheaths at the base of the leaves are conspicuous and persist after the leaves die.

Arrow-grass plants grow in separate tufts often intermingled with rushes and grasses, so they are sometimes difficult to distinguish. From May, however, when they begin to bloom, until late fall, the distinctive flowers and seeds make arrow-grass easy to recognize.

The green, wind-pollinated flowers are only $\frac{1}{32}$–$\frac{1}{16}$ inch (1–2 mm) across. They are widely spaced along a stalk that ranges from 8 to 32 inches (20–80 cm) tall and usually stands above the leaves. The flowers have two rows of cup-shaped petal-like structures that enclose 3–6 stamens and 3–6 ovaries that are surmounted by silvery

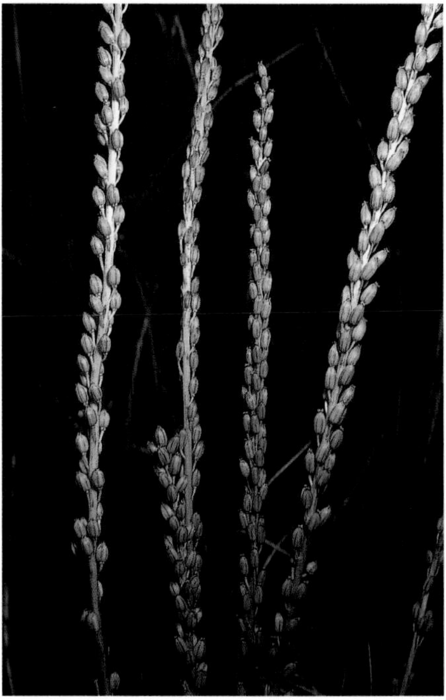

Seaside arrow-grass,
Triglochin maritimum

stigmas resembling tinsel stars. The flowers are followed by elongated 12-winged fruits.

Arrow-grass has been known to cause cyanide poisoning in sheep and cattle. Although some toxicity may be lost when the plants are dried for hay, the hydrocyanic acid that remains is in a chemical form that is more accessible than that in fresh material; however, it dissipates after several months of storage. Unlike poisonous plants that are distasteful to animals, the green plants of arrow-grass are not especially unpalatable and may be readily eaten by hungry sheep or cattle. Many species of ducks eat the seeds of arrow-grass, apparently without ill effects.

Southern arrow-grass (*Triglochin striatum* Ruiz & Pavón) is a tropical species that grows in salt and brackish marshes as far north as Maryland and Delaware. It is smaller than seaside arrow-grass, with leaves up to 16 inches (40 cm) in height. The flower stalks are usually shorter than the leaves, and the fruit is rounded in shape.

Although it is rare in this book's range, slender arrow-grass (*Triglochin palustre* L.) is a northern species that may be found in brackish marshes south to New York. It is also a smaller plant than seaside arrow-grass, reaching only 8–16 inches (20–40 cm) in height. The fruit is an elongated three-winged capsule.

American Beachgrass

Ammophila breviligulata Fern.
Grass Family, Poaceae

RANGE: Along the Atlantic coast from Newfoundland south to North Carolina; inland around the Great Lakes and Lake Champlain.
HABITAT: Dunes and sandy shores.

Unlike other common grasses, which die if the growing point is covered by only a few inches of soil or sand, American beachgrass has the unique ability to survive and grow when the growing point is deeply covered after a storm. In addition to being able to survive burial, American beachgrass sends out thick horizontal rhizomes just below the surface of the soil and quickly stabilizes the sand. The name of this genus, *Ammophila*, means "to love sand."

Even the most stable dune may not be able to withstand a violent storm. If a severe storm breaches a stabilized dune, however, the cut will show a dense three-dimensional mesh of tough rhizomes, stems, and roots that reveals why this grass is so effective in building dunes.

The stalks of American beachgrass usually range in height from 20 to 40 inches (50–100 cm). They grow in tufts containing several stalks each and are connected by tough rhizomes that spread in several directions from the base of the plant.

The leaf blade is dark green, contains tough fibers, and is rough on the upper surface. It extends into a fibrous sheath that continues to the base of the plant. When the leaves are mature, the outer edges are rolled under, making them appear cylindrical. Unrolled, the leaves are $5/32$–$5/16$ inch (4–8 mm) wide, with the ligule between the sheath and blade no more than $1/8$ inch (3 mm) wide.

When beachgrass blooms in the summer, each stalk carries a snow-white plume of massed stamens that are borne in a somewhat

American beachgrass, *Ammophila breviligulata*

compressed panicle 4–16 inches (10–40 cm) long, with the base often partially enclosed in the upper sheath.

In the places where it grows best, American beachgrass is sometimes cultivated, and mature stalks are transplanted to eroded areas. This gives better results than planting seed. When transplanting was first attempted, it was quickly found that leaving ample space between the transplants not only was more economical but also restored the dunes to a more natural state. Thick plantings resulted in dense growth that was more easily washed away by storms because the water could not run between the plants.

The effectiveness of European beachgrass (*Ammophila arenaria* [L.] Link) for binding sand on high windswept dunes was recognized in England in the sixteenth century. The water-resistant character of the plant was well known, and large quantities were cut and used to make mats to keep haystacks dry, for thatch, and for baskets. The erosion that resulted from excessive cutting became so severe that Queen Elizabeth I restricted destructive cutting and encouraged planting.

Dune sandbur, *Cenchrus tribuloides*

Dune Sandbur, Sandspur

Cenchrus tribuloides L.
Grass Family, Poaceae

RANGE: Southern New York south to Florida and west to Louisiana.
HABITAT: Dunes and sandy fields in the outer coastal plain.

Of the several species of sandbur that grow within this book's range, this is one of the largest and most vigorous. *Cenchrus tribuloides* is a semierect or trailing annual with profuse branches that may be up to 40 inches (1 m) long. The burs that contain the seeds are arranged along stalks and have 5–40 irregular, flattened, barbed spines almost hidden in a mass of woolly white hair. These spines are usually less than ¼ inch (7 mm) long, but if stepped on, they can cause painful wounds.

Another species, common sandbur (*Cenchrus longispinus* [Hack.] Fern.), is also a spreading or ascending annual grass but is usually somewhat smaller than dune sandbur and tends to be a weed growing in disturbed soils rather than a dune plant. It is found from Maine south to Florida and west to Texas, California, and Oregon.

The most obvious difference between the two species is that the burs on common sandbur each have 45–75 spines and lack the shaggy hair characteristic of those on dune sandbur. The spines of common sandbur are also more slender but are equally sharp pointed.

In the southern parts of this book's range, two other *Cenchrus* species may be found. *Cenchrus echinatus* L., aptly named Hedgehog-grass, grows in sandy fields, dunes, and the edges of forests from North Carolina south to tropical America and west to California. It grows in sprawling clumps, with stems up to 40 inches (1 m) tall. The burs of this species tend to be less crowded along the stalks than those of the former two species, and a ring of bristles circles the base of each bur.

Coastal sandbur (*Cenchrus carolinianus* Walt., which includes *Cenchrus incertus* M. A. Curtis) may also be found in sandy soils from southeastern Virginia south to tropical America and west to the Central Plains and California. The burs of this species are smaller than those of the others described here and have few spines; the body of each bur is densely covered with fine hairs.

Sandbur fruits no doubt are an effective mechanism for dispersing seeds as they become attached to fur and clothing and travel to new sites, serving as another example of nature's many hitchhikers.

Saltgrass, Spikegrass

Distichlis spicata (L.) Greene
Grass Family, Poaceae

RANGE: Along the Atlantic coast from Nova Scotia south to Florida and west along the Gulf coast through Texas and to tropical America; also on the Pacific coast and inland in salt flats and marshes in every state west of the Mississippi River except Arkansas.
HABITAT: Upper levels of both tidal and inland salt marshes and flats.

Saltgrass is a perennial grass that occupies relatively less space in most marshes than either smooth cordgrass (*Spartina alterniflora*) or salt hay grass (*Spartina patens*). It can grow in areas that may be dry most of the summer, and it may also move into wetter areas, such as sites occupied by tall reed (*Phragmites australis*) or hightide bush (*Iva frutescens*). Sometimes it grows in patches next to other plants such as black rush (*Juncus gerardii*), or it may be mixed with salt hay grass. The late botanist and author Bill Niering called salt-

Saltgrass, *Distichlis spicata*

grass "the red maple of the tidal marsh" because of its broad tolerance for wetness.

Saltgrass plants may be 6–18 inches (15–45 cm) tall, depending on growing conditions, and may grow erect or prostrate. The plants have spike-shaped seed heads that taper at both ends; relatively short, two-ranked gray-green or blue-green leaves; and overlapping leaf sheaths. The leaves are 2–4 inches (5–10 cm) long and may be flat or rolled inward. The name *Distichlis* refers to the ranking of the leaves, which are arranged alternately in two rows along the vertical axis.

The flower spikes of saltgrass are ½–3⅛ inches (1.2–8 cm) long and up to ¾ inch (2 cm) wide, with male and female flowers on separate plants. The spikes are composed of smaller two-ranked spikelets that are compressed into a spindle-shaped head that tapers at both ends. In bloom, the male flower heads are covered with numerous conspicuous anthers that are either creamy white or bright purple.

Saltgrass produces small, flat, brown seeds, but reproduction takes place more often by tough rhizomes that push into stands of other species. These rhizomes enable saltgrass to colonize salt pannes, creating shade and lowering the temperature and salinity of the pannes so that plants like salt hay grass and black rush can move in.

Saltgrass has salt-secreting glands at the tips of the stems. These are not conspicuously in use at the salinities found in tidal salt marshes. In areas such as around Great Salt Lake with high levels of salt that inhibit the growth of everything but green algae, however, saltgrass excretes salt with these glands and builds hummocks of soil with a salt content low enough that other plants can colonize and grow in the area.

Stands of saltgrass are usually more common and more vigorous in marshes that were ditched extensively for mosquito control in the 1930s or diked for production of salt hay. Because saltgrass is able to thrive in continuously saturated soil, some marshes with wide mosquito-control ditches and spoil banks that keep water impounded in the ditches may have almost solid stands of saltgrass from ditch to ditch. Saltgrass is also able to move quickly into former upland and freshwater areas that are flooded due to rising sea level. In undisturbed marshes, little or no saltgrass may grow, even at the upper edges.

It would be hard to mistake saltgrass for any other species in northern salt marshes, but in the South, it might be confused with coastal dropseed (*Sporobolus virginicus* [L.] Kunth). This species grows as far north as Virginia and can also be found in the upper area of salt marshes. An erect plant that may grow to 2 feet (60 cm) in height, it also has two-ranked, inwardly rolling leaves with overlapping sheaths. Its flower spike is generally longer and more narrow than that of saltgrass, however, and the leaves on the upper portion of the stem are much shorter than the lower leaves.

Wild Rye, Terrell Grass

Elymus virginicus L.
Grass Family, Poaceae

RANGE: Newfoundland south to Florida and west to Alberta and Arizona.
HABITAT: Borders of salt, brackish, and freshwater marshes; also in thickets, damp meadows, and moist shores.

Wild rye is a perennial that varies in height from 12 to 48 inches (30–120 cm) and grows in clumps or tussocks. The plants do not have rhizomes (although the base of the stem may sometimes grow horizontally for a short distance), and they reproduce entirely from

Wild rye,
Elymus virginicus
var. *halophilus*

seed. Since they are tufted perennials, their size increases with time and varies considerably according to the age of the plants.

Most of the stems have 6–10 leaves, which are 5⁄32–½ inch (4–12 mm) wide, rough on both sides, and usually rolled inward on the upper surface. The flowers are terminal and arranged in a stiff, erect, unbranched spike 1½–8 inches (4–20 cm) long. They are packed closely together, and each flower has a straight hairlike awn that projects above the flower. The flowers bloom from June to October.

The ripe seeds resemble grains of rye. They are hairy at the upper end and retain the layers of chaff when they are shed. The seeds remain on the plants into the late fall and winter, making them a valuable food for birds and other wildlife.

Like other plants that grow over a large area, this species is variable both in physical characteristics and in physiological adaptations. Although most varieties of wild rye grow in upland habitats, one, *Elymus virginicus* L. var. *halophilus* (Bickn.) Wieg., grows in tidal salt marshes and brackish areas from Nova Scotia to Virginia and in alkaline soils in Minnesota. The variety name *halophilus* comes from the Greek word meaning "salt-loving."

The plants that grow in saline soils are usually blue-green and have a waxy coating like the bloom on a blueberry. In addition, the flower spikes have white stripings between the stripes of green, and the leaves tend to be coiled rather than flat. Other varieties of *Elymus virginicus* are green throughout and lack the bluish bloom and white stripings. *Elymus virginicus* var. *halophilus* grows best at the edges of tidal marshes that are high in organic matter, in association with salt hay grass (*Spartina patens*), but is rarely found growing in sandy soils or in areas of salt marshes inundated by daily tidal flow. Some forms of wild rye grow in brackish soils on the margins of tidal salt marshes, particularly those that have been modified by roads or have been augmented with fill soil.

Elymus virginicus var. *halophilus* resembles both American dunegrass (*Leymus mollis* [Trin.] Hara, formerly *Elymus mollis* Trin.) and lyme grass (*Leymus arenarius* [L.] Hochst, formerly *Elymus arenarius* L.), but both of these species are dune grasses and do not grow in tidal marshes. In this book's range, American dunegrass grows only as far south as Massachusetts. Lyme grass is a native of Europe that has naturalized around the shores of the Great Lakes.

Sweet Grass

Hierochloe odorata (L.) Beauv.
Grass Family, Poaceae

RANGE: Circumboreal, as far south as New Jersey and Maryland in this book's range.
HABITAT: Freshwater and brackish marshes, meadows, shores, and swales.

Sweet grass is the first grass to bloom in the spring in tidal marshes. In late April, flowering stems push up through the dead leaves left from the previous year. By early May, the new stems are 12–24 inches (30–60 cm) long and have two or three short leaves and a pyramid of creamy white flowers at the upper end.

Individually, the flowers are small and inconspicuous, but in mass, they make a striking lacy border around the brackish marshes where they often grow. By the time the flowering stalks fade, long

Sweet grass,
Hierochloe odorata

vegetative stems have developed from buds on the rhizomes, and the leaves on the stems, unlike those on the flowering stalks, are soft and pliable and, in the northern part of the range, may be 30 inches (80 cm) long and ¼–½ inch (7–12 mm) wide.

These long leaves are glossy and extremely fragrant. The odor of even two or three leaves in an automobile on a hot summer day is almost overwhelming with the fragrance of coumarin, which is similar to vanilla. Another common name for this species is vanilla grass.

For years, the Micmacs in northern Maine and Canada have made baskets from the long leaves of this grass. They are frequently twisted into slender cords and woven over dry oak splints. A common shape is a round basket with a cover and no handle. The fragrance of the leaves will last for years and is especially noticeable on damp foggy days.

In Europe, this species of grass is known as holy grass, and on certain Christian festival days, its leaves are strewn before church doors. The leaves have also been used to flavor vodka in Poland.

Southern sweet grass, *Muhlenbergia capillaris*

Southern Sweet Grass, Purple Hairgrass

Muhlenbergia capillaris (Lam.) Trin.
Grass Family, Poaceae

RANGE: Along the Atlantic coast from Massachusetts south to Florida and the West Indies and west along the Gulf coast to Texas; inland to Indiana, Kansas, and Oklahoma.
HABITAT: Moist flats between coastal dunes, stabilized dunes, and salt shrub thickets as well as inland; usually on clay, sandy, or rocky soils.

Southern sweet grass is a perennial that grows in round clumps or tussocks 20–40 inches (50–100 cm) wide. The leaves are rolled inward and arched outward like water in a fountain. The leaves begin to roll when very young, with the outer edges curling toward the midrib on the upper surface of the leaf; when mature, the leaves appear to be round rather than flat.

The flower stalks are slightly longer than the leaves and stand erect in a clump in the middle of the tussock. The flowers have the simple structure of grasses, with anthers that are pink when they bloom in October but darken to purple by November.

In the seventeenth century, this species of *Muhlenbergia* was used on southern rice plantations to make the large, round, flat-bottomed winnowing baskets in which rice grains were separated from the chaff. As the rice was tossed upward, the wind would blow away the lighter chaff and the heavier grain would fall back into the basket.

These baskets were made in the tradition of a coiled type of basketry brought from Africa. They are similar to the coiled baskets of the Native Americans of the Southwest, but the two types can be easily distinguished. To make the baskets, several strands of *Muhlenbergia* were coiled tightly and secured with strips of cabbage palm (*Sabal palmetto*) leaves or the flattened stems of needlerush (*Juncus roemerianus*).

In modern times, these baskets are valued as works of art and are very much in demand. They come in many shapes and sizes and often have decorative patterns made with plain or knotted needles of long-leaf pine (*Pinus palustris*). The demand for the baskets has so depleted the native stands of southern sweet grass that conservation groups around Charleston, South Carolina, and Savannah, Georgia, are trying to develop methods of cultivating it.

Most of the more familiar coastal grasses, such as American beachgrass (*Ammophila breviligulata*), sea oats (*Uniola paniculata*), the *Spartina* species, and common reed (*Phragmites australis*), propagate primarily vegetatively rather than by seed. Since *Muhlenbergia capillaris* is one of the few species of this genus that does not produce stolons, cultivating it may be a challenge.

The system of nomenclature used in this book includes *Muhlenbergia filipes* M. A. Curtis in *Muhlenbergia capillaris*.

Switchgrass

Panicum virgatum L.
Grass Family, Poaceae

RANGE: Quebec and Nova Scotia south to the West Indies and west to Manitoba, Montana, Arizona, and Mexico.
HABITAT: Primarily a freshwater species of dry or moist sandy soils in open woods, fields, and roadsides; in this book's range, often found on the landward side of brackish marshes, shores, and dunes.

Switchgrass is a handsome grass that is seen frequently along the coast landward of areas that are permanently saline. Occasional drenching by salt water during a storm will kill the leaves, but the

Switchgrass,
Panicum virgatum

plant itself will usually survive. It is not adapted, however, to living in permanently saline soils.

Although switchgrass often grows in solid stands, near the ocean it is usually found in clumps with hard rhizomes and a vigorous root system. The clumps are 2–3 feet (60–90 cm) wide with stiff, erect, flowering stalks that may rise 5–6½ feet (1.5–2 m) above the arching leaves. The leaves have somewhat hairy sheaths and a ring of hairs where the sheath and blade join.

The leaf blades are ½ inch (12 mm) wide and 6–12 inches (15–30 cm) long, tapering to a slender point. The leaves are thin, glossy, and bluish-green overlaid with purple on the upper surfaces and edges and dull on the underside, with an inconspicuous midrib.

The flower stalks bear delicate panicles with widely spaced brown flowers in midsummer. By late August, the seeds have ripened and are shed, providing food for migrating birds.

Switchgrass is most conspicuous in October when the saltmarsh grasses have faded to gray and switchgrass has turned a brilliant golden-brown. In spite of the delicate texture of the leaves, they resist weathering and persist through the winter and into the following growing season. Dead leaves and stems from the previous year may be found among the current season's growth as late as September.

Seaside panicum (*Panicum amarum* Ell.), another perennial member of this genus, is found on coastal dunes and in sandy coastal soils from Rhode Island (where it is very rare) and Connecticut south to Florida and west to Texas. The stems of seaside panicum, which range from 16 inches (40 cm) to 8 feet (2.4 m) in length, may grow in a cluster or take an elongated solitary form and root at the lower nodes. Unlike switchgrass, which has an open, loose inflorescence, seaside panicum has a very compressed panicle of flowers. The whole plant is smooth and has a whitish cast. Along with American beachgrass (*Ammophila breviligulata*) and sea oats (*Uniola paniculata*), seaside panicum is considered one of the most important grasses for stabilizing dunes.

Some authorities separate beachgrass (*Panicum amarulum* A. S. Hitchc. & Chase) from this species, but according to the system used here, beachgrass is included in *Panicum amarum*.

As a group, the *Panicum* species are very important plants for wildlife, providing seed and forage for numerous species of birds and mammals.

Common or Tall Reed, Phragmites

Phragmites australis (Cav.) Trin. *ex* Steud.
Grass Family, Poaceae

RANGE: Nearly cosmopolitan, on all continents except Antarctica; in this book's range, most common from Massachusetts to Virginia and spreading from North Carolina south to Florida.
HABITAT: Tidal brackish marshes, freshwater marshes and wet shores, streambanks, damp roadside ditches, and sand dunes.

Phragmites is probably the most widely distributed flowering plant in the world. Natural stands are found in Europe, Asia, Africa, North and South America, and Australia and are probably absent only in Antarctica, New Zealand, Polynesia, the Arctic, and some oceanic islands. It grows from Finland to the humid lowlands of the

Common reed,
Phragmites australis

equator in freshwater wetlands, salt deserts, and salt marshes and at elevations of up to 10,000 feet (3,000 m) in Tibet.

It is a perennial grass that grows 4–12 feet (1.2–3.7 m) tall (sometimes up to 18 feet [5.5 m]) and spreads rapidly. Common reed can produce seeds, but it usually propagates vegetatively through a network of underground rhizomes or through stolons that run along the surface of the ground and root at the nodes. These stolons can elongate as much as 20 feet (6 m) during a single growing season in the cool climate of New England and grow even faster in the Tropics.

The leaves of phragmites are 6–20 inches (15–50 cm) long and 1⅛ inches (3 cm) wide and taper to a slender point. Both surfaces are smooth, but the margins are rough to touch. The sheaths are overlapping, also smooth with rough edges, and hairy where the leaf and sheath join. The flowers are borne in an elongated panicle at the upper end of the stalks. They may be white or dark red and fertile or sterile.

Even though common reed has some tolerance for salt water (up to 25 parts per thousand salt), it grows most frequently and vigorously in freshwater wetlands or in the transition zone between freshwater marshes and salt marshes where the salt content ranges from fresh to brackish. Large brackish marshes may become solid stands of phragmites in a very short time. Vigorous growth of phragmites in or near a salt marsh is an indication that large quantities of fresh water are entering the marsh at that point either from a stream or an underground source or as runoff from a road.

Roads or dikes built across salt marshes often change the salinity of the water in certain areas of the marsh and cause a sudden dramatic invasion of common reed into those areas. The degree of tolerance to salinity is demonstrated by the fact that stolons of the reed may grow 10 feet (3 m) or more across a salt marsh but fail to root because the roots are stunted by the salt water. The stand of reeds will stop at the edge of the marsh, where salinity becomes higher than 25 parts per thousand.

Although common reed does provide shelter and nesting sites for some birds and other wildlife, it supplies much less food than a healthy, more diverse salt marsh. Where common reed has encroached into salt marshes as a result of the construction of roads, drainage ditches, or floodgates and dikes, the marsh has become much less productive of animals and has lost plant diversity as well. For these reasons, methods of controlling the reed, including treatment with herbicides, burning, or flooding, are being investigated. Cultivation of other plants to prevent the growth of phragmites has not been especially effective. In areas of Scotland that have been cultivated for a hundred years, common reed is reportedly still growing vigorously among the crop plants.

Common reed has never been cultivated as a crop plant, but it has had economic importance in many parts of the world. In Europe, it is still considered to be the best material for thatched roofs and for mats to cover cold frames. People in various parts of the world, including Native Americans, have used it to make mats and screens, fences and shelters of various types, cordage, nets, baskets and fish traps, lattices to strengthen adobe, and arrow shafts. In addition to using the stems as building material, some Native American tribes in California ate the roots and rhizomes and made candy out of the sweet gum that exuded from the stems.

The scientific name *Phragmites* is from the Greek word meaning "growing in hedges," referring to the dense, hedgelike growth of this plant. Some authorities list it as *Phragmites communis* Trin.

Little Bluestem

Schizachyrium scoparium (Michx.) Nash
Grass Family, Poaceae

RANGE: New Brunswick and Quebec south to Florida and west to Alberta, Montana, Texas, and Mexico.
HABITAT: Backdune areas, dry woods, open fields, and roadsides.

Little bluestem grows in loose or dense clumps 16 inches–5 feet (0.4–1.5 m) tall. The stems are stiff and hard and arch outward from the base. The upper half of the stems is usually branching, and the nodes are bluish or somewhat purple. The leaves are 1⁄16–1⁄4 inch (2–7 mm) wide and folded and are shorter than the flowering branches. The leaf sheaths may be smooth or shaggy and are clear green or have a dull waxy coating.

The flowers are borne along the upper edges of the branches either singly or in small groups. They bloom from August to October. They are not conspicuous until they set seed; in the fall, when the plants are covered with seeds hanging from long, glistening, white hairs, they are one of the most beautiful plants in the landscape.

Little bluestem was formerly classified as *Andropogon scoparius* Michx. but has since been moved to the genus *Schizachyrium* because of its flower structure. Authorities have divided the species into many varieties and subspecies. Other common names for it include wiregrass, beardgrass, and broom.

Little bluestem is not so little, growing as tall as 5 feet (1.5 m). But it is short in comparison with its relative big bluestem (*Andropogon gerardii* Vitman), which can grow up to 10 feet (3 m) tall. The dominant plant of the tallgrass prairie of the Central Plains, big bluestem may also be found in open fields from Quebec south to Florida and west to Saskatchewan and Arizona. The inflorescence of big bluestem is at the end of the flowering stalk and has two to six racemes of closely spaced flowers. Because the inflorescence resembles a bird's foot, another common name for this species is turkeyfoot. The young foliage of both little and big bluestem has a bluish-green cast, which gives them the common name bluestem. Later in

Little bluestem,
Schizachyrium scoparium

the season, however, they turn lovely shades of brown, tan, and purplish-red.

Several other close relatives of little bluestem may be found in this book's range, most of them known by the common name broomsedge or splitbeard. They include *Andropogon glomeratus* (Walt.) B. S. P., *Andropogon gyrans* Ashe, *Andropogon longiberbis* Hack., *Andropogon mohrii* (Hack.) Hack. *ex* Vasey, *Andropogon ternarius* Michx., *Andropogon virginicus* L., *Schizachyrium stoloniferum* Nash, and *Schizachyrium tenerum* Nees. They are identified primarily by technical characteristics of the flowers. To make matters more complicated, they have been treated in a variety of ways by different authorities.

The seeds of the bluestems and broomsedges are eaten by songbirds and small mammals, and the entire plant is browsed by deer. Most are also good forage grasses for cattle.

Smooth cordgrass,
Spartina alterniflora

Smooth Cordgrass, Saltwater Cordgrass

Spartina alterniflora Loisel.
Grass Family, Poaceae

RANGE: Newfoundland and Quebec south to Florida and west to Texas; naturalized along parts of the Pacific coast; also in South America and northern Europe.
HABITAT: Salt marshes.

Smooth cordgrass is the first grass to become established on tidal flats when enough sediment has been deposited to support growth and to allow the surface to be exposed for at least six hours between tides. Not only is smooth cordgrass a pioneer, but when mature, it will also tolerate longer periods of partial submergence by sea water than other saltmarsh grasses. It is the dominant plant species at lower elevations in the salt marsh, but it occurs in abundance at higher elevations as well.

Smooth cordgrass varies in height from 1 foot (30 cm) at its northern limits in Canada to 5–10 feet (1.5–3 m) in marshes from South Carolina to Florida. The leaves may be up to 16 inches (40 cm) long and ½ inch (12 mm) wide and taper to a twisting tip. In texture, they are rather coarse and fibrous and hard to break. They are blue-green in color and have a smooth, somewhat waxy surface.

At its base, where it meets the sheath, the leaf has a ring of hairs (the ligule) that can be seen clearly when the blade is folded back against the sheath.

Smooth cordgrass is most conspicuous when in bloom. The white anthers are massed in a graceful spike at the top of the flowering stalk and curve slightly as they wave in the breeze. The blooming period extends from July to October and may vary from year to year. One year, all of the flowers may bloom at the same time, but another year, the plants may bloom sporadically over an extended period.

Smooth cordgrass does propagate from seeds, and seeds and seedlings can occasionally be seen in November. The major propagation, however, is vegetative, occurring when a clump of sod breaks off of a creek bank and is carried by the water to another area where it can grow. The ability to produce vigorous vegetative growth and withstand long periods of inundation enables smooth cordgrass to move into tidal flats ahead of other kinds of plants.

Earlier research identified "tall" and "short" forms of smooth cordgrass. As sediment is deposited and the level of the marsh rises, the roots and rhizomes of smooth cordgrass proliferate, forming a dense sod. Like other sod-forming grasses, the stand eventually reaches a stage of low productivity referred to as "sod-bound" (an agricultural term applied to pastures and hayfields when they are no longer productive and need to be reseeded). When the plants are in this state, the roots, rhizomes, and stems are crowded, and the plants are less productive, have fewer flowers, and are shorter than those growing along tidal creeks where there is more aeration.

This is a natural stage in the development of salt marshes. Short smooth cordgrass is usually at a slightly higher elevation in the marsh than the taller, more productive plants. It may be found in a pure stand or mixed with other kinds of plants, especially salt hay grass (*Spartina patens*), sea lavender (*Limonium carolinianum*), and annual glasswort (*Salicornia virginica*). At later stages of saltmarsh progression at higher elevations in the marsh, the short form of smooth cordgrass is replaced by other kinds of grass.

Although smooth cordgrass usually grows in areas of the marsh that are exposed for at least six hours between tides, it can also grow in standing water for extended periods—for example, in shallow pools that hold water for weeks at a time between moon tides.

Spartina alterniflora is a species of great importance to wildlife. Waterfowl, shorebirds, marshbirds, and songbirds eat the seeds; geese and muskrat eat the rhizomes; and deer eat the entire plant. Stands of smooth cordgrass also provide food, nesting sites, and shelter for many other animals, both above the ground and in the soil below.

Big Cordgrass, Salt Reed-grass

Spartina cynosuroides (L.) Roth
Grass Family, Poaceae

RANGE: Southern Massachusetts south to Florida and west to Texas.
HABITAT: Tidal salt, brackish, and freshwater marshes.

Big cordgrass varies in height from 3⅓ to 13 feet (1–4 m). The plant is much more rough-textured than freshwater cordgrass (*Spartina pectinata*) and has thicker rhizomes that are covered with white scales. The rhizomes are often deeply buried in the muck of the marshes where big cordgrass grows.

The primary leaves have blades up to 30 inches (75 cm) long and $^{3}/_{16}$–1 inch (5–25 mm) wide. Their rough edges are sharp enough to inflict serious cuts.

The panicles of seeds are borne at the top of the stalks and are dense rather than open. They may be up to 1 foot (30 cm) long and usually have more than 30 lateral branches on each stalk. The branches bearing seeds tend to be longer at the base and decrease in length as they ascend the stem, so that the branches at the top may have fewer seeds than those at the bottom.

The spikelets producing the seeds resemble those of freshwater cordgrass but do not have the long, sharp bristle tip that is conspicuous on the spikelets of freshwater cordgrass.

Big cordgrass is rare at the northernmost end of its range but

Big cordgrass, *Spartina cynosuroides*

may form dense colonies in coastal marshes south of New England. Geese and muskrat eat the stout rhizomes of this plant, and its seeds are consumed by many species of birds.

Salt Hay Grass

Spartina patens (Ait.) Muhl.
Grass Family, Poaceae

RANGE: Quebec south to Florida and the West Indies and west to Texas; also inland in saline situations in the northern Midwest. HABITAT: Salt and brackish marshes, wet beaches, sandflats, and interdune and backdune areas.

Salt hay grass, also known as salt-meadow cordgrass and highwater-grass, usually occupies areas of higher elevation on tidal salt marshes than does smooth cordgrass (*Spartina alterniflora*). Studies have shown that smooth cordgrass is flooded virtually every day of the growing season in the lower elevations of the marsh, but salt hay grass is flooded 50–75 percent of the time during the growing season. When conditions are favorable (such as in parts of southern New Jersey and around Delaware Bay), salt hay grass may cover many square miles of salt marsh, just above the level of a normal high tide.

Salt hay grass,
Spartina patens

Salt hay grass is easily identified because both leaves and stems are extremely slender in comparison with those of the other two common tidal marsh grasses, smooth cordgrass and saltgrass (*Distichlis spicata*). A stand of salt hay grass also tends to be brighter green in midsummer than stands of the other two species.

The diameter of the stems seldom exceeds ⅛ inch (3 mm), and the length of the slender leaves may vary from 1½ to 24 inches (4–60 cm). Both stems and leaves tend to be longer in the southern part of the range, where the entire plant may grow to over 3⅓ feet (1 m) in height. Taller plants also occur on wet sandy beaches and in interdune swales.

The leaves are bluish-green to yellowish-green (becoming more yellowish late in the growing season), tough and fibrous, and rough on the upper surface and along the margins but smooth on the lower surface. Always slender in proportion to their length, they are widely spaced along the stems, are attached at a 45-degree angle, may be flat or rolled inward, and taper to a pointed tip.

Two or more flower stalks project from each stem at the same angle as the leaves and are conspicuous when the flowers are in bloom. The anthers are large in proportion to the size of the flowers and may be a creamy white or a deep rose-pink. On plants with pink flowers, the upper portions of the stems are usually wine-red. The plant blooms from late June to October, depending on the location.

The slender stems seldom remain erect for more than a few weeks before they are flattened by the winds and tides. A special ball-and-socket joint at the base of the stem allows the stem to move in any direction without being broken. As a result, by midsummer, most stands of salt hay grass have developed a thick green mat with a "cowlick" surface resembling a recently grazed pasture.

Below the green surface of the current year's growth lie the dead stems and leaves of older plants in a resilient tangle often more than 6 inches (15 cm) thick. Dead plants of salt hay grass are extremely resistant to decay and remain in place several years before they disintegrate enough to be washed away. Utilized by numerous bacteria, fungi, and small animals, the decaying leaves are a very important component of the food web of a salt marsh.

The basal portion of the stems of the current year's growth remains green all winter, no matter how severe the weather, protected by the mat of dead vegetation above it. The plants also have slender rhizomes, and in the spring, new shoots develop, either from buds on the rhizomes or from the green bases of the stems. The new shoots push up through the mattresslike cover of dead grass to become the current year's new growth.

The first settlers in New England were told that the local salt hay would be good feed for their cattle. By the end of the first year, however, many of the salt hay marshes were being drained and planted with English grass seed. The farmers had quickly discovered that the silica content of the local salt hay made it unsuitable feed for cattle. The best use for it was as weed-free mulch for gardens and strawberry beds and bedding for cattle. It has also been used as padding in coffins because it is less expensive than excelsior.

Freshwater cordgrass,
Spartina pectinata

Freshwater Cordgrass

Spartina pectinata Link
Grass Family, Poaceae

RANGE: Newfoundland and Quebec south to North Carolina and west to Alberta, Washington, and Texas.
HABITAT: Coastal brackish and freshwater marshes, as well as inland freshwater marshes and in soils of moderate moisture.

Freshwater cordgrass is a rather coarse perennial grass that may be 6½ feet (2 m) tall. In the prairie states, it is called prairie grass or sloughgrass. Although it is primarily a freshwater wetland species, along the East Coast, freshwater cordgrass extends into the upper edge of tidal brackish marshes.

The leaves, which may be up to 4 feet (1.2 m) long and ⅝ inch (16 mm) wide, are rough but not as abrasive as those of big cordgrass (*Spartina cynosuroides*). The leaf blades taper to a very fine slender tip and roll into a cylinder when even slightly dry. The flower clusters at the tops of the stems are 16 inches (40 cm) long and usually have fewer than 20 (although sometimes more than 30) lateral branches that are all about the same length and alternate up the stem. The spikelets are one-flowered, overlap one another, and are somewhat flat with noticeably sharp, stiff bristles on the two scales at the base of the seed. When the flowers bloom—from July to September, depending on the location—the anthers are large enough to be showy and are a rich orange-tan color.

Freshwater cordgrass spreads by underground stems as well as by seed. In the prairie states, the stands are usually dense, but along the East Coast, the stems are more likely to be widely spaced and the number of plants low at a single site. Freshwater cordgrass is conspicuous due to its height, its exceptionally long leaves, and its handsome flower heads.

Gama Grass

Tripsacum dactyloides (L.) L.
Grass Family, Poaceae

RANGE: Massachusetts south to Florida and west to Michigan, Iowa, Nebraska, Oklahoma, and Texas; also in the West Indies and Mexico.
HABITAT: Freshwater and brackish marshes, swamps, wet meadows, and banks of ponds and streams.

Gama grass is a tough perennial that spreads by coarse, knotty rhizomes into colonies 12–30 feet (3.5–9 m) wide, with stalks up to 10 feet (3 m) tall. The leaves are widely spaced along the stems and are usually more than 1 foot (30 cm) long and up to 1 inch (2.5 cm) wide, with wide midribs. The edges of the leaves and sheaths are rough to the touch, but except for a few hairs on the upper surface at the base of the leaves, all other surfaces are smooth and hairless.

Lateral branches develop from the axils of the leaves, making it a bushy plant, especially when both primary and lateral branches produce flower spikes at the upper ends.

The flower spikes are slender stalks 4–12 inches (10–30 cm) long, the upper two-thirds of which are occupied by the staminate or male flowers and the lower third by the female or pistillate flowers. The male portion of the flowering branches resembles the branches of a corn tassel. The female flowers are set within openings in

Gama grass,
Tripsacum dactyloides

curiously jointed structures that have the texture of horn or cartilage. Each joint is approximately ⅜ inch (1 cm) long. The structure of the inflorescence is suggestive of the flower structure of corn or maize (*Zea mays* L.), which also has separate male and female flowers.

The horny covering of the female flowers is bright green, and the anthers of the male flowers are wine-red. The flowers bloom from July to October, depending on the location.

Gama grass is a nourishing forage grass, but it has never been common enough, either wild or cultivated, to be of economic value as forage or hay.

Sea oats, *Uniola paniculata*

Sea Oats

Uniola paniculata L.
Grass Family, Poaceae

RANGE: Southeast Virginia south along the Atlantic coast to Florida and west along the Gulf coast to Texas; also in the West Indies and Mexico.
HABITAT: Drifting sands and stabilized dunes near the ocean.

As a sand binder on southern dunes, sea oats is the counterpart of American beachgrass (*Ammophila breviligulata*), which grows on northern dunes. The two species overlap for a relatively short distance from southern Virginia to Cape Hatteras, North Carolina. If these species did not overlap sufficiently to stabilize the drifting sand there, Cape Hatteras would not exist.

Sea oats, like many coastal grasses, are strongly rhizomatous. They grow in large clumps or elongated stands on or between dunes near the ocean. The plants are 3⅓–8 feet (1–2.5 m) tall and have leaves both at the base of the plant and along the stems. The leaves are slender, 4–24 inches (10–60 cm) long, and up to ⅜ inch (1 cm) wide; they tend to roll inward as they mature. Each stem leaf has a sheath wrapped around the lower end of the stem and a ligule with a ring of hairs where the blade and sheath connect. All surfaces of the plant, including the leaves and stems, are smooth.

The masses of basal leaves appear to be crucial to the ability of sea oats to stabilize sand. The plants grow well on the first row of dunes above the beach, where the waves may be exceptionally high even on calm days in summer and where few other species can survive. The basal leaves apparently break the force of the water, which then flows more gently over the dune below without disturbing the sand.

The flowering panicles of sea oats are 8–24 inches (20–60 cm) long and are produced at the tips of the stems above the leaves. In shape, they resemble the panicles of oat plants, making sea oats undoubtedly the most beautiful of the coastal grasses, in the North or South.

In fact, the beauty of the panicles of sea oats makes them so popular for bouquets that most beaches accessible to the general public have nearly as many signs proclaiming "Don't Pick the Sea Oats" as stalks of sea oats, and the plants that remain lack the size and vigor of sea oats growing on undisturbed dunes.

Awl-sedge

Carex stipata Muhl. *ex* Willd. var. *stipata*
Sedge Family, Cyperaceae

RANGE: Newfoundland south to Florida and west to Alaska, New Mexico, and California.
HABITAT: Shallow freshwater wetlands and low ground; also in brackish wetlands adjacent to coastal waters.

The sedge family is large, with at least 5,300 species globally, and its members are usually difficult to identify, but the old rule "sedges have edges, grasses are round" is a useful clue for distinguishing members of this family from other grasslike plants. Sedges also lack the jointed stems that are prominent in the true grasses. Similar to the flowers of grasses, most sedge flowers are not showy and are pollinated by the wind.

Awl-sedge plants tend to grow in clumps, and the stems are filled with spongy white tissue; they are not round and hollow like the stems of grasses. The sharp-edged stems are triangular in cross section and somewhat thicker in proportion to the plant's height than the stems of most sedges. The plants are 1–4 feet (30–120 cm) tall, depending on the growing conditions.

The leaves of awl-sedge are coarse in texture and usually long,

Awl-sedge,
Carex stipata

with the sheaths extending beyond the base of the blade. The fragile sheaths have a corrugated appearance.

The flowers grow at the ends of the stems in short, compact clusters. The male and female flowers are in the same spikelet, with the male flowers above the female flowers. Each flower is enclosed in a thin bulb-shaped membrane that tapers to a slender point. Like the height of the plants, the length of the inflorescence varies with location, from 1$\frac{3}{16}$ to 4 inches (3–10 cm).

When the flowers are in bloom, the spikelets are pale yellowish-green. As the flowers fade and the seeds ripen, they change to glossy brown, but the stems remain a bright green. The seeds fall soon after they ripen, leaving bare, hairlike stalks for the rest of the summer.

Around the world, there may be as many as 2,000 species of sedges in the genus *Carex*, with at least 500 found in North America north of Mexico. Of these, over 100 species may be found growing in coastal habitats within the range of this book, far too many to attempt to describe here. Anyone with an eye for detail and a fondness for microscope work, however, will find the study of sedges very rewarding and discover that a great deal of beauty can be found in tiny packages.

Carex plants have had little economic importance except as ornamentals and occasionally as bedding for livestock. Among western Native American tribes, a few species are used in basket making, both for fiber and for the creation of dyes, and a few have ritual significance.

The ecological impact of *Carex* is far greater. Sedges are an important component of many wetlands and provide cover and nesting sites for wildlife. Many mammals, including muskrat, deer, and rodents, browse on the leaves and roots, and the seeds are eaten by small mammals, ducks, shorebirds, marshbirds, gamebirds, songbirds, and turtles. Moths have been observed eating the pollen of sedges, and a variety of other insects use sedges for food and shelter.

Beach Umbrella-sedge

Cyperus polystachyos Rottb. var. *filicinus* (Vahl) C. B. Clarke
Sedge Family, Cyperaceae

RANGE: Southern coastal Maine south to Florida and west to Louisiana; also in the West Indies.
HABITAT: Brackish marshes, ditches, interdunes, and sandy coastal beaches; occasionally found on freshwater shores and in wet pinelands.

Umbrella-sedge, nutsedge, flatsedge, sweetrush, chufa, and galingale are among the common names for plants in the genus *Cyperus*, which contains as many as 600 species worldwide. They may be found in a variety of habitats, from swamps, marshes, and wet shores to dunes, dry woodlands, and fields. Papyrus (*Cyperus papyrus* L.), the bulrush that sheltered Moses in the Bible, is one of the most famous members of this group; it was once used to make paper and continues to be grown as an aquatic ornamental. Other species, such as yellow nutsedge or chufa (*Cyperus esculentus* L.), can be troublesome agricultural weeds as well as important food sources in some parts of the world.

Beach umbrella-sedge is a grasslike annual that grows in small tufts. The whole plant may be 4–16 inches (10–40 cm) tall, with

Beach umbrella-sedge,
Cyperus polystachyos

three-sided stems and very narrow (less than ⅛ inch [3 mm] wide) linear leaves that are shorter than the flowering stems.

The inconspicuous flowers are arranged in elongated, flattened spikelets that may be up to ¾ inch (2 cm) long and ⅛ inch (3 mm) wide (the flattened spikelets are what give this genus the common name flatsedge). A scale covers each flower, which has both male and female parts but no petals or sepals. The scales are initially green but become tawny when mature.

The spikelets are clustered in groups of 5 to 10. The clusters or spikes are sometimes sessile or may be on stalks up to 4 inches (10 cm) long. One or more spikes form an umbel at the end of the flowering stalk. Several leafy bracts, which may be up to 10 inches (25 cm) long and ⅛ inch (3 mm) wide, rise from the base of each umbel.

Some authorities treat this variety as a separate species, *Cyperus filicinus* Vahl.

The seeds and tubers of *Cyperus* are eaten by many different species of birds and mammals. Chufa is of particular importance to wildlife and is found throughout this book's range and in most tropical and temperate areas of the world. In some parts of the world, chufa is cultivated and known as earth almond. The tubers are high in fat, sugar, and starch and are eaten as a cooked vegetable, made into flour, and used as a coffee substitute.

A number of other members of this genus can be found in coastal habitats in this book's range. They can be differentiated by technical characteristics such as the shape of the fruits (achenes), the arrangement of the spikelets, the number of flowers in the spikelets, and the shape and nerve patterns of the flower scales. Although it can be difficult to distinguish the individual species, the flattened spikelets immediately reveal that they all belong to the genus *Cyperus*.

White-topped Sedge

Rhynchospora colorata (L.) H. Pfeiffer
Sedge Family, Cyperaceae

RANGE: Southeastern Virginia south to Florida and west to Texas; also in the West Indies and eastern Mexico.
HABITAT: A coastal plain species in this book's range, common in savannas, swamps, ditches, damp roadsides, and similar sunny areas.

Wide colonies of white-topped sedge are common along sunny highways in the South. Sedges usually resemble grasses and are difficult to identify, but this species can be easily recognized. The stems are 4–24 inches (10–60 cm) tall, with leaves shorter than the stems, but the most conspicuous features are the very unequal bracts at the top of the flowering stalk. The portion nearest to the flowering head, ranging from one-third to one-half of the bract, is glistening snowy white, whereas the outer portion is a rich bright green. Hundreds of these stalks in bloom at once are quite noticeable!

The showy bracts probably serve to attract the insects that pollinate this plant, which is not wind pollinated like most species of sedges. The colorful bracts are visible from May to September.

Rhynchospora colorata usually has fewer than seven bracts. Another species of white-topped sedge, *Rhynchospora latifolia* (Baldw. *ex* Ell.) Thomas, usually has more than seven bracts, and the bracts are somewhat wider in proportion to the length (hence the name

White-topped sedge,
Rhynchospora colorata

latifolia, which means "broad leaf"). This species reaches only as far north as North Carolina and may be found south to the Gulf states and west to southeastern Texas. Both of these species were formerly listed under the genus *Dichromena*.

Chairmaker's Rush, Olney Three-square

Scirpus americanus Pers.
Sedge Family, Cyperaceae

RANGE: Nova Scotia south to South America and west to the Pacific coast.
HABITAT: Brackish marshes, upper edges of tidal salt marshes, inland saline marshes, and (less frequently) tidal freshwater marshes.

A colony of chairmaker's rush is an arresting site, the tall, dark green plants standing stiffly erect, with the small flower head near

Chairmaker's rush,
Scirpus americanus

the tip of each plant seeming strangely out of proportion to the height of the plant. The plants may grow as tall as 6½ feet (2 m). The stiff bearing of this species has lent it another common name, swordgrass.

Chairmaker's rush grows from a perennial rhizomatous root, often forming large colonies on the upper edges of salt marshes. The base of the stem may be at least ⅜ inch (1 cm) thick and is sharply triangular, with each of the three sides deeply concave. Leaves are seldom apparent, although there may be a few short leaves, usually less than 4 inches (10 cm) long, near the base of the stem.

The inconspicuous flowers are arranged in small brown spikelets that are 3⁄16–¾ inch (5–20 mm) long. The spikelets may be solitary, but more often they are in clusters of 2 to 15, attached directly to the stem with no stalks. Growing from the base of the flower cluster is a single leaflike bract that appears to be a continuation of the main stalk. The bract may be ⅜–2 inches (1–5 cm) long and ends in a somewhat blunt tip.

Some authorities have used the synonym *Scirpus olneyi* Gray for *Scirpus americanus*, but according to the system used here, *Scirpus olneyi* is included in *Scirpus americanus*.

A similar species, common three-square (*Scirpus pungens* Vahl), was long called *Scirpus americanus* due to a misunderstanding of the original herbarium specimen. Common three-square grows in brackish marshes and tidal fresh waters as well as inland wetlands and is found throughout this book's range from the Canadian maritime provinces south to Florida and west to Texas and the Pacific coast.

Scirpus pungens also has a triangular stem, but the sides are only slightly concave or bulge outward a little. There are usually several leaves near the base of the plant, some of them long enough for the tips to reach the middle of the main stem, which is sometimes twisted. It grows as tall as 5 feet (1.5 m).

Like the spikelets of chairmaker's rush, the brown spikelets of common three-square are sessile, with as few as one or as many as six spikelets in a cluster. Each spikelet is ¼–¾ inch (7–20 mm) long. An erect, sharply pointed bract, ⅜–6 inches (1–15 cm) long, rises from the flower cluster.

Both *Scirpus americanus* and *Scirpus pungens* have been called chairmaker's rush because in colonial days and into the early decades of the 1900s they were used to make the backs and seats of chairs. Native Americans also used these bulrushes to make mats, baskets, toys, and even small boats (thanks to the waterproof nature of the leaves).

Nearly 60 species of *Scirpus* grow in North America and form a very important component of wetland habitats. Bulrush colonies provide nesting sites and protective cover for mammals, birds, fish, reptiles, amphibians, and invertebrates. The rootstocks and stems are eaten by muskrat and wading birds, and the seeds are utilized by many species of birds and mammals. People have also used bulrushes for food. The tubers have been cooked like potatoes or dried and ground into a nutritious flour. Bulrush pollen and seeds have also been used to make flour, and the young shoots have been eaten as well.

Leafy bulrush,
Scirpus robustus

Leafy Bulrush

Scirpus robustus Pursh
Sedge Family, Cyperaceae

RANGE: Nova Scotia south to Florida and the West Indies and west to Texas; also in California.
HABITAT: Tidal salt and brackish marshes.

At a distance, bulrushes may resemble grasses because of their leafiness, but even casual inspection shows that the stems are sharply triangular in cross section rather than round and tend to be thicker in proportion to height than the stems of grasses. The stems of *Scirpus robustus* are good examples.

Leafy bulrush is a perennial that grows from tuberous rhizomes. It is a rather coarse, vigorous, leafy plant 2–5 feet (0.6–1.5 m) tall. The dark green stem leaves are 5⁄32–3⁄8 inch (4–10 mm) across. Most of the leaves grow above the middle of the flowering stalk, and the ends of the longest ones conspicuously overtop the flower heads. In

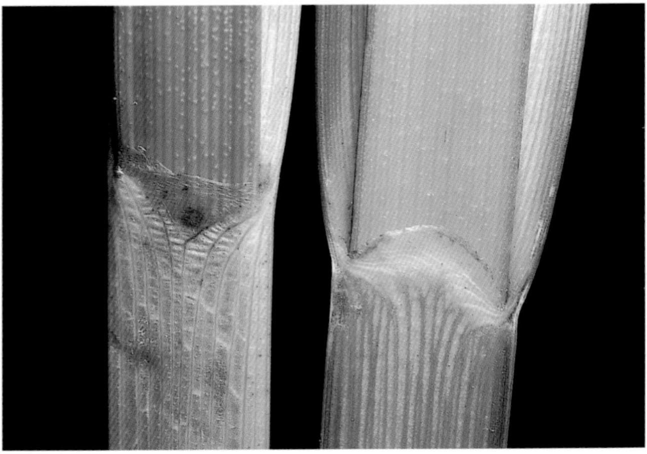

Ligules of *Scirpus maritimus* (left) and *Scirpus robustus* (right)

addition to the stem leaves, the inflorescence of leafy bulrush has up to four leaflike bracts of unequal lengths that extend well above the inflorescence. The bracts tend to be erect rather than drooping.

The ligule where the leaf blade and sheath join is rounded at the top, with conspicuous veins descending below it.

The inconspicuous flowers of leafy bulrush are arranged in stout oval or cylindrical spikelets that vary in length from ½ to 1½ inches (1.2–4 cm) and may be solitary or in small clusters. Most of the spikelets or spikelet clusters are sessile, but a few may have stalks. When the flowers are in bloom, yellow anthers dangle from the scales on the surface of the flower heads. After the pollen is shed, the bright reddish-brown color of the flower heads darkens and may become gray.

A similar perennial bulrush, saltmarsh bulrush (*Scirpus maritimus* L.), is found in coastal freshwater and saline marshes and swamps from Nova Scotia south to Virginia and westward. This species is native both to Europe and North America, and some specimens found in marshes around North American seaports may have originally come from Europe. In the northern part of its range, saltmarsh bulrush is usually no more than 2–3 feet (60–90 cm) tall, but farther south, it may reach 5 feet (1.5 m) in height. Some authorities have divided *Scirpus maritimus* into various species and subspecies, but according to the system used here, they are lumped under a single species, without varieties.

Leafy bulrush and saltmarsh bulrush can be distinguished fairly easily. Saltmarsh bulrush is more leafy below the middle of the stems, and when the plants are in bloom, the tips of the longest leaves are usually below the flower heads. Few of the two to five floral bracts of saltmarsh bulrush extend far above the inflorescence, and the spikelets of saltmarsh bulrush are more slender in proportion to the width. The ligule is distinctly V-shaped and tends to be made of thinner tissue than that of leafy bulrush. The mature spikelets of saltmarsh bulrush are yellowish or tawny.

Both leafy bulrush and saltmarsh bulrush tend to grow in brackish areas at the upper edges of salt marshes where fresh water enters the marsh. They also grow along the edges of river marshes that are less saline than marshes closer to the ocean. Saltmarsh bulrush grows in inland freshwater situations as well, especially in more alkaline waters (hence another common name for this plant, alkali bulrush).

River bulrush (*Scirpus fluviatilis* [Torr.] Gray) may be found in tidal freshwater marshes and other freshwater habitats from Canada and the north-central United States south to Virginia and west to California. It is also a stout, leafy, perennial bulrush that may grow as tall as 5 feet (1.5 m). It has long leafy bracts that vary in length, but unlike the previous two species, the bracts are drooping rather than erect. The pale brown spikelets may be sessile, or they may droop or be erect on long stalks. Similar to the spikelets of saltmarsh bulrush and leafy bulrush, the spikelets of river bulrush may be solitary or in clusters. The ligule is slightly rounded.

Blue-stem palmetto, *Sabal minor*

Blue-stem Palmetto, Dwarf Palmetto

Sabal minor (Jacq.) Pers.
Palm Family, Arecaceae

RANGE: Dare County, North Carolina, and coastal plain south to South Carolina, Georgia, and Florida and west to south Texas.
HABITAT: Low woods, usually wetter than the sites occupied by saw palmetto.

Two species of shrub palms—blue-stem palmetto and saw palmetto—are native to the Southeast and may be found growing in the same areas. Although they have several features in common, they are distinct enough that distinguishing the two species is not difficult.

The primary difference is that saw palmetto (*Serenoa repens*) has serrate petioles, in contrast to the smooth edges of the leaf stalks on blue-stem palmetto. In addition, the stems of blue-stem palmetto are always underground and the plants tend to grow in clusters, whereas the stems of saw palmetto are always on the surface and the plants usually grow in solid stands.

Occasionally, blue-stem palmetto has fibers hanging from the upper edges of the leaves, but most plants, like saw palmetto plants, have no hanging fibers. Also like saw palmetto, blue-stem palmetto has leaves that usually lack a midrib; if present, the midrib is no more than 1$\frac{3}{16}$ inches (3 cm) long.

Blue-stem palmetto is more widely distributed and more likely to be seen in this book's range than saw palmetto. When the two species are growing in the same area, blue-stem palmetto tends to have somewhat larger, thicker leaves that are more glossy and a richer shade of green. The fan of the blue-stem palmetto is also usually narrow, whereas the saw palmetto forms a very open fan. The flowers and fruit of the two species are similar. Blue-stem palmetto flowers from May to July and bears fruit from September to November. Palmetto fruits are eaten by squirrels, raccoons, and several different species of birds.

Blue-stem palmetto tends to grow as a shrub in the eastern portion of its range, but farther west, it may be as tall as 10 feet (3 m) and have a distinct trunk.

Cabbage Palm

Sabal palmetto (Walt.) Lodd. *ex* J. A. & J. H. Schultes
Palm Family, Arecaceae

RANGE: Brunswick County, North Carolina, south to South Carolina, Georgia, Florida, and the Bahamas; not found growing naturally more than 75 miles from the ocean.
HABITAT: Freshwater and brackish marshes and maritime forests in shade or sun.

When cabbage palm grows in natural stands, several trees are usually found growing together rather than singly. The trees may be as tall as 82 feet (25 m), with the trunks about 2 feet (60 cm) in diameter and of the same diameter from the base of the trunk to the top. The lower part of the trunk is grayish-tan and shows the horizontal scars of the bases of the leaves that have fallen off. The upper portion of the trunk retains the "boot-jacks," which are the petioles of the old leaves that have not yet fallen off.

The leaf blades are fan-shaped and pleated and split partway down each pleat. The tips of the leaf segments have a long filament trailing from the end. There is an arching midrib in the center of each leaf blade, 2–8 inches (5–20 cm) long, where the leaf blade joins the stem. The smooth-edged petioles may be up to 6½ feet (2 m) long.

The upper surface of the leaves is glossy and medium green; the lower surface is dull and gray-green.

Cabbage palm,
Sabal palmetto

Cabbage palm, like the smaller shrubby palms of the Southeast, produces flowers on large, oval, delicate, many-branched, pale green clusters of stems produced in the axils of the leaves. The flowers are greenish-white, with three petals, three sepals, and six stamens. They are fragrant and bloom in June and July. The honey produced by these flowers is considered a delicacy and is sold in some southern markets and roadside stands.

The fruits are globular, ½ inch (12 mm) in diameter, and orange when mature in late summer, but they may remain on the tree until they turn dark brown or black.

Before Florida was overwhelmed by real estate development, cabbage palm, the state tree, was plentiful and harvested commercially. The "cabbage," the bud at the upper end of the tree, was canned and sold; removing this terminal bud killed the tree. The leaves were used to make fans, hats, and mats. The fibers in the "boot-jacks" were made into brushes, and the trunks were used to make log cabins because the wood was resistant to wood-boring insects. The trunks were also used as pilings for docks because they were resistant to boring sea worms.

Although much of their native habitat has been destroyed, cabbage palms are widely used as ornamentals. They are beautiful and easily cultivated.

Saw Palmetto

Serenoa repens (Bartr.) Small
Palm Family, Arecaceae

RANGE: Beaufort and Jasper Counties, South Carolina, south to Florida and west along the Gulf coast to southeastern Louisiana; introduced as an ornamental in western Louisiana and Texas.
HABITAT: Dunes, shady woods, savannas, and other areas.

Saw palmetto is easily recognized by the downward-pointing serrated edges of the petioles, which can inflict painful cuts. Well-trained hunting dogs will not follow game into a saw palmetto thicket.

Although an occasional plant may be treelike and have a short, erect trunk, the stems usually run along the surface of the ground, branching at intervals and sending up clusters of leaves with saw-toothed petioles. These stands form dense thickets with plants 4–6 feet (1.2–1.8 m) tall, although specimens up to 23 feet (7 m) have been recorded.

The leaves have a typical fan shape and may be up to 3⅓ feet (1 m) wide. They have pleated, alternating segments that are folded together when the leaves are young and open as they mature. The segments of the leaves are attached directly to the tip of the stem without a midrib and have no fibers hanging from the upper tips. The color of the leaves varies from yellow-green to blue-green, depending on the location.

Flowers are produced on large, many-branched clusters of delicate pale green stems arising from the axils of the leaves. The flowers bloom from May to July. They are cream-colored and have a musty odor. Each flower has three petals ⅛–3/16 inch (3–5 mm) long; three sepals, which are slightly smaller than the petals; and six stamens. The fruits are oval or round and ⅝–¾ inch (1.5–2 cm) in diameter; when ripe, they are orange in color. If the fruits remain on the plant, they turn dark brown and then black as they age. The fruits of

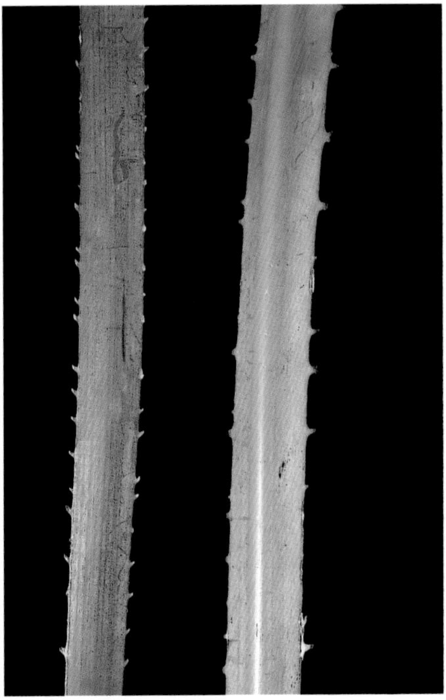

Saw palmetto,
Serenoa repens

saw palmetto were relished by Native Americans and are an important source of food for wildlife, including raccoons and white-tailed deer. An extract of the fruit has been extensively marketed as a remedy for prostate problems.

Saw palmetto is extremely resistant to fire and remains green even after other plants around it are destroyed by fire. Although it tends to grow in fairly dry habitats rather than in swamps or poorly drained soils, it will survive in soils that are waterlogged for short periods.

Field trips should never be taken through saw palmetto thickets unless the thickets line roads or wide trails. Not only will the participants be subject to painful cuts, but rattlesnakes are much more likely to be encountered in the brush than on the trails.

Sweetflag,
Acorus americanus

Sweetflag, Calamus

Acorus americanus (Raf.) Raf.
Sweetflag Family, Acoraceae

RANGE: Prince Edward Island, Nova Scotia, and Quebec south to Florida and west to Alberta, Minnesota, eastern Washington, Texas, and Colorado.
HABITAT: Freshwater and tidal freshwater marshes, swamps, wet ditches, and other shallow waters.

Sweetflag comes by its name fairly: all parts of the plant are fragrant when crushed. Because of its sweet odor and the volatile oils it contains, this plant has been used for many edible and medicinal purposes, even to make perfume. Indeed, it would be hard to find another herbaceous plant that has been used in so many different ways. If the "sweet calamus" mentioned in the Bible (Exodus 30:23, Song of Solomon 4:14, and Ezekiel 27:19) is the same as sweetflag—and many authorities believe it is—then its use is ancient.

Sweetflag is a perennial wetland plant that grows from stout, fleshy rhizomes that form a thick layer just beneath the soil's surface. Its swordlike, yellowish-green leaves may reach over 6½ feet (2 m) in height but are more commonly 2–3 feet (0.6–1.2 m) tall and 3⁄16–1 inch (5–25 mm) wide. The pronounced midvein of the leaf is sometimes off center, and the leaf edges may be crinkled.

The flowering stalk or scape is three-sided. The fingerlike spadix, which may be 1½–4 inches (4–10 cm) long and somewhat curved, juts off the scape at a sharp angle and bears numerous tiny greenish-yellow flowers. The spathe forms a leaflike structure that appears to continue the flower stalk above the spadix.

Chinese herbalists have used sweetflag for centuries; on the Chinese New Year, they hung sweetflag leaves over doorways to keep away evil influences. Many Native American tribes also had ritual uses for the plant. Europeans and American settlers strewed the sweet-smelling leaves on floors to mask unpleasant odors and perhaps to repel insects. Many cultures made a candy from the rhizomes of sweetflag, which was believed to ward off contagious diseases.

Sweetflag has been traded as a commodity in Asia and Europe (and its colonies) and among Native American tribes. In Europe, it was probably introduced from Asia; some believe it was brought to Poland by the Tartars, and it is known to have become abundant in Germany by 1588.

Many authorities do not separate the North American sweetflag from the Eurasian species and list them both as *Acorus calamus* L. Some place it in the same family (Araceae) as skunk cabbage (*Symplocarpus foetidus*) and Jack-in-the-pulpit (*Arisaema triphyllum*), whereas others place it in a separate family, the Acoraceae, as in this book.

Golden club, *Orontium aquaticum*

Golden Club

Orontium aquaticum L.
Arum Family, Araceae

RANGE: Massachusetts south to Florida and west to western Louisiana.
HABITAT: Tidal freshwater marshes and shallow coastal ponds and streams; sandy, peaty, and muddy shores.

Golden club is related to skunk cabbage (*Symplocarpus foetidus*) and Jack-in-the-pulpit (*Arisaema triphyllum*), but it is very different in appearance from the other members of the arum family. It is an aquatic perennial with thick rhizomes that are deeply rooted to the bottom of shallow coastal ponds and streams.

The structure of the plant is rather simple. The leaves have parallel veins and are narrowly oblong, 4–16 inches (10–40 cm) long and 1½–6 inches (4–15 cm) wide. Long, slender petioles extend from the leaves down to the rhizomes, and the leaves float flat on the surface of the water or sometimes extend above the water. The leaves have plain edges with no teeth and are smooth on both surfaces. The whole plant may grow as tall as 2 feet (60 cm). Golden club plants grow much larger in the southern states than they do farther north and consequently are popular as ornamentals in pools and water gardens.

The bright yellow flowers are borne at the upper end of a special organ called a spadix, which develops on a stem that extends from the base of the plant. The spadix corresponds to the "Jack" in Jack-in-the-pulpit. The "pulpit" or spathe is reduced to a leaf sheath wrapped around the stem.

The spadix of golden club is tubular, somewhat fleshy, and dazzlingly white. The contrast of the white with the yellow flowers is quite striking. The flowers have no petals. The lower ones are composed of six concave sepals and six stamens, and the upper ones have four of each. Golden club flowers from March to June, and the fruit is a single seed inside a bladderlike structure.

The leaves of golden club shed moisture entirely when they are removed from the water; for this reason, one of its common names is never-wet.

Like its relatives Jack-in-the-pulpit, skunk cabbage, and arrow arum (*Peltandra virginica*), golden club has been used for several medicinal and edible purposes. However, all of these species contain calcium oxalate crystals, which may cause life-threatening swelling of the throat and mouth if the plants are eaten raw or improperly prepared.

Arrow Arum, Tuckahoe

Peltandra virginica (L.) Schott
Arum Family, Araceae

RANGE: Southern Quebec and Ontario south to Florida and west to Michigan, Missouri, and Texas.
HABITAT: Swamps, bogs, marshes, pond shores, muddy edges, and shallow waters, including slightly brackish and tidal freshwater areas.

Arrow arum is a plant of muddy edges, its shiny, smooth, deep green leaves emerging from the shallow waters where it thrives, often in large colonies. It is called arrow arum because the shape of the leaf often resembles an arrowhead. The leaves can have a number of other shapes, however, so it is best to learn other ways to identify it in order to distinguish it from the arrowheads (*Sagittaria* spp.), which also have a confusing variety of leaf shapes.

When arrow arum is full-grown, the blades of the leaves can be as long as 2 feet (60 cm) and as wide as 1 foot (30 cm). Since the leaves

Arrow arum,
Peltandra virginica

grow on long stalks, the whole plant may reach as much as 3–4 feet (0.9–1.2 m) in height, although 1–2 feet (30–60 cm) is more common. The leaves may be oblong, with no lobes at the base; have two long, sharply pointed basal lobes; or have basal lobes that are broad and rounded.

Whatever the shape of the leaves, the patterns of the veins on the leaves are clearly different from those of arrowheads. In *Sagittaria*, the narrow major veins all radiate out from the point where the petiole meets the leaf blade. In *Peltandra*, three broad veins radiate from the junction of the petiole and blade, one going to each of the basal lobes and one going upward toward the tip of the leaf. Secondary veins run almost perpendicular to these wide veins, with a network of parallel smaller veins between them. Another slim vein follows the margin of the leaf, outlining it entirely. *Peltandra* shares this marginal vein patterning with its relatives Jack-in-the-pulpit (*Arisaema triphyllum*) and skunk cabbage (*Symplocarpus foetidus*), but *Sagittaria* lacks the outlining venation.

The flower structure of arrow arum is similar to that of Jack-in-the-pulpit. The flowers form on a long stalk (8–16 inches [20–40 cm] long) that rises directly from the perennial root. At the end of the stalk is the spadix, a cylindrical structure 4–8 inches (10–20 cm) long, which may be white or golden-yellow. The male flowers develop on the upper four-fifths of the spadix, and the female flowers on the lower fifth.

The narrow, long-pointed, green spathe rolls inward, wrapping at least three-quarters of the way around the upper male portion of the spadix and almost completely enveloping the bulging lower section where the female flowers bloom and the fruit develops. The margins of the spathe are pale and have distinct wavy edges, giving it the decorative look of a fancy bonnet. A close look inside the spathe will show flies or other pollinating insects on the surface of the spadix.

As the fruit matures, the upper male portion of the spadix withers away, leaving a cluster of dark berries wrapped in the remains of the spathe. This pod settles into the muck and decays, eventually releasing the slime-coated seeds. Wood ducks are reputed to eat large quantities of the fruits of arrow arum.

White arum (*Peltandra sagittifolia* [Michx.] Morong) may be encountered in coastal plain swamps from North Carolina (where it is rare) south to Florida and west to Mississippi. The white spathe of this species does not wrap so tightly around the spadix but is broad and flaring at the base and comes to a long, sharp tip, a striking contrast with the golden spadix. The berries are red.

The common name tuckahoe is an Algonquian name for arrow arum, as well as for several other plants and fungi collected for food and medicine.

Spanish Moss

Tillandsia usneoides (L.) L.
Bromeliad Family, Bromeliaceae

RANGE: Coastal plain from Virginia south to Florida and west to Texas; also in Central and South America.
HABITAT: Epiphytic on trees, telephone lines, and fences in moist woods, swamps, and coastal forests.

Dangling in tangled gray masses from trees and telephone wires, Spanish moss is a familiar sight in moist southern coastal forests.

Spanish moss, *Tillandsia usneoides*

Contrary to its common name, Spanish moss is not a moss but a flowering plant in the same family as pineapple.

Spanish moss is an epiphyte or air plant, a plant that grows on other plants or surfaces for physical support but manufactures its own food. It does not have roots that penetrate the surface it grows on, so it does not harm the host by taking nutrients from it. Spanish moss is capable of photosynthesis; although superficially it appears gray, after a rain it takes on a faint green glow, revealing the presence of chlorophyll.

The branching, wiry stems of Spanish moss are no wider than $\frac{5}{32}$ of an inch (4 mm). The threadlike leaves are $\frac{3}{4}$–$2\frac{3}{8}$ inches (2–6 cm) long and can barely be distinguished from the intertwined stems. Both the stems and the leaves are densely covered with gray scales. It is these scales that give Spanish moss the ability to live without roots since they are specialized to absorb water and nutrients.

The flowers are borne singly on short side branches and bloom from late February to June. They are $\frac{3}{16}$–$\frac{3}{4}$ inch (5–20 mm) long and have three sepals and three green petals that fade to yellow. Although inconspicuous, they produce a nectar that attracts the insects and hummingbirds that pollinate them.

The fruit of Spanish moss is a cylindrical capsule about 1 inch (2.5 cm) long. When ripe, it releases tufted, sticky seeds that travel on the wind and stick to branches, where they may develop new plants.

A single Spanish moss plant may reach as much as 16½ feet (5 m) in length. Although it is not parasitic, it sometimes harms host trees by blocking off light to the leaves; this can be especially problematic in citrus orchards. People have found many uses for Spanish moss, including stuffing mattresses and padding upholstered furniture.

Two other species of *Tillandsia* may be found in southern Georgia and northern Florida. Ball moss (*Tillandsia recurvata* [L.] L.) grows from Florida and southeasternmost Georgia west to Arizona and forms dense clumps up to 6 inches (15 cm) wide on trees and telephone lines. Wild pine (*Tillandsia bartramii* Ell.) grows in moist woods, with leaves up to 16 inches (40 cm) long that form a dense rosette.

Pickerelweed

Pontederia cordata L.
Water Hyacinth Family, Pontederiaceae

RANGE: Nova Scotia and Prince Edward Island south to South America and west to Ontario and Minnesota.
HABITAT: Freshwater marshes, shallow ponds, and quiet streams, including tidal freshwater streams.

Pickerelweed is an aquatic perennial that sometimes forms dense stands. The leaves are shiny and dark green, usually heart-shaped at the base and gradually tapering to a blunt tip. The flowers grow in a spike and generally stand slightly above the main visible leaf; other leaves lie flat on the water and are often overlooked. The flowers themselves are a soft shade of violet-blue, with a pair of yellow spots on the upper lobe of each flower. When young, they may be covered with glandular hairs. The whole plant may be as much as 40 inches (1 m) tall.

Bees, flies, butterflies, and moths pollinate the showy flowers of pickerelweed; the bright yellow spots on the upper lobe of the flower help to guide them to the nectar and pollen. The seeds of pickerelweed are eaten by ducks, and the plant is considered an important food source for muskrat.

Pickerelweed may grow vigorously enough to block ditches and small ponds. Its growth habits seem slow, however, when compared to its tropical relative, water hyacinth (*Eichhornia crassipes* [Mart.] Solms). Water hyacinth was introduced into the United States from

Pickerelweed, *Pontederia cordata*

South America in 1884. It escaped its original site of introduction and has now become one of the most aggressive aquatic plants in the United States. It is found in fresh and occasionally brackish waters from Florida north to Maryland and west to Missouri and Texas and is spreading in central California.

Water hyacinth flowers resemble those of pickerelweed but are broader, are pale purple in color, and have fewer flowers on each flowering stalk. The leaves are rounded and form a cuplike shape, and the petioles are inflated so that the plant can float on the water (the plant may also be rooted in mud). Similar to pickerelweed, each flower has a yellow spot on the upper lobe.

Stands of water hyacinth can form a solid covering on ponds and other quiet waters. These stands may crowd out the native aquatic plants and create such dense shade that underwater plants are killed and the temperature and oxygen content of the body of water are affected. This in turn has an impact on the native organisms that live in these waters, so that overall biological diversity may be reduced when water hyacinths take over. The state of Florida alone spends millions of dollars each year trying to control the spread of this species, which affects not only biodiversity but also commercial fishing, recreational fishing and boating, and other activities important to human beings.

Black rush,
Juncus gerardii

Black Rush, Black Grass

Juncus gerardii Loisel.
Rush Family, Juncaceae

RANGE: Irregularly circumboreal, as far south as Virginia in this book's range and inland to Michigan and Minnesota, where it appears to be an accidental introduction.
HABITAT: Coastal salt marshes and inland in disturbed and saline habitats, such as along railways.

Less tolerant of saline conditions than many tidal marsh plants, black rush grows at the upper edge of salt marshes, slightly below the extreme high tide mark. At this elevation, inundation by high tides and deposition of sediment is less frequent. Under these conditions, black rush may be the dominant plant or it may be mixed with arrow-grass (*Triglochin maritimum*), salt hay grass (*Spartina patens*), hightide bush (*Iva frutescens*), and, in peaty soils, seaside gerardia (*Agalinis maritima*). Black rush does grow in sandy soils, but not as vigorously as it grows in mud or saltmarsh peat. It may also grow at comparable elevations along roads and dikes across salt marshes and on the spoil banks along ditches. It is an indicator plant showing extreme high tide levels.

Other common names applied to *Juncus gerardii* are mud-rush, because it is often found in muddy salt marshes, and black grass, because in many respects it is grasslike in appearance. South of Virginia, *Juncus gerardii* is replaced in marshes by needlerush (*Juncus roemerianus*), a larger, coarse rush with stiff needlelike leaves.

Black rush is a perennial that grows in small tufts and has slender dark rhizomes and stolons that spread horizontally. Thanks to its rhizomes, black rush can form dense mats on the high salt marsh. In height, the plants range from 8 to 24 inches (20–60 cm), with the taller plants in the southern part of the range. The stems are slender and wiry, are oval in cross section, and have inconspicuous nodes where the leaf sheaths are attached. Both the leaves and the stems are dark green, and the sheaths extend halfway up the stem. The leaves at the base are much closer together than those toward the top of the stem, and there is often a bractlike leaf at the base of the branched flower cluster. This bract is rarely taller than the flower cluster.

The leaves remain close to the stem rather than projecting out at a sharp angle. In contrast with the thin, flat, fibrous leaves of true grasses, the leaves of black rush are somewhat fleshy, are convex on the lower surface and concave on the upper, and have no midrib. The leaves are rarely more than 1/16 inch (2 mm) wide, vary in length from 4 to 8 inches (10–20 cm), and taper to a slender tip.

The flowers are borne in one-sided groups of three to six along the branches of the flower clusters. The individual flowers are seldom more than 1/8 inch (3 mm) across, but they are so exquisite in detail that they warrant close study under a magnifying lens. Each flower has six tepals that are similar in size and shape. They are triangular and curve slightly inward. They are chocolate-brown on the edges and green through the center. The brilliant orange ovary is perched above the ring of surrounding tepals and is topped with a stigma that has three plumelike rosy-red to purple segments. The six anthers are pale yellow and are borne in a ring below the feathery stigma.

The flowers appear from June to September, and a few weeks after the plant blooms, the shiny dark brown seeds develop. The seeds, which are globular and narrow toward the base, are partially enclosed by the remains of the tepals. The surface of mature seeds is delicately ribbed and cross-lined. When the seeds are fully ripe, they color wide areas of the marsh reddish-brown.

Toad-rush (*Juncus ambiguus* Guss.) may be found in saline habitats from Labrador south to Massachusetts and Rhode Island. This little rush is an annual, seldom reaching more than 6 inches (15 cm) in height and easily overlooked except in mid-June when it blooms.

The inflorescence of toad-rush occupies at least two-thirds of the total plant and is a branched panicle with the flowers scattered along the branches in twos and threes. The anthers are a conspicuous golden-brown and longer than the threadlike filament on which they grow.

Toad-rush was formerly listed as *Juncus bufonius* L. var. *halophilus* Buch. & Fern. Typical *Juncus bufonius* grows in damp to wet freshwater habitats throughout this book's range and is at least twice the height of *Juncus ambiguus*.

Needlerush, Black Rush

Juncus roemerianus Scheele
Rush Family, Juncaceae

RANGE: Southern New Jersey south to Florida and west to southern Texas.
HABITAT: Landward edges of salt marshes, brackish marshes, and tidal creeks.

Needlerush produces vigorous rhizomes and forms dense colonies in the transition zone between regularly flooded salt marshes and upland areas. New growth of needlerush is a deep, dull green, but from a distance, a stand of needlerush, which also contains old growth, appears grayish-tan, making it readily distinguishable from a deep green stand of smooth cordgrass (*Spartina alterniflora*).

Needlerush grows from 15 inches to over 6½ feet (0.4–2 m) tall. Both stems and "leaves" are round and grayish-green, except for the lower portion of the stems, which, like the rhizomes, are reddish. The stem terminates in a cluster of flowers; rising erect above the flower cluster is a bract (often called a "leaf") that appears to be a continuation of the stem. This bract may be 1–3 feet (30–90 cm) long. A sheath wraps around the base of the flower cluster and the bract.

Needlerush, *Juncus roemerianus*

The flowers develop laterally at this sheath. The brown (or sometimes greenish-yellow) flowers are ⅛ inch (3 mm) long and are borne in small branched clusters, with the three outer tepals distinctly longer and more sharp-pointed than the three inner ones. Some plants produce only female flowers, whereas others have flowers that contain both male and female parts. The flowers bloom from March to October, followed by small, globular, dark brown, three-sided seeds.

Like the stems, needlerush bracts are stiff and pungent. In addition, they have a needle-sharp tip at the upper end that is rigid enough to tear skin and clothing. It is advisable to avoid contact with needlerush on field trips.

Needlerush is most abundant in extensive colonies in the marshes of northern Florida but is an important component of coastal marshes as far north as North Carolina and Maryland. It gives a brown-black appearance to the marshes where it grows in large stands (hence its other common name, black rush). It is often associated with *Spartina patens* and *Spartina alterniflora*. Needlerush is a good indicator plant showing the landward extent of salinity in brackish marshes. In estuaries in the South, needlerush is the dominant plant.

Saw-grass (*Cladium mariscus* [L.] Pohl ssp. *jamaicense* [Crantz] Kükenth, or *Cladium jamaicense* Crantz, according to some authorities) is another grasslike plant that can form dense colonies in brackish marshes. Unlike rushes and grasses, which usually have round stems, saw-grass has the three-sided stem typical of many members of the sedge family (Cyperaceae), to which it belongs.

Saw-grass is a perennial that can colonize large areas of brackish and tidal freshwater marshes with its rhizomes. It grows 3⅓–10 feet (1–3 m) in height. Its leaves are 3⁄16–½ inch (5–12 mm) wide and may be flat or folded down the midrib. It is the leaves that give saw-grass its name: along their margins and the midrib on the lower surface of the leaf are tiny rough projections that make the leaf feel like a saw blade. They can cut like one too, making large stands of this species, like stands of needlerush, places to avoid on field trips.

The inflorescence of saw-grass branches many times, so it is easy to understand how this genus was given the name *Cladium*, which is from the Greek word *cladion*, meaning "branchlet." Saw-grass grows from southeastern Virginia south to the West Indies and west along the Gulf coast to Texas. It is the major component of the "river of grass" of the Florida Everglades, written about so eloquently by Marjory Stoneman Douglas in *The Everglades: River of Grass* (1947).

Twig-rush (*Cladium mariscoides* [Muhl.] Torr.) may also be found along the upper, less saline edges of salt marshes and in freshwater marshes from Minnesota and Nova Scotia south to Texas and Florida. Inland it is typically found in the peaty soils of bogs, fens, and lakeshores. It is more slender than saw-grass, grows only to 3 feet (90 cm) in height, and has narrower leaves that lack the saw blade projections of saw-grass, although they may be slightly rough along the margins.

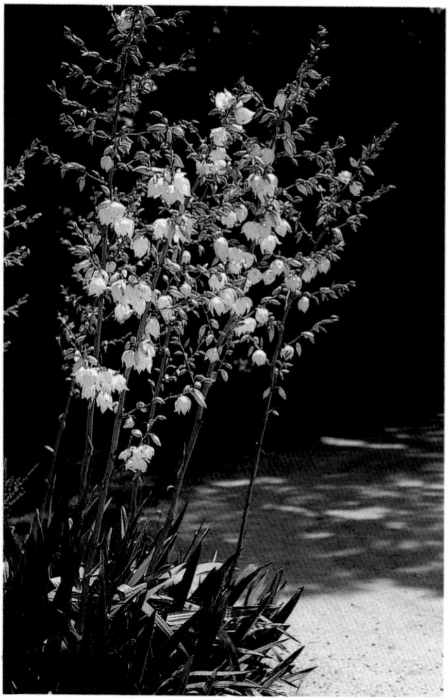

Bear grass,
Yucca filamentosa

Bear Grass, Adam's Needle

Yucca filamentosa L.
Agave Family, Agavaceae

RANGE: Native from Maryland south to Florida and west to Louisiana; escaped from cultivation and naturalized along the coast from Maryland north to Massachusetts.
HABITAT: Sand dunes and other dry soils in open areas and thin woods.

Yucca plants are famous for their tough leaves and sharp edges, which give these plants such colorful common names as Adam's needle, bear grass, and Spanish bayonet.

Yucca filamentosa may occasionally have a short trunk but usually grows as a cluster of leaves emerging directly from a short perennial base underground. The plants may grow as isolated clumps or as a mass of clumps crowded together. From Maryland north, where

Yucca filamentosa has escaped from cultivation, it appears to be spreading and bears watching as a potentially invasive ornamental.

The leaves are dark green, leathery, and tough. Most of them have strong, white, curling fibers hanging from the margins; these fibers give this species another common name, silkgrass. The leaves are up to 32 inches (80 cm) long and 2¾ inches (7 cm) wide in the middle, narrowing to ¾ inch (2 cm) at the base and tapering abruptly to a firm sharp point at the upper end.

The flowering stems may be up to 10 feet (3 m) tall and have a massive panicle of flowers 2–6 feet (0.6–1.8 m) long at the top. Each branch of the panicle bears a large number of bell-shaped white flowers that are rounded at the top, open at the bottom, and 2–2¾ inches (5–7 cm) long. The flowers are composed of five to seven tepals.

The fruits are small cylindrical pods 1³⁄₁₆–2 inches (3–5 cm) long, ¾ inch (2 cm) in diameter, and constricted around the middle. When ripe and dry, they are tan to gray in color and have a papery texture.

The blooming period of this species of yucca is from late April to September, depending on the location.

Other species of yucca found in coastal habitats in this book's range include Spanish bayonet (*Yucca aloifolia* L.) and mound-lily yucca (*Yucca gloriosa* L.). Spanish bayonet is a native of Mexico that has escaped from cultivation north to southern coastal North Carolina in this book's range. Growing as a shrub or small tree with a stout trunk and one or more branches, it may reach up to 16½ feet (5 m) in height. Each stiff leaf is tipped with a very sharp point, and the leaf margins have sharp teeth that can inflict painful cuts. This species grows in open areas on sandy soils, including sand dunes and the edges of brackish marshes.

The native mound-lily yucca is found in similar habitats from Louisiana to the central coast of North Carolina. It may also grow as a shrub or a small tree, reaching up to 16½ feet (5 m) in height, although it is usually no more than 6½ feet (2 m) tall in this book's range. The leaf tips of this species are also very sharp, but the leaf edges are neither filamentous nor serrated, instead having a narrow brown margin. Both this species and Spanish bayonet have fruits that droop downward, unlike bear grass, which has erect fruit.

Yucca flaccida Haw. is sometimes treated as a separate species, but in the system used here, it is included under *Yucca filamentosa*.

Yucca flowers attract hummingbirds and many insects, but they have a particularly interesting relationship with moths of the genera *Tegeticula* and *Parategeticula* in the family Incurvariidae. When a female moth visits a yucca flower, she gathers pollen and rolls it into a ball. After collecting pollen masses from several flowers, she finds a flower at the appropriate stage, bores holes in its ovary, and deposits eggs. After she deposits the eggs, she climbs up the stigmas of that flower and stuffs a pollen ball into the tube created by the united stigmas, thus pollinating the flower. The moth eggs develop within the fruit capsule and hatch just as the yucca seeds are ripening. Although some of the seeds are eaten by the larvae before they emerge and fall to the ground to pupate, enough remain to form new yucca plants.

Native Americans have used yucca in many different ways. The leaves are intertwined to make cords that can be woven into baskets, mats, and other products. The roots, which contain saponins, are used to make soap for washing clothing as well as for ceremonial bathing in some tribes. The plants have had many edible and medicinal uses as well.

Starry False Solomon's Seal

Maianthemum stellatum (L.) Link
Lily Family, Liliaceae

RANGE: Newfoundland south to New Jersey; inland to Virginia, Indiana, and Missouri; and west to British Columbia and California.
HABITAT: Sandy or gravelly soils of coastal thickets and shores, coastal bluffs, hedgerows, and open fields and woodlands.

Starry false Solomon's seal is an attractive spring-blooming plant. It is an erect or slightly arching perennial that grows 8–24 inches (20–60 cm) tall with a terminal cluster of starry white flowers.

The thick lance-shaped leaves are sessile or slightly clasping and are 2⅜–6 inches (6–15 cm) long and ¾–2 inches (2–5 cm) wide. The leaves tend to be stiffly ascending, although they are sometimes arching, and they are often crowded along the stem. They appear smooth, but close inspection may reveal the presence of fine hairs on the undersides of the leaves and on the stems. The stems may be green or a deep reddish color.

Starry false Solomon's seal, *Maianthemum stellatum*

The flowers are borne on short stalks at the end of the stem in an unbranched cluster that may contain as few as five flowers or as many as 20 or more. Each snowy-white flower is approximately ⅜ inch (1 cm) across and has six tepals, a single central pistil, and six white stamens tipped with a yellow anther.

The berries that form after the plants have bloomed are initially green with blackish stripes, ripening to dark red or almost black. The berries are not considered a major food for wildlife, but they are eaten by grouse, songbirds, and small mammals.

Some authorities call this species *Smilacina stellata* (L.) Desf. and separate it into two varieties, the coastal variety being *Smilacina stellata* var. *crassa* Victorin.

Solomon's plume or false Solomon's seal (*Maianthemum racemosum* [L.] Link) and Canada mayflower (*Maianthemum canadense* Desf.) may be found in coastal woodlands in the northern portion of this book's range, but from Maryland south, they are primarily plants of piedmont and mountain habitats.

Solomon's plume, which grows in woodlands from Nova Scotia south to Georgia and west to British Columbia and Arizona, may become as tall as 3 feet (90 cm), with a stem that tends to form a strong arch. It has elliptical leaves that extend horizontally from the stem, and both the stem and the undersides of the leaves are finely hairy. The branching inflorescence contains numerous tiny white star-shaped flowers, each usually no more than 5⁄32 inch (4 mm) across. The fruits are red when ripe and may be mottled with purple. An alternate name for this species is *Smilacina racemosa* (L.) Desf.

Canada mayflower or wild lily-of-the-valley is a diminutive woodland plant that may grow in large patches. It can be found from Labrador and Newfoundland south to the mountains of North Carolina and west to British Columbia, Kentucky, and Iowa. Each flowering plant has a heart-shaped leaf halfway up the stem and then one or two other smaller smooth leaves above, topped with an unbranched cluster of six or seven starry white flowers no more than ¼ inch (7 mm) across. The entire plant is usually no more than 3 inches (7.5 cm) tall, although specimens nearly 8 inches (20 cm) tall have been recorded. The flowers are fragrant, and a wide expanse of these plants gives the woodlands a fragrance that proclaims, "Springtime!" By July, the flowers have been replaced by berries that are at first cream-and-red speckled and then by August are solid red. The red berries may remain on the plants into the winter and provide a lovely contrast with the snow.

The scientific name *Maianthemum* is derived from the Latin word *Maius* for the month of May and the Greek word *anthemon*, meaning "a flower." *Maianthemum* species usually bloom in May and sometimes into June. The common name Solomon's seal, which is used for several of these species, refers to circular scars on the elongated rootstocks. Each scar represents a year's growth and resembles a king's seal.

Atamasco Lily

Zephranthes atamasca (L.) Herbert
Lily Family, Liliaceae

RANGE: Piedmont and coastal areas from southern Virginia to Alabama.
HABITAT: Moist meadows and wet open woods.

Atamasco lily is one of the most conspicuous spring flowers, blooming from mid-March to May depending on the location; it looks more like a cultivated plant than a wild one. The flowers resemble a translucent Easter lily and are 2¾–4 inches (7–10 cm) long, rising bare-stemmed from a bulb. They are usually white but sometimes

Atamasco lily,
Zephranthes atamasca

rose-pink; generally there is only one flower per bulb, but occasionally a bulb will produce two or three flowers. The leaves appear after the plant blooms.

In the areas where they are adapted, atamasco lilies appear to grow exceptionally well under large live oak trees (*Quercus virginiana*) where the grass is mowed regularly and other vegetation is rather sparse, so that the atamasco lilies have little competition. Large colonies of atamasco lilies are likely to be found at such sites, and the ratio of white to pink flowers is usually about 50 to 1.

The generic name *Zephranthes* is from the Greek words *zephyr*, for the west wind, and *anthos*, meaning "flower." "Atamasca" is apparently what Native Americans called this lily. Another common name for it is naked lady, referring to the bare, leafless stem from which the flower grows. The plant is known to be poisonous to livestock and should not be eaten by people as well.

Redroot, *Lachnanthes caroliana*

Redroot

Lachnanthes caroliana (Lam.) Dandy
Bloodwort Family, Haemodoraceae

RANGE: Nova Scotia south to Florida and the West Indies and west to Louisiana; also in a few sites in the south-central United States.
HABITAT: Acidic swamps, bogs, wet ditches, pond borders, and low woodlands.

Lachnanthes caroliana is the only representative of the bloodwort family in the United States and Canada. It is primarily a coastal plain species, although isolated populations can be found far from the coastal plain in Tennessee and West Virginia. It is rare in New England but more common from New Jersey south. Apparently this plant has spread into commercial cranberry bogs in some regions, where it can be an aggressive weed.

Redroot is a perennial with slender rhizomes and stolons that yield a red sap. It grows 8–30 inches (20–80 cm) in height. The longest leaves, which may be up to 16 inches (40 cm) long, are near the base of the plant; scattered, progressively shorter leaves may be found along the flowering stalk. The base of each leaf forms a sheath around the stalk, and the leaf remains folded inward along the midvein; a short distance from the stalk, the two leaf margins fuse and remain fused to the leaf tip. The leaves and base of the flowering stalk are smooth, but the plant becomes hairy near the top of the flower stalk, where the stalk and flower cluster are densely covered with matted, woolly hairs. The genus name *Lachnanthes* refers to these hairs: *lachne* is the Greek word for "wool," and *anthos* means "flower."

The rounded or flat-topped flower cluster is composed of several alternate branches, each branch with numerous small, short-stalked, dull yellow flowers. Each flower is about 3/8 long (10 mm) with six tepals (three longer and three shorter ones) that are covered with woolly hairs and with three stamens. The hairy tepals persist as the fruit develops.

Redroot is well known for its use as a dye, as a synonym for the scientific name, *Lachnanthes tinctoria* (J. F. Gmel.) Salisb., attests. It has also been used medicinally. The Seminoles of Florida made a tonic with *Lachnanthes* root that reportedly gave its users the impetus to perform heroic deeds and make fine speeches. In the South, redroot is reputed to be poisonous to hogs.

A similar plant, goldcrest (*Lophiola aurea* Ker-Gawl.), also has a similar geographic range and habitat. Like redroot, goldcrest has folded, fused leaves and is densely covered with woolly hairs. The leaves of goldcrest, however, are narrower, the flowers are a brighter yellow, the hairs extend most of the way down the flower stalk, and there is a tuft of hairs at the base of the stamens and pistil. Its six tepals are closer to one another in length, and it has six rather than three stamens. The plant grows 1–2 feet (30–60 cm) tall. Some authorities have placed *Lophiola* in the bloodwort family, but recent study shows that it is more closely allied with members of the lily family.

Slender Blue Flag

Iris prismatica Pursh *ex* Ker-Gawl.
Iris Family, Iridaceae

RANGE: Near the coast from Nova Scotia south to Georgia, as well as inland.
HABITAT: Freshwater, brackish, and saline swamps, marshes, meadows, and shores.

"Iris" means rainbow in Greek, an apt name for this very showy group of flowers. There are four species of blue flag iris that grow

Slender blue flag, *Iris prismatica*

along the Atlantic coast in this book's range. The most widespread is slender blue flag, a narrow-leaved perennial with striking violet-blue flowers. It grows up to $2\frac{1}{3}$ feet (70 cm) in height and has leaves that are $\frac{1}{8}$–$\frac{1}{4}$ inch (3–7 mm) wide. In many respects, it is a smaller and overall more slender version of common blue flag (*Iris versicolor* L.), which may reach $3\frac{1}{3}$ feet (1 m) in height and has leaves that are $\frac{3}{16}$–$1\frac{3}{16}$ inches (5–30 mm) wide.

The easiest distinction, however, is by habitat. Common blue flag grows in fresh water, whereas slender blue flag is more likely to be found in brackish to saline habitats, often in sight of salt water, where it frequently associates with narrow-leaved cattail (*Typha angustifolia*) and marsh fern (*Thelypteris palustris*). The other two species, southern blue flag (*Iris virginica* L.) and purple flag (*Iris tridentata* Pursh), are also more likely to be found in freshwater habitats on the coastal plain, southern blue flag from Maryland south to Texas and purple flag from North Carolina south to northern Florida. Common blue flag grows from Canada south to Virginia and inland to Minnesota.

Iris flowers are beautifully designed to attract the insects and birds that pollinate them. Each flower has nine showy petal-like structures. The outermost parts—the sepals or falls—are longer and broader than the other segments and are flat or arch downward. In the innermost layer are the three petals or standards, which are erect or arch outward and are shorter and narrower than the sepals. Between the falls and the standards are the pistils, which have long styles that form a passageway with each sepal, ending in a flaplike stigma that bends upward. Hidden beneath the pistils are the stamens. The falls often have a "beard" of hairs, lines that serve as nectar guides, and sometimes a yellow or white spot to help advertise the presence of nectar.

When an insect lands on the colorful fall, the lines guide it toward the nectar at the center of the flower, and it progresses into the tube formed by the pistil and the sepal. As it moves down this passageway, it deposits pollen from another iris flower onto the receptive area of the stigma and then picks up fresh pollen from the anthers. As the insect leaves the flower, it moves over the nonreceptive area of the stigma, which ensures that the insect does not pollinate the plant with its own pollen.

Among other differences, the four species mentioned above vary in color (the shades of blues and purples in the flowers), shape and size of the falls and standards, type of hairs (or absence of hairs), color of the showy spot, and degree of venation on the falls. They also exhibit significant differences in the shape of the fruit capsules. Of the four, only slender blue flag has a sharply three-angled fruit capsule.

Green-fly Orchid

Epidendrum conopseum Ait. f.
Orchid Family, Orchidaceae

RANGE: Rare in southeastern North Carolina and a narrow strip south along the coast to Georgia and Florida, where it is more common; occasional along the Gulf coast to westernmost Louisiana.
HABITAT: Epiphytic on the bark of old trees, especially southern magnolia and live oak but also on sweet gum, black gum, red cedar, and bald cypress, and occasionally on sandstone and in swamps and forests.

Green-fly orchid is the only epiphytic orchid that grows north of Florida, and it has a more northerly range than any other epiphytic orchid in the Western Hemisphere because of its ability to with-

Green-fly orchid, *Epidendrum conopseum*

stand temperatures as low as 38°F. Its scientific name, *Epidendrum*, means "growing on trees," reflecting its epiphytic habit. The second half of its name, *conopseum*, translates from the Greek as "gnatlike," perhaps referring to the small size of the flowers.

The plant has no pseudobulbs, which are enlarged areas on the stem found in some species of orchids. The stems are slender, smooth, either erect or vinelike, and 2⅜–16 inches (6–40 cm) long, with one to three (or sometimes more) leaves growing in two ranks above the middle of the stem. The leaves are pale green, a narrow oblong in shape, and 1³⁄₁₆–3½ inches (3–9 cm) long. They have a leathery texture and taper to an abrupt point that may or may not end in a firm bristle. The leaves have no petiole but extend into tightly pressed sheaths around the stems. The sheaths are ⅛–¼ inch (3–7 mm) long.

The fragrant flowers are pale yellow-green, are occasionally tinged with purple, and are never more than 1 inch (2.5 cm) in diameter and often less. They have a lip, two slender petals, and two sepals that are somewhat wider than the petals. The number of flowers per plant varies from a single flower to more than 100 on large plants cultivated in a greenhouse. It flowers year-round but mainly from January to September.

Although this species of orchid is relatively rare and its habitat is often far above the ground or in inaccessible wet places, it may be seen on field trips to preserves where the plants are protected. Information about these field trips can be obtained from local botanical societies.

Lizard's Tail

Saururus cernuus L.
Lizard's Tail Family, Saururaceae

RANGE: Southern Quebec and New England south to Florida and west to Minnesota and Texas.
HABITAT: Swamps and marshes (including tidal freshwater wetlands), margins of lakes and ponds, and low wet woods.

Lizard's tail grows best in black muck more than 3⅓ feet (1 m) deep, so be sure to measure the depth before exploring a large vigorous stand of lizard's tail—it is easy to get stuck in one! Although it is uncommon or rare in coastal areas at the northern end of its range, lizard's tail is much more common in coastal habitats south of New Jersey. It is also known as swamp lily or water-dragon.

Lizard's tail is a perennial that grows from aromatic rhizomes and is often found in large colonies. The jointed stems grow closely together, reaching up to 4 feet (1.2 m) tall, and are sparsely branched. The entire, alternate leaves have long petioles, are heart-shaped, are 2–6 inches (5–15 cm) long and up to 3½ inches (9 cm) wide, and taper to a slender point.

The flowers are white and bloom from May to September, depending on the location. The flowers are produced toward the ends of the jointed stems, each flower stalk being opposite a leaf stalk. The flowering stalk is 2⅜–8 inches (6–20 cm) long, with the white flowers closely packed together at the upper end. The flowers have a pistil, three to eight stamens, and an ovary but no petals or sepals.

The top flowers are the first to bloom, and as they wither and droop, the end of the flower stalk also droops, making the flowering spike look like the letter J upside down or a lizard's tail. The scientific name also refers to this characteristic: *Saururus* comes from the Greek words *sauros*, meaning "lizard," and *oura*, meaning "tail"; *cernuus* means "nodding." When the fruits mature, the spike once again becomes erect.

Lizard's tail,
Saururus cernuus

Saururus can be easily recognized since only two species exist in the world—the species described here and a similar one that grows in Asia.

Northern Bayberry

Myrica pensylvanica Loisel.
Bayberry Family, Myricaceae

RANGE: Newfoundland south to North Carolina (where it is rare), and, less frequently, inland to southern Ontario and Ohio.
HABITAT: Acidic soils, from wet to dry, of sand dunes, coastal thickets, open woods, upper edges of coastal marshes, bogs, and moist shores.

Northern bayberry is an important component of coastal thickets in the northern half of this book's range; to the south, it is replaced

Northern bayberry,
Myrica pensylvanica

by wax-myrtle or southern bayberry (*Myrica cerifera* L.). Northern bayberry thrives in soils with a wide range of moisture, whereas wax-myrtle grows best in wet soils.

Myrica pensylvanica is a many-branched shrub that is typically about 3–4 feet (0.9–1.2 m) in height, although it may reach 10 feet (3 m) or more. The deep green alternate leaves tend to be clustered near the ends of the twigs and are usually 1½–3⅛ inches (4–8 cm) long and ½–1³⁄₁₆ inches (1.2–3 cm) wide. The leaf has an elliptical shape, with a wedge-shaped base and often a few small teeth near the tip of the leaf, which comes to a tiny point. The leaves, which often appear twisted at the midpoint of the blade, may be either dull or glossy and appear to be smooth, but close inspection with a magnifying lens reveals short, scattered hairs across the upper surface and hairs along the midvein on the lower surface as well as along the margins of the leaves. A lens will also show the tiny golden (or sometimes brown) resin dots on the lower leaf surface. These resinous glands produce the oils that give bayberry its distinctive fragrance.

Bayberry is usually dioecious, with inconspicuous male and female flowers borne on separate plants. The round fruits that form on the female plants are initially green but turn a dusty gray-blue as they mature. They are ⅛–3⁄16 inch (3–5 mm) across with a bumpy surface and are covered with hairs when young. Recent evidence indicates that in some species of *Myrica*, individual plants may not remain either male or female throughout their life spans but may be female in some years and male in others.

The fragrant fruit of bayberries is the source of the famous bayberry candles, which require 40 pounds (18 kg) of ripe berries to produce 1 pound (0.45 kg) of wax. The berries are boiled in water until the wax floats to the surface; then the wax is strained through a cloth while still hot to remove the solids. Wicks are then dipped into the kettle of hot water with the wax floating on top, and the dipping process is repeated until the candles are the desired thickness. Bayberry candles are considered a luxury because of the effort involved in producing them and because their fragrance is much more pleasant than that of ordinary tallow candles.

Wax-myrtle grows from New Jersey south to Florida and the West Indies and west to Arkansas, Texas, and Mexico. It may grow as a colony of short plants reaching only 3⅓ feet (1 m) tall or take the form of a tree and grow to over 33 feet (10 m) in height. Unlike northern bayberry, which has mostly deciduous leaves, the leaves of wax-myrtle are evergreen, up to 6 inches (15 cm) long, and about 1 inch (2.5 cm) wide. They may have a few teeth on the upper third of the leaf and have golden or brown resin glands on both leaf surfaces. The gray-blue fruit is hairless and usually less than ⅛ inch (3 mm) in diameter.

A third species of bayberry can be found in coastal plain habitats from New Jersey south. Swamp candleberry (*Myrica heterophylla* Raf.) is a shrub or small tree that grows as tall as 6½ feet (2 m). Its leaves are up to 4¾ inches (12 cm) long and 2 inches (5 cm) wide, have resin dots only on the lower surface, and may persist through the year. This species also grows in damp or wet habitats.

As a group, the bayberries are well adapted to acidic, nitrogen-poor soils. Like members of the bean family, their roots develop a relationship with certain bacteria in the soil. These bacteria, which grow in nodules on the plant's roots, are able to convert nitrogen from the atmosphere into compounds that the plants can absorb and use to make amino acids, the basis of proteins. In return, the plants provide carbohydrates that the bacteria use for food.

The myrtle or yellow-rumped warbler thrives on bayberry fruit during the winter months. This may explain why myrtle warblers can spend the winter farther north than many other wood warblers, which seem to lack the necessary enzymes to digest the waxy coating on this fruit. Bobwhite also eat large quantities of bayberries, and tree swallows rely heavily on them during migration and in the winter.

Dwarf Chestnut Oak, Dwarf Chinquapin Oak

Quercus prinoides Willd.
Beech Family, Fagaceae

RANGE: Southern Maine south to North Carolina (mountains and piedmont only) and inland to the Midwest and Oklahoma.
HABITAT: Dry sandy soils near the coast; inland on dry rocky slopes.

On the Atlantic coastal plain from Massachusetts south to New Jersey, the dwarf chestnut oak is associated with pitch pine barrens and dry sandy thickets near the coast. It is a slender shrub 3⅓–10 feet (1–3 m) (occasionally up to 16½ feet [5 m]) tall and often grows in colonies. The alternate leaves are oblong or slightly wider at the upper end. They are 1½–6 inches (4–15 cm) long and have five to eight veins on either side. The sinuses of the leaves are rounded, but each vein ends at the edge of the leaf in a sharply pointed tip. The upper surface of the leaf is bright green, and the lower surface is covered with fine gray hairs.

The acorns are ⅝–1 inch (1.6–2.5 cm) long, with thick cups that are half the length of the acorns, and they are reputed to be edible. This species is among the oaks that have relatively sweet acorns.

Bear oak (*Quercus ilicifolia* Wangenh.) is another small oak that may be found on dry rocky or sandy soils on the northern coastal plain from southern Maine south to New York, as well as inland to Ohio, West Virginia, and the mountains of North Carolina. A shrub or small tree that rarely reaches 15 feet (4.5 m) in height, it typically has short leaves no more than 4¾ inches (12 cm) long and one-half

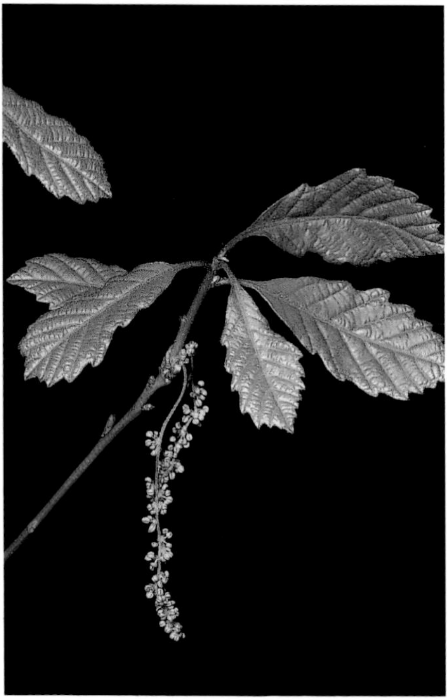

Dwarf chestnut oak,
Quercus prinoides

to two-thirds as wide as they are long; each leaf has two to seven bristle-tipped lobes. The leaves are green on top and covered with fine gray hairs on the undersurface. The name *ilicifolia* means "leaf like holly," which refers to the fact that the leaves bear a resemblance to the leaves of American holly (*Ilex opaca*).

A number of other small oaks may be found on the coastal plain of the southern states. Sand live oak (*Quercus geminata* Small) grows on coastal dunes and in sandy areas inland from North Carolina to Mississippi (some authorities list it as *Quercus virginiana* P. Mill. var. *maritima* [Michx.] Sarg.). It can be a shrub or small tree, reaching up to 33 feet (10 m) in height. Its thick, oblong, evergreen leaves are usually entire, roll under at the margins, have prominent veins, and are covered with tiny hairs on the undersurface; some of these hairs lie flat against the leaf, but others stand straight up. It usually flowers two or three weeks after live oaks (*Quercus virginiana*) in the same vicinity. Its descriptive name *geminata*, meaning "twins," refers to the fact that the acorns are usually found growing in pairs.

Turkey oak (*Quercus laevis* Walt.) is an important component of coastal plain plant communities on poor sandy soils from southeastern Virginia south to Florida and west to Louisiana. It is often found growing alongside long-leaf pine (*Pinus palustris*) and other oaks that can tolerate dry sterile soils. It can grow up to 66 feet (20 m) tall (but is usually shorter), and its leaves may be as much as 12 inches (30 cm) long and 8 inches (20 cm) wide, with deeply cut sinuses and three to seven long bristle-tipped lobes; the longest lobes are near the center of the leaf. The leaves are shiny on top and have tufts of hairs in the axils of the main veins on the underside. The acorns are up to 1 inch (2.5 cm) long, are on short stalks, and have cups that cover about one-third of the nut.

Sand post oak (*Quercus margarettiae* Ashe *ex* Small) is a colonial shrub or small tree that grows up to 33 feet (10 m) tall in dry sandy soils on the coastal plain from southeastern Virginia south to Florida and west to central Texas and Oklahoma. It is often found in mixed long-leaf pine and scrub oak woodlands or in areas that have been burned over or heavily logged. Its short-stalked leaves have from three to five irregular blunt lobes, are 1½–4 inches (4–10 cm) long and ¾–2 inches (2–5 cm) wide, and, when mature, are smooth on the upper surface and softly hairy beneath.

Myrtle oak (*Quercus myrtifolia* Willd.) may also be found on dunes and in sandy scrub oak and pine woodlands from South Carolina south to Florida and west to Louisiana. Usually a shrub but occasionally a small tree, it may grow to over 40 feet (12 m) in height and often forms thickets. Its entire, evergreen leaves are no more than 2 inches (5 cm) long and are rounded at the tip, losing the terminal bristles very early in their growth.

Live Oak

Quercus virginiana P. Mill.
Beech Family, Fagaceae

RANGE: Coastal plain from southeastern Virginia south to Florida and west to Texas and northeastern Mexico.
HABITAT: Maritime forests and sandy soils in both dry and moist situations.

An April dawn is a grand time to visit a live oak grove. The new leaves form a haze of pale green overhead, and the old brown leaves

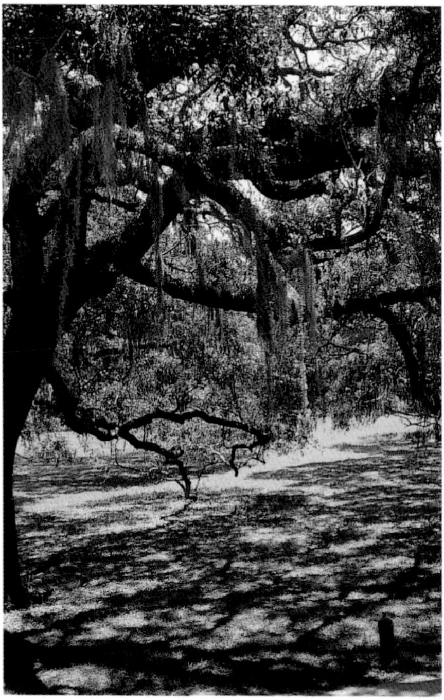

Live oak,
Quercus virginiana

crackle underfoot beneath the great boughs. Columns of resurrection fern trail along the broad branches, and the sunlight casts lacy patterns through the Spanish moss onto the forest floor. High in the branches, wood warblers flitter in search of the insects that also thrive on these oaks.

The classic image of a live oak is of a large tree with a short stout trunk and huge, widely spreading branches dripping with Spanish moss. A live oak may grow as tall as 66 feet (20 m), with a crown much wider than the tree is tall and a diameter as much as 9 feet (2.7 m). It can also take the form of a shrub in some situations.

Live oak has alternate, oblong, evergreen leaves that are thick and shiny on the upper surface and covered on the undersurface with very fine gray to whitish hairs that lie flat. They are usually entire, are 1½–4¾ inches (4–12 cm) long and ⅜–2⅜ inches (1–6 cm) wide, and have a very short petiole, although occasionally new leaves will have sharp tips and even a few teeth along the margins. The veins of the leaves are not very noticeable, and often the margins curl under slightly. The leaves are shed after a year as new leaves emerge.

The male flowers of live oak are on clusters of slender, hairy, dangling catkins, and the inconspicuous, wind-pollinated female flowers may be found in the axils of the leaves of the current year's growth. The shiny, dark brown acorns are on stalks 1–5 inches (2.5–12.5 cm) long, either solitary or in clusters of two to five. Each acorn is up to 1 inch (2.5 cm) in length, with a hairy gray cup that may cover one-quarter to one-half of the cylindrical nut. Live oak acorns are low in tannic acid and are considered to be among the sweetest of the oak nuts, relished by people and many species of animals. The trees also shelter a great variety of plants and animals, comprising entire communities in southern coastal plain ecosystems.

Live oaks are planted as ornamentals and harvested for firewood. Although they are usually a component of forests behind coastal dunes (and inland), they are remarkably tolerant to salt spray and high winds.

Black oak (*Quercus velutina* Lam.) is an important barrier beach species north of New Jersey; it grows in dry soils and on dunes from southern Maine south to Florida and west to Minnesota and Texas. A number of other large and medium-sized oaks may be found in coastal plain habitats in this book's range, all of them native with one exception. English oak (*Quercus robur* L.) is a cultivated European oak that occasionally naturalizes in eastern Canada and the northeastern United States. In southern New England, naturalized English oak is seen only near the coast. The leaves resemble those of white oak (*Quercus alba* L.), but the petiole is very short, and the base of the leaf ends in two short earlobe-shaped projections. The acorns are borne in pairs on long stalks. English oak is easily recognized from a distance in autumn since its leaves remain green long after the glowing golds and russets of the native oaks have turned to dull brown.

There are more than 80 species of oaks in North America north of Mexico, as well as numerous hybrids. Oaks in northern climates are deciduous, but many southern species are evergreen. As a group, they are one of the most important components of North American forests. Forest types are often defined by oaks, as in oak-hickory forests and pine-oak scrublands. In one system of categorizing eastern North American forests, oaks are named in 64 out of 90 categories.

It would be difficult to overestimate the importance of oaks to wildlife. Over 90 species of birds and mammals are known to rely heavily on acorns as a fall and winter food source; countless other animals, both vertebrates and invertebrates, use oaks for food, shelter, and breeding sites. Oaks have also had great economic importance to people as lumber, firewood, shade trees, and livestock feed; many Native American tribes have also relied heavily on oaks as a source of food.

Sand Jointweed

Polygonella articulata (L.) Meisn.
Buckwheat Family, Polygonaceae

RANGE: Southern Quebec and Maine south on the coastal plain to northeastern North Carolina; also on the shores of the Great Lakes and inland dunes in Illinois, Iowa, and Minnesota.
HABITAT: Dry, acidic, sandy soils, backdunes, and open woods.

Coming across this wiry little plant in a pine barren forest or on the back of a dune is always a treat, a reminder of the beauty all around us.

Growing from 4 inches to 2 feet (10–60 cm) tall, this slim annual stands erect, with its branches mostly pointing upward. The stems are smooth and jointed. The small leaves roll in on the underside and are usually no more than 1 inch (2.5 cm) long and very narrow; they soon drop off and may be gone by flowering time.

Sand jointweed blooms from July to October, the tiny flowers often crowded on slender racemes. Although they have no petals, each stalked flower has five showy sepals that range in color from white to pink to deep rose. Initially the flowers open outward, but after pollination, they nod and take on a bell-like shape, becoming pinker with age.

The scientific name means "little *Polygonum*." *Polygonum* comes from the Greek words *poly*, meaning "many," and *gonu*, meaning "joint" or "knee," and refers to the jointed stems of these species. *Articulata* also alludes to the jointed nature of the stems.

Several other species of *Polygonella* may be found in the southern part of this book's range. October-flower (*Polygonella polygama* [Vent.] Engelm. & Gray) and knotweed (*Polygonella americana* [Fisch. & C. A. Mey.] Small) are both perennials with a woody base

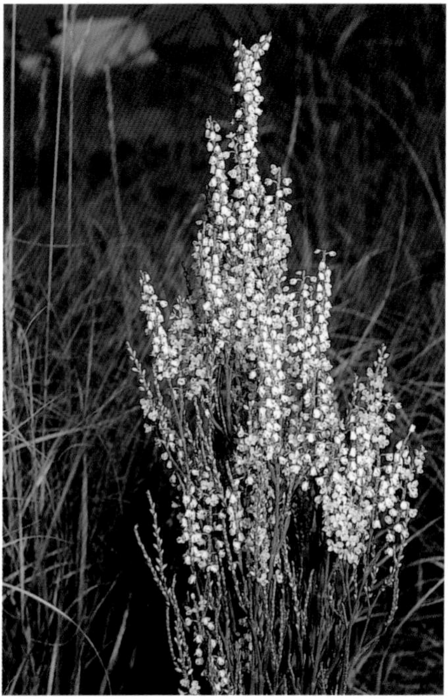

Sand jointweed,
Polygonella articulata

and often have branches that spread broadly near the ground. Fringed polygonella (*Polygonella fimbriata* [Ell.] Horton) and slender jointweed (*Polygonella gracilis* Meisn.) are erect annuals. Characteristics of the leaves, sepals, joint sheaths, and fruits help differentiate them.

Seabeach Orach, Spearscale

Atriplex pentandra (Jacq.) Standl.
Goosefoot Family, Chenopodiaceae

RANGE: Coastal New Hampshire south to Florida and the West Indies and west to Texas; also in South America.
HABITAT: Sandy seashores, dunes, and edges of tidal salt marshes.

The goosefoot family contains numerous species of fleshy or succulent herbs and shrubs. These plants are well adapted to dry and/or saline habitats, and thus many—such as the genera *Chenopodium*,

Seabeach orach, *Atriplex pentandra*

Atriplex, *Salsola*, *Suaeda*, *Salicornia*, and *Bassia*—are found in coastal and desert ecosystems. Although this group is not known for its showy flowers, the family does contain important food species, including spinach (*Spinacia oleracea* L.) and beets and Swiss chard (both cultivars of *Beta vulgaris* L.), and some plants with foliage of ornamental value, such as summer cypress (*Kochia scoparia* [L.] Schrad.).

Seabeach orach is a widely branching annual herb that may be erect or spread out on the ground. It grows as tall as 20 inches (50 cm) in this book's range. The alternate short-stalked or sessile leaves are $3/8$–$1\,3/16$ inches (1–3 cm) long and vary in shape from oblong to oval; the tips may be rounded or come to a point. The leaves are entire or may have margins that undulate or possess a few scattered teeth. Often there are clusters of smaller leaves at the base of the larger leaves or at the base of the flower clusters. The whole plant has a silvery-gray appearance because of the mealy scales that cover it, although the stems may be quite red, especially as autumn approaches.

Seabeach orach blooms from June until frost, with flowers that are green and inconspicuous. The male flowers are on a spikelike inflorescence at the end of the stem, and the female flowers are in rounded clusters in the leaf axils.

It is the fruits that most readily distinguish *Atriplex* species from other close relatives, such as *Chenopodium*. The female flowers and fruit of *Chenopodium* are enveloped in a four- or five-part calyx, whereas the female flowers and fruit of *Atriplex* are enclosed in two small bracts that may have very unusual shapes. In seabeach orach, these bracts are broadest in the middle, with several large teeth along the upper margin and a wedge-shaped base. Three or four smaller protuberances can be found near the base.

The name orach is a corruption of the generic name, *Atriplex*, which is the ancient Latin name for this genus. Some authorities separate *Atriplex arenaria* Nutt. from *Atriplex pentandra*. According to such a designation, *Atriplex arenaria* is the species in this book's range (and is the plant described here), and *Atriplex pentandra* occurs from southern Florida west to Texas and south to the Tropics.

Orach, Spearscale

Atriplex prostrata Bouchér *ex* DC.
Goosefoot Family, Chenopodiaceae

RANGE: Newfoundland south in this book's range to South Carolina and west to British Columbia, Oregon, and California.
HABITAT: Coastal beaches, edges of dunes, tidal salt and brackish marshes, and in saline soils inland.

Orach or spearscale is a widely distributed member of the goosefoot family. It grows along the coast in salt marshes and brackish areas that are occasionally flooded by salt water and in both saline and highly fertile soil inland.

Orach is a many-branched annual with weak stems and a sprawling habit of growth. Small plants may grow erect, but a plant of any size can cover an area 3–4 feet (0.9–1.2 m) in diameter and be no more than 10 inches (25 cm) tall. With support, it will grow like a vine.

There is considerable variation in orach leaves. The length may be 1–3 inches (2.5–7.5 cm), and the lower leaves are stalked and sometimes opposite, but the upper leaves are alternate and usually attached directly to the stem. The leaf shape ranges from long and slender to broadly triangular with a base that may be rounded, heart-shaped, arrowhead-shaped, or straight. The edges of the leaves may be entire, wavy, or somewhat serrate, and the color is a medium blue-green. When young, the leaves are covered with fine

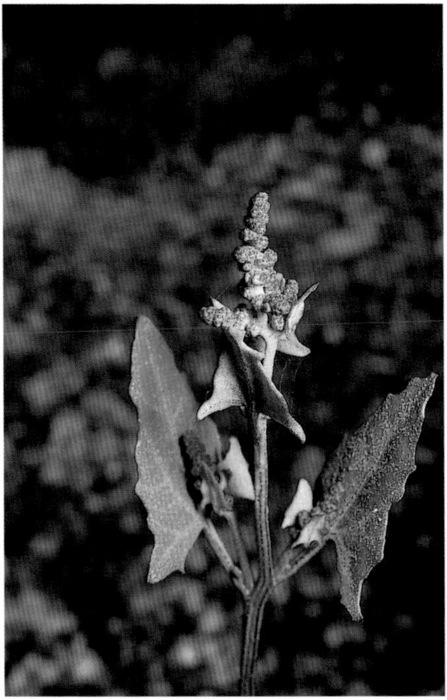

Orach,
Atriplex prostrata

white granules that sometimes may also be seen on the stems and bracts surrounding the seeds.

The flowers appear from June until frost and consist of masses of minute green or rosy flowers that grow in interrupted clusters along the upper ends of even the smallest branches. The individual flowers cannot be distinguished without a magnifying lens.

As the seeds develop, the triangular bracts that enclose them expand to ¼ inch (7 mm) in length and become fleshy, sometimes with protuberances on the sides. At this stage, they are conspicuous, and by autumn, when both the seed heads and the leaves have turned rosy-red, they provide a striking contrast with the color and texture of the marsh grasses.

The genus *Atriplex* is complex, and taxonomists differ on its treatment. In the system used here, *Atriplex prostrata* includes what some authors variously call *Atriplex hastata sensu* Aellen, *non* L. or *Atriplex patula* L. var. *hastata auct. non* (L.) Gray; the description in this book is based on *Atriplex patula* var. *hastata*.

Hairy bassia,
Bassia hirsuta

Hairy Bassia

Bassia hirsuta (L.) Aschers.
Goosefoot Family, Chenopodiaceae

RANGE: Massachusetts south to Virginia.
HABITAT: Salt marshes and saline shores.

Hairy bassia is a sprawling, bushy-branched annual 20–30 inches (50–80 cm) in diameter. The leaves are fleshy, round, and velvety, tapering slightly at either end, and are usually no more than ½ inch (12 mm) long. Like other members of the goosefoot family, hairy bassia turns bright pink or red in autumn and, at this stage, is usually glossy and smooth rather than hairy.

The flowers are so small that they are hardly visible without a magnifying lens. They contain only the organs required to produce seeds and five almost invisible sepals.

As the fruits mature, the sepals elongate and become fleshy. Two opposite sepals elongate more than the others and develop pointed ends. As a result, the ripe fruit is a fleshy, segmented oval with pointed ends and a bright red spot in the center. Ripe fruits seldom exceed ⅛ inch (3 mm) in length, and the seeds are almost invisible.

Hairy bassia is commonly found in disturbed areas on tidal salt marshes or areas where the predominant grass is salt hay grass (*Spartina patens*) and the sediment is high in organic matter rather than sand. At Cape May, New Jersey, where vigorous stands of salt hay grass cover miles of tidal salt marsh, hairy bassia is almost the only other species present. Masses of it grow along the saltmarsh creeks where black marine sediment has been exposed by the continuous traffic at boat landings.

A native of Europe, hairy bassia was apparently introduced into the United States early in the twentieth century. A reference book published in 1914 mentioned only in a footnote that it had been found in Massachusetts and New Jersey. The 1991 edition of the same reference noted that hairy bassia could be found from Massachusetts to Virginia.

Hyssop-leaved bassia (*Bassia hyssopifolia* [Pallas] Volk.), a native of Eurasia, may also be found naturalized along the seashore from Massachusetts south to New Jersey and in alkaline areas of the Southwest. It is a very hairy plant with short, fine hairs covering most surfaces and long, white, silky hairs in the floral axils. The leaves are flat and slender, 2–2⅜ inches (5–6 cm) long and only ⅜ inch (1 cm) wide. They are somewhat wrapped around the stem at the base and taper to a sharp point at the upper end. Like hairy bassia, this species has five sepals, but unlike hairy bassia, each sepal at maturity has a slender hooked spine on the dorsal surface, giving this species a second common name, five-hook bassia.

The genus *Bassia* is named in honor of Ferdinand Bassi, curator of the Botanic Garden of Bologna, Italy, in the eighteenth century.

Dwarf glasswort, *Salicornia bigelovii*

Dwarf Glasswort

Salicornia bigelovii Torr.
Goosefoot Family, Chenopodiaceae

RANGE: Nova Scotia south to Florida and the West Indies and west to Texas, Mexico, and California.
HABITAT: Tidal salt marshes with organic soils.

Dwarf glasswort is the least common of the species of glasswort that grow along the Atlantic coast, and like annual glasswort (*Salicornia virginica*), it is an annual. It usually grows on tidal salt marshes that contain high amounts of organic matter.

Dwarf glasswort may be found growing alone or in association with either annual glasswort or perennial glasswort (*Sarcocornia* spp.), but the species can be easily distinguished. It is also often associated with saltgrass (*Distichlis spicata*) and black rush (*Juncus gerardii*).

Like the other glassworts, dwarf glasswort has fleshy, jointed stalks. They tend to be club-shaped with rounded tops and taper toward the base. They vary in height from 4 to 16 inches (10–40 cm) and are usually about 3⁄16 inch (5 mm) thick. A plant may have only a single unbranched stalk or a stalk with two or three branches. The joints, which are obviously shorter than they are broad, are set at a sharp angle rather than horizontally, which makes the individual joints appear wedge-shaped. The scales (modified leaves) at the joints are pointed rather than blunt, with a bristle at the tip.

The flowers appear in depressions at the joints and are pale yellow structures similar to the flowers of annual glasswort. They are produced almost over the entire plant rather than only around the middle.

The seeds, like those of annual glasswort, germinate in the spring during the neap tides, but only after having floated around for a number of days.

In New England in autumn, the upper portions of dwarf glasswort turn dark red, but the lower portions remain green. Farther south, the plants remain green until frost.

Annual Glasswort

Salicornia virginica L.
Goosefoot Family, Chenopodiaceae

RANGE: New Hampshire south to Florida.
HABITAT: Tidal salt marshes, saline swales, and similar sites.

Annual glasswort is a succulent plant that ranges from 4 to 20 inches (10–50 cm) tall and is composed of either single or branched fleshy, jointed, jade-green stems. The joints are usually ⅛ inch (3 mm) thick and four times as long as they are wide.

Like many plants that are adapted to living in a saline environment, annual glasswort has anatomical features that differ from those of plants living on dry land. The leaves are reduced to blunt scales at the joints, and the flowers are tiny yellow dots. Each flower has two pistils and two stamens, and the flowers are produced in clusters of three in depressions at the joints of the stems. The two outer flowers are often sterile, and the center one produces seeds.

Large stands of annual glasswort are often found in shallow, sandy tidal salt marshes in New England, where the plant is associated with salt hay grass (*Spartina patens*). It is most conspicuous in October when it takes on autumn colors ranging from orange to rosy-red.

The seeds of annual glasswort germinate best at low salinities when exposed to air. These conditions exist during the neap tides in April. At this time, the tides are the lowest of the year and heavy rains lower the salinity of the marsh soils. The seeds have only about

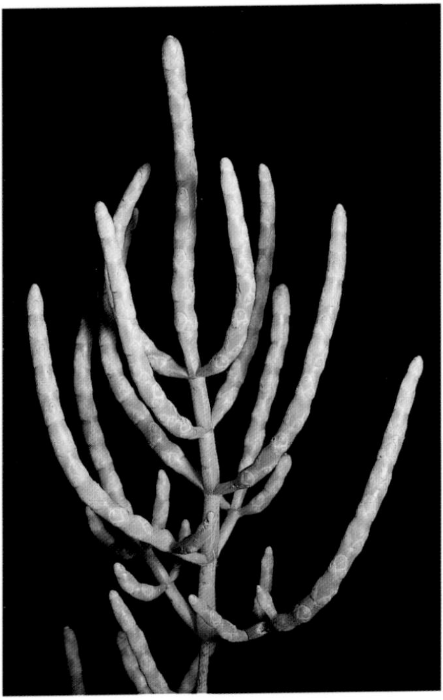

Annual glasswort,
Salicornia virginica

four days to germinate and produce a root long enough to attach the seedlings firmly to the substrate on which the plants grow. Seedlings that are not well established will be washed away by the next high tide. Under some circumstances, the seeds are not shed but remain on the plants and germinate as the plant decays.

Farther south, annual glasswort is less common. It is rarely found in the large salt hay grass marshes of New Jersey or the larger smooth cordgrass (*Spartina alterniflora*) marshes of Georgia, which are covered with water even at low tide. Annual glasswort has been reported in all of the coastal counties of Georgia, where it usually grows in saline dune swales and similar saline habitats but is not common.

Taxonomists have recently conducted genetic studies on the genus *Salicornia* and suggest that the species be differentiated taxonomically by chromosome count rather than anatomical characteristics, which are heavily influenced by the environment. These experts have proposed that the diploid annual be named *Salicornia maritima* Wolff & Jefferies and the tetraploid annual be named *Salicornia virginica* L. According to this scheme, *Salicornia maritima* extends only as far south as southern New England and Long Island, and *Salicornia virginica* is the widespread annual species in this book's range. To further complicate matters, both of these species have been called *Salicornia europaea* by some authors.

Common Saltwort

Salsola kali L. ssp. *kali*
Goosefoot Family, Chenopodiaceae

RANGE: Newfoundland south to Florida and west to Louisiana; more common in the northern portion of its range.
HABITAT: Coastal beaches, both sandy and cobble.

Anyone who has ever had the misfortune of stepping on a prickly saltwort plant knows why wearing shoes is a good idea when walking at the shore and may also have gained a new respect for the defenses that have evolved in many plants.

Common saltwort is well designed for living in exposed, salt-drenched habitats. It has a well-established root system, fleshy leaves that can retain water, and a physiology that can tolerate high concentrations of salt. Its scientific name, *Salsola*, comes from a Latin word meaning "salty." In spite of the protective modifications, however, saltwort will not survive prolonged immersion in sea water.

Saltwort is a widely branched plant and tends to be more or less prostrate rather than stiffly erect. Its diameter may vary from a few inches to as much as 3 feet (90 cm). The leaves are alternate, fleshy, and stiff and may be downy or smooth. They are slightly flattened when young, but when mature, they have a definite awl shape with a stiff sharp point at the upper end. The leaves at the base of the stem are the longest, but they are no longer than 1 3/16 inches (3 cm). They are progressively shorter from the base to the top of the stem and into the branches, where the upper leaves may be no more than 1/4 inch (7 mm) in length. The prickles at the tips of the leaves may inflict painful injuries.

The tiny green flowers appear in mid- to late summer and are borne singly in the axils of the leaves. They are composed of a pistil, stamens, and a calyx but no petals. The calyx has converging lobes

Common saltwort,
Salsola kali

that cover the fruit and spreading wings at the base. By the time the ripe fruit is ready to fall in early October, the calyx has turned either rosy-red or lead-gray.

Seedlings of saltwort develop along the driftline of oceanic or estuarine beaches, where vegetative debris tends to be deposited by the highest tides. This flotsam provides enough protection and nutrition to make it possible for the seeds of a few salt-tolerant annuals, such as common saltwort and sea rocket (*Cakile edentula*), to germinate and become established.

Before 1850, saltwort was collected on beaches in England and burned for its ash, which has a high sodium carbonate content. This ash was called barilla and was sold to make soap.

Russian thistle or tumbleweed (*Salsola kali* L. ssp. *tragus* [L.] Aellen, or *Salsola tragus* L., according to some authorities) may also be found in this book's range, although it tends to grow inland, not near salt water. A native of the arid lands east of the Mediterranean—Algeria, Turkey, Pakistan, Iran, and south-central Russia—it was first introduced into the United States in 1877 as an impurity in a shipment of flaxseeds to South Dakota. It soon became established as an invasive weed and continues to pose a serious problem, especially in parts of the western United States.

The leaves of Russian thistle are threadlike and somewhat longer than those of common saltwort. The plant is bushier and more rounded and has been given the name tumbleweed because when blown by the wind, dead plants roll like balls across the landscape.

Russian thistle was especially troublesome to the small town of Mobridge, South Dakota, in the fall of 1989. A lake near Mobridge had dried up because of drought, and an exceptionally vigorous stand of Russian thistle grew on the fertile lake bottom. Many of the plants exceeded 4 feet (1.2 m) in diameter. One night, a strong wind snapped the stems of the dead plants and sent them rolling toward town. When the townspeople awoke the next morning, their houses, cars, and streets were covered with tumbleweeds. Many people could not even open their doors.

Residents feared the possibility of fire because dry tumbleweeds are exceedingly flammable and burn with an explosive force. Because the plants are prickly and extremely hard to handle, however, they were difficult to dispose of. The problem was solved by crushing the plants, piling them in windrows, and baling them, which produced an estimated 30 tons (27.2 metric tons) of tumbleweeds.

Perennial Glasswort

Sarcocornia perennis (P. Mill.) A. J. Scott
Goosefoot Family, Chenopodiaceae

RANGE: Massachusetts south to North Carolina.
HABITAT: Tidal salt marshes, saline swales, shores, and other saline locations.

Recently, taxonomists have been taking a fresh look at the glassworts and have now divided the genus *Salicornia* into two genera, *Salicornia*, which contains the annual species, and *Sarcocornia*, which contains the perennial species in this book's range. Some experts have divided the former perennial glasswort (*Salicornia virginica* L.), into two species, *Sarcocornia perennis*, as described here, and *Sarcocornia fruticosa* (L.) A. J. Scott. Under this system, *Sarcocornia perennis* may be found from New England south to

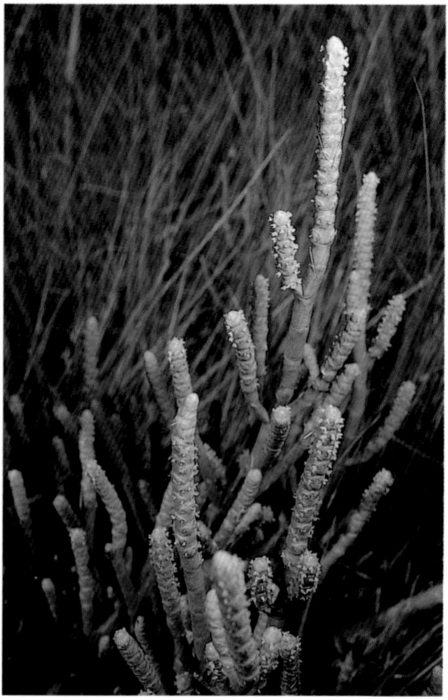

Perennial glasswort,
Sarcocornia perennis

North Carolina. It tends to have a prostrate or decumbent growth form. *Sarcocornia fruticosa* is the perennial species that occurs from North Carolina to Texas and tends to have a more erect growth form.

In New England, perennial glasswort may grow in mats as large as ¼ acre (0.1 hectare) or as small mats or single plants composed of three to four stalks. In mats, the stems are close together, seldom branched, and usually partially decumbent. In South Carolina and Georgia, however, the plants often occur singly and may have only one or two stalks.

In size and shape, it resembles annual glasswort (*Salicornia virginica*), with relatively slender, jointed, fleshy stems about ⅛ inch (3 mm) wide and 4–12 inches (10–30 cm) tall. The plants may be erect or somewhat decumbent, but unlike annual glasswort, the base of the stems is woody, not succulent. Even in small plants, the stem is slightly woody and may run along the ground for an inch or two and be firmly rooted in the substrate.

The flowers of perennial glasswort are borne on the upper third of the vegetative stalk where the joints are only ⅛ inch (3 mm) long. The flowers are similar to those of the other species of glassworts, with one or two stamens and two pistils, but are white and crescent-shaped and just long enough to be visible to the naked eye. The autumn color is orange to rosy-red, very much like that of annual glasswort.

Perennial glasswort grows best in the high marsh, along with saltgrass (*Distichlis spicata*) and salt hay grass (*Spartina patens*). It also grows in salt pannes and with sea lavender (*Limonium carolinianum*) in disturbed areas of marshes or along the upper edges of marshes and beaches bordering salt marshes.

The name glasswort comes from the sound the plants make when stepped on: like breaking glass. Similar to other species of glasswort, this one was once used in cooking because of the high salt content, although most people today would probably avoid it for the same reason. Ducks and geese feed on the stems and seed-bearing tips of *Salicornia/Sarcocornia* species, especially during the autumn.

In the South, another succulent plant sounds like glasswort when stepped on and grows in similar habitats. Known as saltwort (*Batis maritima* L.), it is in the saltwort family (Bataceae). It is found from southern South Carolina south to Central and South America and west to Texas and often grows alongside the glassworts in salt and brackish marshes and other saline areas. Similar to perennial glasswort, its old stems are woody, but the stems are trailing and root at the nodes, forming arches from which the erect flowering branches grow.

Tall Sea Blite

Suaeda linearis (Ell.) Moq.
Goosefoot Family, Chenopodiaceae

RANGE: Maine south to Florida and west to Texas; also in the West Indies.
HABITAT: Coastal salt and brackish marshes and moist edges of beaches and dunes.

The few annuals that are found on salt marshes are nearly always from the goosefoot family. The sea blites join the ranks of other members of this family, such as the genera *Atriplex*, *Bassia*, and *Salsola*, that are able to tolerate saline habitats.

Tall sea blite,
Suaeda linearis

Tall sea blite grows 8–30 inches (20–80 cm) in height. The plants usually have erect central stems with profuse ascending lateral branches, but small plants may have few if any side branches, and plants washed by the tides may sprawl, with the lateral branches prostrate.

The fleshy blue-green leaves of tall sea blite are simple, entire, and arranged alternately along the stem. They are flat on top and rounded on the lower surface and usually have a gray waxy coating like that of a blueberry, although sometimes they lack this coating and may be a bright green. The longest leaves are at the base of the stem and are rarely longer than 1½ inches (4 cm), decreasing in length toward the top.

The rudimentary wind-pollinated flowers are borne in the axils of the leaves along the upper several inches at the tips of the branches. They have five stamens, two styles, no petals, and five sepals. The flowers are almost invisible when the plants begin blooming in late summer, but by late September or early October, the sepals assume a

Low sea blite,
Suaeda maritima

rosy-purple color as the seeds develop. At that time, the fruits are less than 1⁄16 of an inch (1.5 mm) across but so profuse that they are conspicuous. The seeds are disk-shaped, shiny, and bright brown and are entirely enclosed in the fleshy sepals.

When the fruits are mature, they resemble irregular stars. The upper sepals are longer than the lower ones and are keeled on the back.

Low sea blite (*Suaeda maritima* [L.] Dumort.) is a native of Eurasia and Africa that has naturalized from eastern Quebec south to Virginia. It is also reported in Florida and Louisiana. In this less common species of sea blite, the sepals are all the same length, one of the most easily recognized differences between the two species. Other differences are the shorter, rounder, and brighter green leaves of low sea blite (although they may sometimes have a waxy coating), as well as the coarser stems, which are often red by midsummer. The seeds may be twice as large as those of tall sea blite.

A subspecies of low sea blite, *Suaeda maritima* ssp. *richii* (Fern.) Bassett & C. W. Crompton (or *Suaeda richii* Fern., according to some authorities), is believed to be native to salt marshes from Nova Scotia and Newfoundland south to northeastern Massachusetts.

Suaeda is an Arabic name for this group of plants.

Sea Purslane

Sesuvium portulacastrum (L.) L.
Fig Marigold Family, Aizoaceae

RANGE: North Carolina south to Florida and west to Texas; also in the West Indies and Central and South America.
HABITAT: Sandy beaches, dunes, and the upper edges of salt and brackish marshes.

Sea purslane often forms sprawling mats on dunes and coastal shores. The delicate appearance of this coastal plant belies its tough nature: few other plants can tolerate the harsh environment at the ocean's edge where sea purslane thrives. The fleshy leaves of sea purslane are a clear sign that it is well adapted to saline habitats.

There are two species of sea purslane in this book's range. *Sesuvium portulacastrum* is a perennial plant that branches freely as it grows and forms roots at some of the nodes; patches up to 7 feet (2.1 m) across have been recorded. The smooth, thick leaves are arranged opposite one another, but often one member of the pair is larger than the other. They are ⅜–2⅜ inches (1–6 cm) long, are up to ¾ inch (2 cm) wide, tend to be broadest in the upper third of the leaf, and come to a pointed tip. The wedge-shaped bases of the leaves clasp the stem and often overlap one another.

The flowers of sea purslane resemble pink-purple stars tucked among the green leaves. They are generally ½–¾ inch (1.2–2 cm) in diameter. Although the flowers lack petals, the calyx is showy, divided into five sepals that are green outside and pink inside. Each sepal has a tiny, fleshy, green projection (often called a horn) at the tip. The flower is attached to the stem with a distinct pedicel, ½–¾ inch (1.2–2 cm) long. There may be as few as 5 or as many as 60 stamens. The fruit capsule is up to ⅜ inch (1 cm) long and contains smooth, shiny, black seeds.

Another species of sea purslane, *Sesuvium maritimum* (Walt.) B.S.P., grows from coastal New York (where it is very rare) south to Florida and the West Indies and west to Texas; it also grows in a few inland locations in Oklahoma and Kansas. An annual plant, it does

Sea purslane, *Sesuvium portulacastrum*

not root at the nodes and may have either an ascending or a sprawling growth habit. Like *Sesuvium portulacastrum*, this species has smooth, fleshy, generally opposite leaves in subequal pairs, but the leaves are usually no more than 1½ inches (4 cm) long and 3⁄16 inch (5 mm) wide. They are rounded at the tip, with a clasping base. The flowers resemble those of *Sesuvium portulacastrum* but tend to be no more than ⅜ inch (1 cm) across, have only five stamens, and are sessile or have a very short (less than 1⁄32 inch [1 mm]) pedicel. The fruit capsule is approximately ⅛ inch (3 mm) long and contains smooth brownish-black seeds.

Both species of sea purslane bloom from spring until frost, and in frost-free areas, they may be found blooming year-round.

Sea Chickweed

Honckenya peploides (L.) Ehrh. ssp. *robusta* (Fern.) Hultén
Pink Family, Caryophyllaceae

RANGE: Circumboreal, as far south as southeastern Virginia in this book's range.
HABITAT: Sandy, cobble, and shingle beaches.

Sea chickweed, also called seabeach sandwort, is a trailing succulent perennial that can grow as a few stalks together or as a spreading

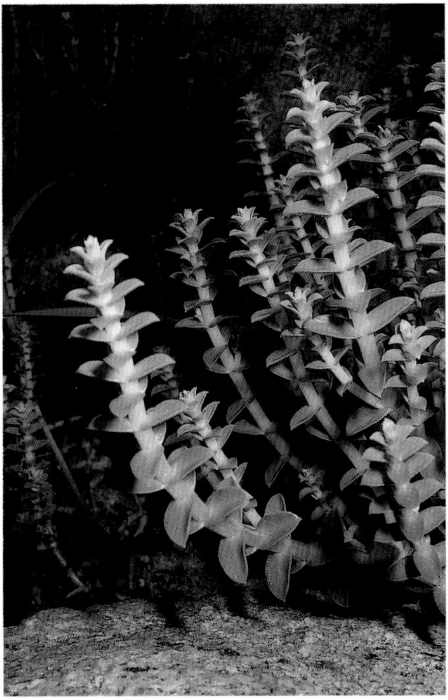

Sea chickweed,
Honckenya peploides

mat. Until recently, it was fairly common on beaches along the northern Atlantic coast, growing in huge mats as much as 30 feet (9 m) in diameter. As more people are using the beaches, however, the plants are frequently trampled and have become much less common; the mats are much smaller in disturbed areas, rarely growing more than 2–3 feet (60–90 cm) in diameter.

Both the stems and the leaves of sea chickweed are quite fleshy. The stems are about ⅜ inch (1 cm) thick and pale yellowish-green. The leaves are about ½ inch (1.2 cm) long, are pointed ovals, and are a deeper shade of yellow-green. They are attached to the stem in opposite pairs, each successive pair stacked at a 90-degree angle to the pair above it. The stems of the current year tend to creep along the ground, rooting at the nodes the first year and producing erect stalks and a few branches the second year. From the side, they often look like a mass of columns, especially on cobble beaches.

The plants are said to be unisexual or bisexual: the flowers on an individual plant may be male or female or may have both stamens and pistils. The flowers are borne in the axils of the upper leaves and are ¼–⅜ inch (7–10 mm) in diameter, with five greenish-white, entire petals. The petals of the female flowers are shorter than the fleshy sepals; those of the male flowers are equal in length to the sepals. The seed capsules are round to oval. Sea chickweed blooms from May to July, earlier than many seashore plants in northern beach habitats.

The plant is named in honor of the German botanist Gerard August Honckeny (1724–1805). An older name for this plant is *Arenaria peploides* L. The generic name, *Arenaria*, is derived from the Latin word *arena*, which means "sand," reflecting the habitat in which many plants in this genus grow. The second part of the scientific name, *peploides*, means "resembling peplis," a kind of purslane.

Saltmarsh Sand Spurrey

Spergularia salina J. & K. Presl var. *salina*
Pink Family, Caryophyllaceae

RANGE: Quebec south to Florida and west to British Columbia and Baja California; also in South America and Eurasia.
HABITAT: Coastal saline and brackish marshes and flats, as well as saline areas inland, including along salted highways.

The delicate saltmarsh sand spurrey is a many-branched annual with stems up to 14 inches (35 cm) long. The branches may be either erect or spread out over the ground and are slightly thickened at the nodes (the place where the leaves meet the main stem). At the base of each node is a thin, triangular, ⅛-inch (3 mm) tall, papery, almost transparent, leaflike structure called a stipule.

The leaves are fleshy, opposite, and bright green and may be smooth or downy. They are attached directly to the stem without an intervening stalk. The longer leaves may reach 1½ inches (4 cm) in length, but most of the leaves, especially those produced from the axils of the longer leaves, are less than 1 inch (2.5 cm) long. The leaves are linear and less than 1/16 inch (2 mm) wide throughout their length, and their rounded tips bear a tiny sharp point. The leaves are visibly flat on the upper surface and rounded on the lower (although this characteristic may be lost once the plants are pressed and dried).

Saltmarsh sand spurrey,
Spergularia salina

The flowers are borne singly on short stalks from the axils of the leaves. These stalks vary in length from ¼ to ¾ inch (7–20 mm), with the longer stalks found at the base of the plant and the shorter ones at the tips of the branches. Each flower has five fleshy, oval sepals that, like the leaves, may be smooth or downy with blunt tips. The sepals are always longer than the petals. The petals are white or pinkish and oval in shape. At the center of each flower are two to five bright yellow stamens and a yellow pistil, a beautiful contrast with the white or pink petals. When fully expanded, the flowers seldom exceed ¼–⅜ inch (7–10 mm) in diameter.

The flowers begin blooming in June and continue through the summer until the first frost. After the flowers fade, globular seedpods develop on the stalks that supported the flowers, and the fruiting stalks tend to arch downward. The seed capsule may equal or exceed the length of the sepals that enclose it. When mature, the capsule is papery thin and brittle and contains numerous tiny pale brown or reddish-brown seeds.

Saltmarsh sand spurrey is essentially a plant of disturbed soils. It is seldom encountered on marshes that are covered with a dense grass sod, but large, solid stands may be seen in areas where the soil is frequently disturbed either because of trampling or by the action of winds and waves. Parts of Monomoy Island off of the Massachusetts coast have wide expanses of saltmarsh sand spurrey in areas where the sandy soil is swept frequently by winds and tides.

Some authorities list this species as *Spergularia marina* (L.) Griseb.

Saltmarsh sand spurrey can be confused with common sand spurrey (*Spergularia rubra* [L.] J. & K. Presl). Common sand spurrey, however, grows only in dry, sandy, or gravelly sterile soils, whereas saltmarsh sand spurrey is restricted to brackish, saline, or alkaline soils. The flower petals of common sand spurrey are pink, and the leaves are flat and not so fleshy and tend to grow in tufts of more than two. Common sand spurrey is a native of Europe and has naturalized in this book's range; along the Atlantic coast, it grows from Newfoundland south to Maryland.

In recent decades, two other European species of sand spurrey have naturalized in maritime habitats in this book's range. Greater sea spurrey (*Spergularia maritima* [All.] Chiov., or *Spergularia media* [L.] K. Presl *ex* Griseb., according to some authorities) may grow as tall as 16 inches (40 cm), with some of its leaves in pairs and some in tufts. It usually has white flowers with 7–10 stamens, and its seeds are dark brown with winged margins. It has been found in salt marshes and salt flats in coastal New York, as well as inland along salted roads.

Spergularia diandra (Guss.) Held. & Sart. has been reported on Cape Cod as well as along the Pacific coast. It is the only sand spurrey in the region to have black seeds.

Spatterdock, *Nuphar lutea*

Spatterdock, Yellow Pond-lily

Nuphar lutea (L.) Sm.
Water-lily Family, Nymphaeaceae

RANGE: Newfoundland south to Florida and the West Indies and west to Alaska, California, the central United States, Texas, and northern Mexico.
HABITAT: Freshwater ponds, slow streams and quiet waters, swamps, and tidal fresh waters.

Throughout this book's range, the rounded, bright yellow flowers of spatterdock can be seen on many ponds and quiet streams in the summertime.

Spatterdock flowers and leaves grow from large rhizomes that are rooted at the bottom of a body of water. The leaves are borne on stiff petioles and may be submerged beneath the surface of the water; lie flat on the water's surface, especially during periods of high water; or emerge above the surface of the water during low tides or in nontidal low-water situations.

The leaves may have a variety of shapes, but they are all thick, smooth on the upper surface, and green on both surfaces, and they have a large triangular slit at the junction of the leaf stem and blade. In some forms, the leaf is oval and about two times as long as it is wide, whereas in others, it is almost as wide as it is long. In another type, the leaf has an arrowhead shape and may be four or five times as long as it is wide. The leaves may be 2–16 inches (5–40 cm) long.

Unlike the flowers of white water-lily (*Nymphaea odorata*), which float on the surface of the water, the flowers of spatterdock stand above the water on stout stalks. The yellow outer portion of the flowers is formed by 6–12 sepals. Inside the circle of inwardly curved sepals are numerous yellow, scalelike petals that are difficult to distinguish from the stamens. The petals and stamens surround the thick, disklike stigma. Nectar glands at the base of the petals attract the flies, beetles, and other aquatic insects that pollinate the flowers. The seeds are dispersed by the water. At the end of the growing season, the leaves die, and new leaves grow from the submerged roots the following year.

Spatterdock seems to be able to tolerate a variety of water levels and can survive periods of low water, recovering from such disturbances more quickly than many other aquatic plants. Although spatterdock is eaten by muskrat, deer, and a few other mammals, its seeds are consumed by some ducks and rails, and it no doubt provides shelter for aquatic animals, it is not considered to be of high value for wildlife.

The name *Nuphar* is derived from the Arabic name for this group of plants. Because of the variety of leaf shapes, growth habits, and characteristics of the flowers and fruits, some authorities divide *Nuphar lutea* into a number of subspecies, whereas others separate the North American group into as many as eight different species.

White Water-lily

Nymphaea odorata Ait.
Water-lily Family, Nymphaeaceae

RANGE: Newfoundland south to Florida and west to Manitoba, Minnesota, and Texas.
HABITAT: Shallow freshwater ponds, marshes, and quiet streams, including tidal fresh waters.

Water-lilies are true aquatic plants. The roots emerge from thick rhizomes embedded on the bottom of quiet ponds and streams. Both leaves and flowers float on the surface of the water attached to long stems that develop from the rhizomes. Each stem contains four large air canals.

White water-lily, *Nymphaea odorata*

Almost circular in shape and connected to the petiole in the center, the leaves have a deep, narrow notch extending from the point of attachment to the petiole to the margin; in diameter, the leaves vary from 4 to 12 inches (10–30 cm). The leaves are smooth and bright green on top and often red or purple on the bottom.

Water-lilies are among the most beautiful wildflowers. They bloom from April to September (depending on the location), opening in the morning and closing around noon on sunny days. On dark days, they may not open at all. The flowers have a large number (17–30) of spreading, pointed petals that are usually a dazzling white but sometimes rose-pink. The center of the flower is filled with a large number (up to 100) of bright yellow stamens. In the center of the stamens, the globular pistil is topped by a flat stigma.

Each flower has four green sepals that wrap tightly over the tops of the fruit as ripening begins. The ripening process continues after the whole mass drops to the bottom of the pond, where the seeds will eventually germinate.

Water-lilies rarely grow in water deeper than 6 feet (1.8 m), and small plants may often be found in water only a few inches deep during the summer. Water-lilies appear to grow equally well in many kinds of soil, ranging from almost pure sand to deep muck.

Europeans sometimes eat the underground rhizomes of the European water-lily (*Nymphaea alba* L.). In North America, *Nymphaea* species have been used for a variety of medicinal and edible purposes by Native Americans. Ducks, shorebirds, and marshbirds eat the seeds and roots of water-lilies, and beaver, muskrat, porcupine, and moose feed on the whole plants.

More than a dozen species or varieties of native water-lilies have been described in the older literature, but current nomenclature combines all of them into the single species described here.

Sweet Bay

Magnolia virginiana L.
Magnolia Family, Magnoliaceae

RANGE: Eastern Massachusetts, Long Island, and Pennsylvania south to Florida and west to Texas.
HABITAT: Wet woods, pocosins, savannas, and edges of swamps, chiefly on the coastal plain.

Native species of magnolia are not usually associated with New England, but two native stands of *Magnolia virginiana* have been growing in the town of Magnolia, Massachusetts, since the 1880s. Specimens collected on Long Island and in Pennsylvania have documented the existence of this species in the Northeast for many years. It has never, however, been abundant north of Virginia.

In the nineteenth century, when summer visitors journeyed to the beach by train, children in Magnolia would sell them bouquets of the flowers of the local sweet bay trees. When summer crowds no longer traveled by train, the sweet bays were neglected and almost destroyed by off-road motorcycles that drove over their root systems and weedy species of plants that were more vigorous than the sweet bays. Fortunately, before the stands were lost, two conservation groups took on the responsibility of trying to save them, and they have been remarkably successful.

In general, this species resembles a smaller version of the well-known southern magnolia (*Magnolia grandiflora* L.). The trees of sweet bay are usually less than 50 feet (15 m) in height (rarely up to 65 feet [20 m]), whereas the southern magnolia may reach 80 or even 100 feet (24–30 m); the diameter of the sweet bay trunks is also smaller. The leaves of sweet bay are 2⅜–6 inches (6–15 cm) long, somewhat thick and leathery, dull on the upper surface, smooth to finely hairy and whitish on the lower surface, and fragrant when

Sweet bay, *Magnolia virginiana*

crushed. The leaves of the southern magnolia are usually much larger, evergreen, very thick and leathery, shiny on the upper surface, and covered with rusty hairs underneath. In the North, the leaves of sweet bay are deciduous, but in the South, they are evergreen.

The flowers of sweet bay are also similar to those of the southern magnolia but are only 4 inches (10 cm) across, have shorter petals, and are much less fragrant.

Several magnolia species were formerly used in Native American and traditional medicine. In some areas, extracts from magnolia trees replaced Peruvian bark (*Cinchona* spp.), the South American plants from which quinine is extracted, in the treatment of malaria and other fevers. Sweet bay trees have also been used for a variety of other medicinal purposes.

Horned poppy, *Glaucium flavum*

Horned Poppy, Sea Poppy

Glaucium flavum Crantz
Poppy Family, Papaveraceae

RANGE: Southeastern Massachusetts and eastern Rhode Island south to Virginia; infrequent inland to Michigan.
HABITAT: Upper edges of shingle beaches in New England and sandy beaches south of New England and waste places.

Horned poppy is a native of Europe that has become naturalized in the United States in several places along the Atlantic coast. It is not common in most areas but is conspicuous where it has become established. Horned poppy is beautiful, but it appears to be becoming a nuisance in some states; Massachusetts includes it on its list of undesirable, invasive, naturalized weed species.

A member of the poppy family, horned poppy may be either biennial or perennial, and the plants may vary in size from 1 to 3 feet (30–90 cm) in diameter. They may be erect or sprawling and are often broader than they are tall. A plant may have one or more stems arising from a single root, and the flowers may be terminal, axillary, or both.

The color of the stems and leaves is a distinctive shade of blue-green. The basal leaves are pinnately dissected like those of oriental poppy (*Papaver orientale* L.) and may be up to 6 inches (15 cm) long. The stem leaves are smaller, are somewhat heart-shaped and clasping at the base, and have wavy teeth along the edges. All of the leaves have a slightly crisp texture and a rough, waxy surface.

The flowers are 2–6 inches (5–15 cm) in diameter, with a large number of yellow stamens in the center and four thin, pale yellow, crinkled petals.

The seedpods of horned poppy give it its common name. They are 6–12 inches (15–30 cm) long, 3⁄16 inch (5 mm) thick, and rough. They may be straight or curved and resemble horns. When the seeds are ripe, the pods split open from end to end, leaving the seeds attached to a membrane at the center of the pod. The seeds remain attached to this membrane for a short time before they are shed.

Horned poppy is unusual in that it has stems and leaves that can tolerate the high salinity of sea water and a root system that cannot. This means that the plants can grow where they are washed by ocean water but only on beaches that are exceedingly well drained. Horned poppy grows well in flower gardens because the roots prefer soils with a low salt content.

The juice of horned poppy is deep yellow, and the roots are poisonous.

Sea Rocket

Cakile edentula (Bigelow) Hook.
Mustard Family, Brassicaceae

RANGE: Labrador south to Florida; also along the shores of the Great Lakes and introduced on the Pacific coast.
HABITAT: Sand beaches, dunes, and edges of tidal salt marshes.

Sea rocket is primarily a plant of sandy beaches along the Atlantic coast. The seeds germinate in small drifts of tidal litter deposited at the upper edges of the beach during the time of the highest tides in the spring. It is an annual throughout most of its range; however, in the Deep South, some plants may be perennial and bloom sporadically year-round.

In size, sea rocket may vary from a single stalk 5 or 6 inches (13–15 cm) tall with a few flowers at the upper end to a sprawling, many-branched plant 3 feet (90 cm) tall and 3 feet (90 cm) wide.

The whole plant tends to be fleshy but less so than some of the other plants that grow in saline environments. The stems are slen-

Sea rocket, *Cakile edentula*

der, smooth, and pale green, and the leaves are somewhat fleshy and a darker green. The smaller leaves tend to be linear and entire, but the larger leaves—which range in size from 1 to 4 inches (2.5–10 cm) long—have rounded lobes along the edges. The flowers are borne along the upper ends of the stems. They have the structure typical of the flowers of members of the mustard family, with four rounded petals that vary in color from pale pink or lavender to pure white.

The distinctive seedpods develop soon after the flowers fade. It is not unusual to find half-grown seedpods at the base of the spike and still unopened flower buds at the top.

When mature, the seedpods are about 1 inch (2.5 cm) long and are attached to the plant by a short stalk. Each seedpod has two compartments. The upper section is bulb-shaped, the lower, cylindrical. From New York north, the seedpods tend to contain two seeds, the seed in the upper compartment erect and the one in the lower compartment facing downward. South of New York, the upper compartment usually contains one seed, and the lower compartment is sterile.

Cakile edentula is sometimes divided into two subspecies. *Cakile edentula* ssp. *edentula* is common from Newfoundland south to North Carolina; the dried upper segment of its fruit is four-angled. *Cakile edentula* ssp. *harperi* (Small) Rodman (or *Cakile harperi* Small, according to some authorities) is found from North Carolina south to Florida; the dried upper segment of its fruit is also four-angled, and it has a prominent rib between each angle. Another species of sea rocket, *Cakile lanceolata* (Willd.) O. E. Schulz, is found from Florida south to the West Indies and Brazil. It tends to grow in a more prostrate form and have long branches; its leaves are less toothed and lobed than those of *Cakile edentula* and tend to be more narrow.

When the seedpods of sea rocket mature, they are smooth, waterproof, and buoyant, capable of being transported long distances by water. The buoyancy of the seedpods of sea rocket was probably the reason that it was the first vascular plant to appear on Surtsey, the volcanic island that erupted off the coast of Iceland in November 1963. After the eruption, the island was carefully monitored to document what kinds of organisms appeared. The first vascular plant recorded was the European species of sea rocket, *Cakile maritima* Scop., a native of Iceland and other parts of Europe.

Cakile maritima is occasionally found along the Atlantic coast of the United States but has apparently become naturalized in only a few places around Chesapeake Bay. The European species differs from *Cakile edentula* primarily in the shape of the seedpod and in having leaves that are either linear or deeply dissected to the midrib.

In earlier times, in both America and Europe, the tender young shoots of sea rocket were eaten as greens, either raw or cooked. This rather than the projectile shape of the seedpod gave the plant its common name. The early Romans enjoyed eating sea rocket because of its peppery flavor. They called it *eruca*, derived from a Greek word meaning "to belch." Over the centuries, the word *eruca* evolved into the English word "rocket." Other members of the mustard family are also called rockets, including the common naturalized weed, *Barbarea vulgaris* Ait. f., which is known as yellow rocket.

Thread-leaved sundew,
Drosera filiformis

Thread-leaved Sundew, Dew-thread

Drosera filiformis Raf.
Sundew Family, Droseraceae

RANGE: Southern New England south to Delaware; South Carolina south to Florida and west to Louisiana; rare in all but the most southern parts of its range.
HABITAT: Low, damp, sandy areas on the coastal plain.

A glistening patch of sundews often has an air of mystery about it, but the reality is grim: look closely and you may find the exoskeletons of insects embedded on the sticky leaves.

The margins and upper surfaces of sundew leaves are covered with long reddish-purple hairs. These hairs end in glands that secrete a sticky fluid that shines like dew in the sunlight (the generic name *Drosera* comes from the Greek word *droseros*, meaning "dewy"). When an insect lands on the surface of the leaf, it becomes trapped on the sticky hairs; neighboring hairs react like tentacles and secrete enzymes that digest the insect. In this way, the plant gains the extra protein essential for growth in the usually acidic, wet, nitrogen-poor soils where the sundews thrive.

Thread-leaved sundew is the largest of the sundews in this book's region, growing up to 10 inches (25 cm) in height. The erect leaves develop directly from the woolly cormlike base, uncurling as they grow in much the same way as a fern fiddlehead. They are so narrow that the leaf blades are indistinguishable from the stems.

The flower stalk is 6–8 inches (15–20 cm) tall and may have as many as 16 pinkish-purple flowers arranged along one side of the curled stalk. Each flower is approximately ⅜–⅝ inch (10–16 mm) wide and has five petals and sepals. The sepals are also covered with glandular hairs.

Other *Drosera* species in this book's range have leaf blades that are readily distinguishable from the petioles. The leaves of these species also tend to spread out around the base of the plants, unlike the erect leaves of *Drosera filiformis*.

Round-leaved sundew (*Drosera rotundifolia* L.) is circumboreal and grows in bogs and boggy edges of ponds as far south in this book's range as South Carolina and Georgia. Its leaf blades are up to ⅜ inch (1 cm) across and are broader than they are long; the leaf stalks are ⅜–2 inches (1–5 cm) long. The flowers of this species are white or occasionally pink.

Spatulate-leaved sundew (*Drosera intermedia* Hayne) also has white flowers and grows in bogs and wet sands or peaty places from Canada south to Florida and west to Texas. Some of the leaves of this species are arranged alternately along the main stem. The petioles are ⅜–3⅛ inches (1–8 cm) long, and the spatulate-shaped blades are about ⅜–¾ inch (1–2 cm) long, typically two or three times as long as they are wide.

In coastal plain areas in the South, two other sundews may be found. Pink sundew (*Drosera capillaris* Poir.) has broad spatulate leaves, pink flowers, and petioles that are usually about the same length as the blades and have scattered glandular hairs. The petioles of short-leaved sundew (*Drosera brevifolia* Pursh) are smooth and usually shorter than the spatulate blades; the plant has pink or white flowers. Both species grow as far south as South America.

Shadbush, *Amelanchier canadensis*

Shadbush, Eastern Serviceberry

Amelanchier canadensis (L.) Medik.
Rose Family, Rosaceae

RANGE: Newfoundland south to Mississippi and inland to central New Hampshire and west-central New York; mostly on the coastal plain south of New York.
HABITAT: Stable dunes, damp woods, shores, swamps, and pocosins.

Throughout its range, the shadbush is a welcome sign of spring. Depending on the location, it blooms from March (e.g., in Georgia) into May (e.g., in Massachusetts) and brightens the still-gray hedgerows with its rounded masses of showy white flowers.

A member of the rose family, shadbush has five white petals, five sepals, and numerous stamens in the center of the flower. It may take the form of a multistemmed shrub, growing to 20 feet (6 m) or more, or a small tree. Like all of the shads, it has alternate, toothed leaves that are either rounded or blunt at the base. The leaf tip of the eastern serviceberry comes to an abrupt point, the teeth of the leaves are blunt, and when young, the leaves are covered with downy hairs and may be folded down the midvein.

A number of species of *Amelanchier* grow in the eastern United States, differentiated by technical characteristics. In the Atlantic coastal plain south of New England, coastal plain serviceberry

(*Amelanchier obovalis* [Michx.] Ashe) becomes more common. It has sharp teeth along the margins of the leaves, mostly on the upper half of the leaf margins. Both this species and eastern serviceberry may be found on stable dunes and in open woods near the ocean.

The fruit of shadbush ripens to red, purple, or almost black in May or June, which explains another common name for this group of shrubs, juneberry. Native Americans used this fruit in pemmican, a mixture of wild fruit, dried meat, and animal fat used as a survival food, and it was also once popular in pies and jams. Although few people now eat it, the fruit is relished by many species of songbirds, gamebirds, and mammals, and the twigs are browsed on by deer, moose, and other hoofed mammals.

Shadbush derives its name from shad, a fish that swims upstream to spawn at about the same time the shadbush blooms. The plants are also known as serviceberry (or in the South, sarvisberry). According to one legend, the origin of the name serviceberry goes back to the time of the early New England settlers. Many people died during the harsh winters, but graves could not be dug in the frozen ground. The bodies were stored until the ground thawed and the itinerant preacher could make his rounds to hold services, by which time the shadbush was in bloom. It is a grim legend for a beautiful plant that lets us know that spring is here at last!

Silverweed

Argentina anserina (L.) Rydb.
Rose Family, Rosaceae

RANGE: Circumboreal, as far south as New England and Long Island in this book's range; inland and westward to southern Indiana, Iowa, New Mexico, and California.
HABITAT: Upper edges of salt marshes, gravelly or sandy shores, and open marshy places.

Silverweed is a perennial, low-growing member of the rose family with a habit of growth resembling that of the strawberry (*Fragaria* spp.), another member of the rose family. The leaves and elongated flower stalks are 4–12 inches (10–30 cm) long and arise from crowns or nodes on the runners. The slender runners or stolons emerging from the crowns may connect with other crowns, forming a network over the surface of the marsh; they may also root at the ends

Silverweed, *Argentina anserina*

and produce rosettes of leaves that are much smaller than the leaves of the main crown.

The leaves have 7–31 sharply toothed larger leaflets that may be as much as 1½ inches (4 cm) long; the longest will be found on the upper portion of the leaf. The larger leaflets are interspersed with much smaller leaflets, and all of the leaflets are arranged along either side of the midrib in an irregular fashion, not necessarily in pairs. The upper surfaces of the leaflets are a lustrous rich green, and the undersides are covered with long, silvery, silky hairs that reflect light and give the plant its common name. The silvery underside is most visible after the first frost, when the leaves turn brown and curl, exposing the silvery hairs.

The flower stalks are slender and leafless and may develop from the crown or from nodes on the stolons, and unlike the stalks of several other closely related species that have clusters of flowers, each stalk produces only one flower. The flowers are yellow, range in size from ½ to nearly 1 inch (1.2–2.5 cm) in diameter, and usually have five petals (occasionally more), five sepals, and numerous stamens and pistils. They bloom from May to September, depending on the location.

The fruits of silverweed are clusters of dry dark red seeds that resemble small blackberries in leaflike cups that look like the hull of a strawberry.

Native Americans have used silverweed for a variety of medicinal and edible purposes.

Some authorities name this plant *Potentilla anserina* L. The word *Potentilla* comes from the Latin word *potens*, referring to the supposedly potent medicinal powers of this group of plants. Its newer name, *Argentina*, alludes to its silvery leaves; *anserina* refers to geese, perhaps reflecting the fact that this plant grows in the far North, where many species of geese nest in the summer.

Beach Plum

Prunus maritima Marsh.
Rose Family, Rosaceae

RANGE: New Brunswick south to Delaware and Maryland; also in central Michigan.
HABITAT: Dunes and sandy soils both near the coast and inland.

Beach plums are most conspicuous when they are in full bloom in May, when the plants are covered with masses of creamy white flowers. Each flower has 5 cupped petals and 15–20 stamens. They grow in clusters of two to three and are often so crowded along the sides of the stems that the twigs cannot be seen. The dark green oval leaves are longer than they are broad, usually no more than 3 inches (7.5 cm) long, and have sharp teeth along the edges. The undersurface of the leaves is downy (as are the buds and twigs), but the upper surface is smooth and glistens in the sun.

In especially favorable locations, beach plum may grow as a rounded tree up to 10 feet (3 m) tall, with a short thick trunk and a large number of branches, but more often it takes the form of a thicket of many-stemmed shrubs 3–4 feet (90–120 cm) tall.

The plums that ripen in September are round to oval, ½–1 inch (1.2–2.5 cm) in diameter, and purple in color (or occasionally reddish or yellow) when ripe. The fresh fruit tends to be sour and somewhat bitter even when thoroughly ripe, but beach plum jelly and jam are legendary delicacies.

The early settlers were excellent horticulturists and assumed they could improve the taste of beach plum fruits, as they had with European fruits. In spite of their best efforts, however, the beach plum fruits kept their natural wild flavor.

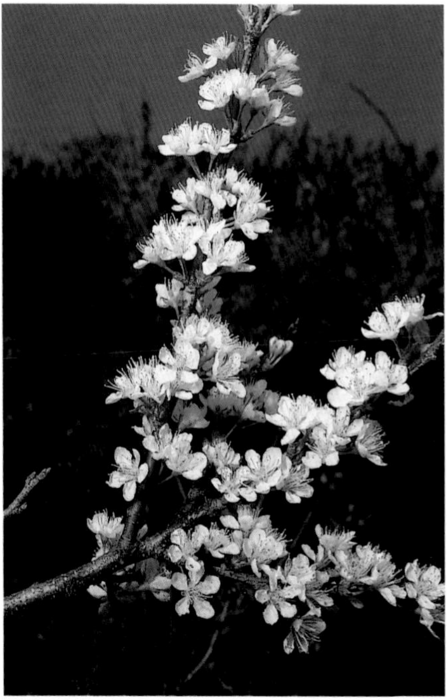

Beach plum,
Prunus maritima,
in flower

In earlier times, beach plums bore abundant fruit, but after the insect, the plum curculio, appeared, very little fruit survived intact. The plum curculio (*Conotrachelus nenuphar*) is one of the snout beetles, in the same family as the infamous cotton boll weevil. When the green plum fruit reaches a certain size, the female plum curculio pierces it with her sharp beak and lays an egg inside it. When the grub hatches, it eats its way into the fruit, all the way to the seed. Even after the fruit falls to the ground, the grub is protected by the remains. Once the grub has fully developed, it leaves the fruit and excavates a cavity in the ground, where it becomes a pupa and, after about a month, an adult. The adult beetle overwinters and starts the cycle all over again the next spring. In addition to beach plums, many other species of wild and cultivated fruits are affected by this beetle.

Beach plums may be cultivated like domestic plums and sprayed to control the plum curculio. As a cultivated crop, they are popular

Beach plum,
Prunus maritima, in fruit

enough to be available from nurseries. Anyone wishing to grow beach plums should buy the plants from a reliable nursery rather than attempt to dig wild plants. Plants grown in a nursery have better root systems than wild plants and are selected from plants that have larger fruits and are more prolific.

Foxes, which are less fussy than people about the presence of insects in their fruit, relish the fruits of beach plum.

In the South, hog plum or flatwood plum (*Prunus umbellata* Ell.) may be found on dunes and in coastal woodlands as well as at inland sites; it grows from North Carolina south to Florida and west to Arkansas and Texas. This plum takes the form of a shrub or small crooked tree up to 20 feet (6 m) tall and is sometimes found in dense colonies. Its white flowers appear from March to April, before the leaves emerge. They are usually in small clusters of two to five blossoms, each flower ⅝–1 inch (1.6–2.5 cm) across on a slim stalk ½–1 inch (1.2–2.5 cm) long. The small round fruits are ⅜–⅝ inch (1–1.6 cm) across, may vary in color from yellow to deep red to black, and are covered with a whitish coating. Like the fruits of beach plum, the sour or bitter fruits are relished for the delicious jams, jellies, and pies that can be made from them.

Wild Black Cherry

Prunus serotina Ehrh.
Rose Family, Rosaceae

RANGE: Nova Scotia south to Florida and west to southern Ontario, North Dakota, Texas, and Arizona; also in Central America.
HABITAT: Maritime forests, stable dunes, coastal thickets, woodlands and woodland edges, old fields and pastures, roadsides, and disturbed sites.

Few trees are as common or widespread as the wild black cherry, which can be found from the cove forests of the Great Smoky Mountains to scrubby coastal woodlands and inland hedgerows.

Although *Prunus serotina* can reach a height of 100 feet (30 m) and a girth of 5 feet (1.5 m), it is rarely half that size in this book's range. Heavily harvested for its beautiful wood, which is prized in cabinetmaking, and cleared away to make room for farms and homes, this once-large tree has dwindled mostly to stunted, crooked trees and sprouts on woodland edges.

The blunt-toothed leaves of wild black cherry are alternate, with petioles ½–¾ inch (1.2–2 cm) long. The leaves come to a sharp tip and are 2⅜–5 inches (6–13 cm) long, usually about three times longer than they are wide. They are shiny on the upper surface, are paler underneath, and often have a row of white to rusty hairs framing the lower half of the midrib on the undersurface.

The white flowers bloom from April to June (depending on the location) in long, drooping, cylindrical racemes at the end of the current year's twigs. Each flower is about ¼ inch (7 mm) across and has five rounded petals, five sepals, one pistil, and numerous projecting stamens. These insect-pollinated flowers are visited by flies, bees, ants, and butterflies eager for the pollen and nectar.

The dark red to black fruits are ¼–⅜ inch (7–10 mm) wide and are on long, drooping clusters. The fruits are thin-skinned, contain a single seed, and may have a bitter taste, although this does not

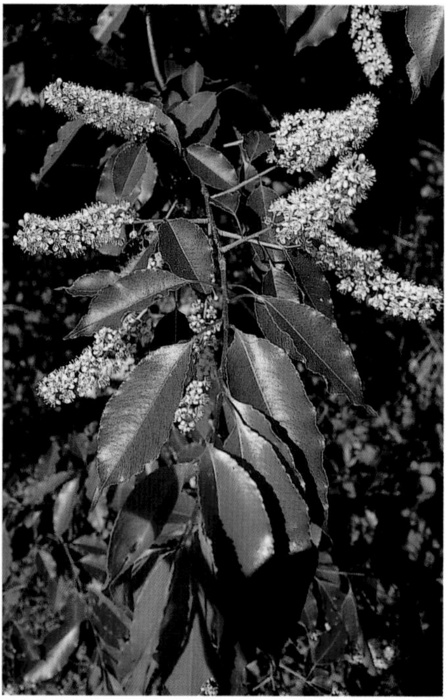

Wild black cherry,
Prunus serotina

seem to deter the many species of birds and mammals that eat the fruit. When the fruits are ripe, American robins have been known to eat so many that they cannot fly.

People also use the fruit of wild black cherry to make jams and jellies. The raw seeds, however, as well as the foliage, bark, and twigs, should not be eaten by people or livestock because they contain toxic cyanide compounds. Cattle rarely eat black cherry unless they are starving, but they relish wilted cherry leaves and may be killed by eating them.

Wild black cherry can often be spotted solely by the pests that infest it. Black cherry knot is a fungal infection of black cherry. Although it is olive-green when it forms in the spring, by fall it becomes black and woody, forming rough, irregular swellings on the twigs and branches. Heavily infested trees may be covered with these knots, making the black cherry identifiable even from a distance in the winter. The eastern tent caterpillar also feeds on wild black cherry, and the tents that house the young colonies are familiar sights on these trees. Both the black cherry knot fungus and the tent caterpillar utilize other plant species, but wild black cherry seems to be especially prone to infestation.

Other species of wild cherry may be found in coastal habitats in this book's range. Choke-cherry (*Prunus virginiana* L.) is a shrub or small tree that grows throughout the northern United States and the southern half of Canada; in this book's range, it may be found from New England south to New Jersey (from there south, it is mostly an inland species). Its leaves are dull on the upper surface and usually about two times as long as they are wide, and they have an elongated tip and sharp teeth on the margins. The flower and fruit clusters are broader and shorter than those of wild black cherry, and it tends to bloom later in May and June.

Carolina laurelcherry (*Prunus caroliniana* [P. Mill.] Ait.) is a small tree or shrub of coastal woodlands, fencerows, and thickets that often blooms as early as February. Widely used as an ornamental, it has apparently naturalized beyond its original range, which extends from North Carolina south to Florida and west to Texas. It has smooth, shiny, thick, evergreen leaves that are entire or have widely spaced sharp teeth on the margins. The white flowers develop on short racemes growing from the axils of the leaves formed the previous year. The dull black fruits may remain until the following growing season.

Salt-spray Rose, Rugose Rose

Rosa rugosa Thunb.
Rose Family, Rosaceae

RANGE: Naturalized from Nova Scotia and Quebec south to New England and New Jersey and west to Minnesota and the Great Lakes.
HABITAT: Sand dunes, beaches, rocky shores, coastal thickets, and roadsides.

Salt-spray rose was introduced from eastern Asia around 1845 and quickly became naturalized near salt water. Although it grows well inland, it is especially vigorous where it is exposed to salt spray in coastal habitats or along salted roadsides, but it cannot grow in saline soils. Unlike many naturalized invasive species, salt-spray rose seems to have fit into the natural successional patterns in New

Salt-spray rose, *Rosa rugosa*

England. When the rose plants reach maturity and die at about 30 years of age, they are often replaced by the native bayberry (*Myrica pensylvanica*), unless other naturalized invasive plants, such as Asian bittersweet (*Celastrus orbiculata* Thunb.), move in first, not by other plants of *Rosa rugosa*. It would be interesting to know what the composition of northern coastal habitats would be today if *Rosa rugosa* had not naturalized along these shores.

Salt-spray rose is a shrub that ranges in height from 3⅓ to 6½ feet (1–2 m). The stems are thick and have a dense cover of sharp brown prickles.

The leaves are compound with 5, 7, or 9 leaflets, 2, 3, or 4 leaflets on each side and one at the upper end. The veins of the leaflets are deeply indented, and the surface is dark green, glossy, and wrinkled. This last feature gives this rose its scientific name, *rugosa*, which means "wrinkled."

The flowers are usually 3⅛–4 inches (8–10 cm) in diameter, with a ring of bright yellow stamens and a stigma like those of other roses. There are many variations in the flower color, from pure white to several shades of purplish-pink to deep rose-red, and an equally wide variation from single to semidouble flowers. They begin blooming as early as May and may continue blooming into autumn.

Rosa rugosa has crossed with some of the native wild roses and produced plants that are intermediate in flowers, foliage, and fruit. The hybrid flowers, however, are always wild-rose pink—they are not white, red, or the purple-pink that is most common in *Rosa rugosa*.

When ripe, the fruits of salt-spray rose are a shiny brilliant scarlet to orange and may be borne singly or in clusters. The single fruits are usually ¾–1³⁄₁₆ inches (2–3 cm) in diameter (although specimens up to 2 inches [5 cm] wide have been observed), somewhat flattened, and less than ¾ inch (2 cm) thick. Fruits borne in clusters tend to be smaller and more globular. The fruits persist into the winter and add color to the landscape as well as providing food for wildlife. They are eaten by many kinds of birds and mammals, and a variety of insects also utilize the flowers and fruits.

The fruits of salt-spray rose are high in vitamin C and are used to make rose hip jam because they have no prickles and are large enough that it is easy to remove the seeds and sepals. For jam, the hips must be picked when they are ripe but before frost.

Several species of native pink-flowered roses may be found in coastal plain habitats in the northern portion of this book's range, often right up to the edge of salt marshes and rocky shores. Distinguished primarily by the characteristics of the leaves and prickles, these include pasture rose (*Rosa carolina* L.), Virginia rose (*Rosa virginiana* P. Mill.), and swamp rose (*Rosa palustris* Marsh.), which grows as far south as Florida. All have fruits that are generally less than ⅝ inch (16 mm) in diameter.

The invasive multiflora rose or hedge rose (*Rosa multiflora* Thunb. *ex* Murr.) is an eastern Asian species that was introduced in the 1860s as an understock for grafting ornamental roses. In the 1930s and subsequent decades, it was widely planted to act as a living fence for livestock, to provide food for gamebirds and songbirds, and to serve as a crash barrier and reduce headlight glare along interstate highways. It has naturalized throughout this book's range and over much of North America. Covered with small fragrant white flowers when in full bloom, this invasive shrub rose is a serious agricultural pest and difficult to eradicate from the pastures, fields, and disturbed edges where it thrives.

False indigo,
Amorpha fruticosa

False Indigo, Indigo-bush

Amorpha fruticosa L.
Bean Family, Fabaceae

RANGE: New Hampshire south to Florida and west to Saskatchewan, Minnesota, Texas, southern California, and northern Mexico; introduced and naturalized from New York into New England.
HABITAT: Tidal freshwater and brackish marshes, margins of salt and brackish ponds, moist woods, riverbanks, and swamps; found especially in calcareous soils.

False indigo is not likely to be associated with snap beans and black-eyed peas, but it is a member of the bean family.

It is a many-stemmed shrub varying from 8 to 16½ feet (2.5–5 m) tall, with alternate compound leaves. The stems are light grayish-brown with a few brown stripes and may be smooth or covered with short velvety hairs.

The leaves are 4–12 inches (10–30 cm) long, compound with 9–

35 leaflets, with half of the leaflets on each side of the midrib and a single leaflet at the upper end. The oval leaflets are rounded at the upper end, and an extension of the midrib projects from the tip to form a 1⁄16-inch (2 mm) bristle. The leaflets usually have distinct stems (petiolules) covered with fine hairs, and at the base of each leaflet is a tiny threadlike stipule. The upper surface of the leaflets is dull, smooth, and a rich green color, and the underside has a velvety cover of soft short hairs.

The shape of the flower is quite different from that of the usual legume. During the evolution of this member of the bean family, the four lateral petals (the wings and keel) disappeared, leaving one large, flat top petal (the standard). This single top petal became tightly rolled around the stamens and the single pistil. The rolled standard is a shade of purple so dark that it appears almost black, and the brilliant deep yellow stamens and pistil project from its outer end. The scientific name for this genus, *Amorpha*, comes from the Greek word meaning "deformed," referring to this plant's lack of the petals usually seen in members of the bean family.

The flowers are packed closely together on erect cylindrical racemes that are 3⁄8–1 inch (1–2.5 cm) in diameter and up to 8 inches (20 cm) long.

Blooming begins with the flowers at the base of the raceme and progresses upward, five or six rows at a time, and lasts for about two weeks. False indigo blooms as early as April in the southern states and into June at the northern end of its range.

While blooming, the bushes are covered with many different kinds of insects feeding on the nectar and pollen in the flowers. Honeybees especially find this plant attractive and fly away loaded with pollen, but several other species of bees, butterflies, and beetles are also commonly found foraging on this plant.

The bell-shaped calyx at the base of the cluster remains on the bush all winter. It contains five curved seedpods that are flattened and covered with resinous dots. Each pod contains one or two oval, shiny, dark gray seeds.

In the northeastern United States, false indigo has escaped from cultivation and is beginning to show up on several states' lists of rapidly spreading invasive species.

Partridge pea,
Chamaecrista fasciculata

Partridge Pea

Chamaecrista fasciculata (Michx.) Greene
Bean Family, Fabaceae

RANGE: Massachusetts south to Florida and west to southern Minnesota and Mexico.
HABITAT: Sandy open areas including dunes, interdunes, and the upper edges of beaches; weedy borders, roadsides, and disturbed habitats.

Partridge pea is an interesting plant throughout the growing season. Children (and the young at heart) love to touch the sensitive leaves and watch them fold and then later in the season see the seedpods project the seeds into the air.

An annual plant, partridge pea may grow 1–3⅓ feet (30–100 cm) in height. Like most members of the bean family, it has alternate compound leaves. The leaves are divided into 5–18 pairs of oblong leaflets, with a tiny bristle at the tip of each leaflet and a pair of small stipules at the base of the petiole. Rising from the middle of the petiole below the leaflets is a tiny saucer-shaped gland that has little or no stem. The plant may be smooth or covered with fine hairs.

The showy, insect-pollinated flowers are 1–1½ inches (2.5–4 cm) across and grow on long stems out of the axils of the leaves. They have 5 bright yellow petals unequal in size, 4 of which are red at the base. Projecting from the center of each flower are 10 stamens with long anthers; 4 of the anthers are yellow, and 6 are deep purple to almost black. The flowers bloom from June to September.

The seedpods that develop after flowering are flat and 1³⁄₁₆–2⅜ inches (3–6 cm) long. The outline of the seeds remains visible as the pods ripen. When the pods are mature, they split lengthwise on both sides and then twist and scatter the seeds some distance away from the parent plant. It is fun to walk through a patch of partridge peas and hear the seeds fly by as you brush against the ready-to-open pods.

The common name, partridge pea, reflects the bobwhite quail's fondness for the seeds of this plant; it is also eaten by mice and rats.

An alternate scientific name for this species is *Cassia fasciculata* Michx. The genera *Cassia*, *Chamaecrista*, and *Senna* form a large complex of plants, with over 500 known species worldwide. In this book's range, and especially in the southern areas, several species may be found in coastal and coastal plain habitats, including wild sensitive plant (*Chamaecrista nictitans* [L.] Moench), another annual that has mostly small, solitary flowers on short stalks off of the main stem, and sicklepod (*Senna obtusifolia* [Link] Irwin & Barneby), a tall, foul-smelling annual with long, slender, curved seedpods.

Beach Pea

Lathyrus japonicus Willd.
Bean Family, Fabaceae

RANGE: Circumboreal along seashores; in this book's range, along the Atlantic coast from New England south to New Jersey.
HABITAT: Upper edges of beaches to the high tide line and in overwash and backdune areas where water is available.

In coastal ecosystems, beach pea is valuable as a soil stabilizer because of its intricate root and stem system. In addition to the stems

Beach pea, *Lathyrus japonicus*

that grow on the surface, a system of rhizomes spreads underground. These rhizomes live over the winter and produce new growth in the spring. Beach pea may be most valuable, however, because of the nitrogen-fixing bacteria that live in nodules on its root system and supply nitrogen in a form that can be used by American beachgrass (*Ammophila breviligulata*) and other plants living on the dunes, where nitrogen is in short supply.

Beach pea usually forms wide mats as runners of over 3⅓ feet (1 m) extend from the original plant and root at intervals. Among these prostrate stems are erect stems 8–12 inches (20–30 cm) tall. The stems are thick, round, and pale green.

The leaves of beach pea are divided into 6–10 oval leaflets. At the base of each leaf is a stipule shaped like a broad-based arrowhead, and at the tip of each leaf is a curling tendril.

The flowers of beach pea are pink and purple, with 3–10 flowers per stem. They resemble the flowers of garden peas or sweet peas in shape and are about ⅝–1 inch (1.6–2.5 cm) long. The flowers are followed by slender seedpods 1–2⅜ inches (2.5–6 cm) long, each containing four or five small seeds.

The peas are supposed to be edible, but the flavor is bitter and they should be avoided to prevent confusing them with the seeds of everlasting pea (*Lathyrus latifolius* L.), a European species that has escaped from cultivation and has also become established on the edges of tidal salt marshes. Everlasting pea has elongated leaflets and stipules and flowers that are bright pink, purple, or white. Everlasting pea plants tend to be larger than those of beach pea, but the seeds and seedpods of the two species look alike and the seeds of everlasting pea are deadly poisonous. Everlasting pea also has wide, flat stems with wings along the edges. This is the most reliable difference between the two species.

Many varieties of beach pea have been described. Some authorities use the name *Lathyrus maritimus* Bigelow for this species.

Trailing Wild Bean

Strophostyles helvula (L.) Ell.
Bean Family, Fabaceae

RANGE: Quebec south to Florida and west to Minnesota, South Dakota, and Texas.
HABITAT: Dunes, upper edges of beaches and sandy brackish areas, and edges of salt marshes; inland in damp thickets, in open woodlands, and along shores.

Trailing wild bean is an annual that can be found twining over other plants on beaches and saltmarsh edges. It has slender green stems that branch horizontally from the base and extend 3⅓–6½ feet (1–2 m) or more where conditions are favorable.

The bright to dark green leaves are triangular and have three leaflets. The terminal one is the largest and is usually 1–2½ inches (2.5–6.5 cm) in length, with a much longer stem than the two side leaflets. The leaflets are broad, are rounded or obtuse at the base, and taper gradually to a pointed tip. They may be unlobed or have a single wide lobe on one or both sides.

The leaves are dull and usually hairless, but scattered hairs are sometimes found on both upper and lower surfaces or sometimes only on the underside.

The flowers are 5/16–½ inch (8–13 mm) across and resemble those of garden peas or beans. The color varies from pale pink to rose-pink to purplish or sometimes greenish. The rounded petal at the back of the flower spreads broadly, and the inner keel petal, which contains the stamens and style, forms an elongated curving beak that is often a much deeper shade of pink-purple than the rest of the flower. The two oblong wing petals frame the base of the keel. At the

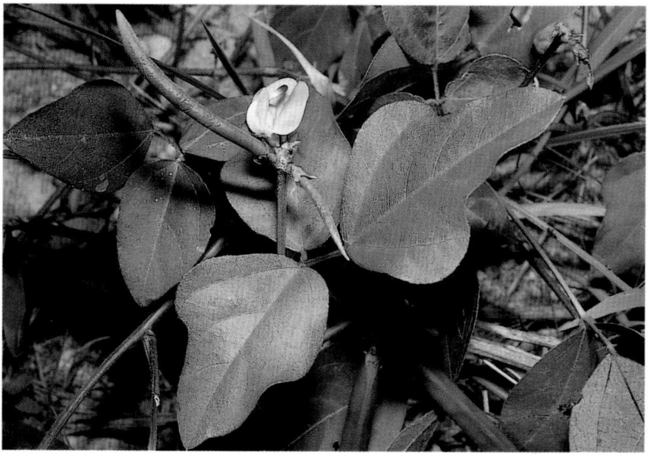

Trailing wild bean, *Strophostyles helvula*

base of the flower are elongated pointed bracts that are as long as the calyx tube.

Trailing wild bean blooms from June to October, and it is not uncommon to find fresh blossoms and mature seedpods simultaneously on a plant. The round seedpods are 1½–4 inches (4–10 cm) long and have a scattering of hairs that press against the pod. The pods contain four to eight oblong seeds that are covered with a dark brownish-gray layer of felted hairs. As the pods open, they twist, flinging the seeds away from the parent plant.

The perennial wild bean (*Strophostyles umbellata* [Muhl. *ex* Willd.] Britt.) may also be found in coastal plain habitats from Rhode Island (where it is very rare) south to Florida and Texas and inland to Oklahoma and Indiana. It grows in sandy soils in woodland clearings, fields, and dunes.

The leaves of the perennial wild bean are also divided into three leaflets, each about ¾–2 inches (2–5 cm) long, with a narrow oblong shape, and rarely lobed. They are hairy on the undersurface and sometimes on the upper side.

The flowers resemble those of the trailing wild bean, but the bracts at the base of the calyx are blunt at the tip and extend no more than half the length of the calyx tube. The seedpod is usually no more than 2½ inches (6.5 cm) long.

Seaside spurge, *Chamaesyce polygonifolia*

Seaside Spurge

Chamaesyce polygonifolia (L.) Small
Spurge Family, Euphorbiaceae

RANGE: Atlantic provinces of Canada south to Georgia and along the shores of the Great Lakes, except for Lake Superior.
HABITAT: Sand and gravel beaches and sand dunes.

Chamaesyce polygonifolia is also known as *Euphorbia polygonifolia* L. It is a member of the spurge family, which contains as many as 7,030 species widely distributed throughout the world but most commonly found in tropical and arid regions. Seaside spurge, however, is restricted to the temperate zone.

One distinguishing feature of many members of the spurge family is the milky, often strongly acrid juice found in the plant. Another is the structure of the flower, which has the appearance of a simple flower but is actually a complex, composite flower, quite different from the composite flower of the daisy or aster. Most members of this family are insect-pollinated, but a few are pollinated by the wind.

Well-known ornamentals that are members of the spurge family include poinsettia (*Euphorbia pulcherrima* Willd. *ex* Klotzsch), crown-of-thorns (*Euphorbia splendens* Bojer *ex* Hook.), and snow-on-the-mountain (*Euphorbia marginata* Pursh). Edible and medicinal plants in this family include cassava (*Manihot* spp.) and castor-bean (*Ricinus communis* L.); other plants yield important commercial substances such as rubber (made from *Hevea* spp.) and tung oil (made from *Aleurites* spp.). Many members of this family are poisonous and can cause severe skin inflammations and internal poisoning in people and livestock.

Seaside spurge is an annual that grows on sandy and gravelly shores above the high tide line and in dune hollows. It is a moderately branched prostrate plant that grows in mats 5–10 inches (12.5–25 cm) in diameter, although it occasionally grows upright.

The stems are a conspicuous rosy-red. The leaves are pale green, narrowly oblong in shape, and about three times as long as they are wide. They are 3⁄16–5⁄8 inch (5–16 mm) long and rounded at the upper end to a short, needlelike point. The lower end has a short petiole at the point of attachment to the stem and may be slightly longer on one side of the midrib. The midrib is prominent only on the underside of the leaf.

The flowers are pale yellow and seldom more than 1⁄16 inch (2 mm) in diameter. They bloom from May until frost, developing at the upper nodes on stalks that are equal in length to or slightly longer than the leaf stalks. Each apparently solitary flower has a composite structure peculiar to the spurge family. A flower is composed of a cluster of 5–14 male flowers, each with a single stamen, surrounding a single female flower that has a three-lobed stigma. The whole cluster is surrounded by a leafy-textured cup called an involucre that may or may not have bracts that resemble petals. The flowers of many members of the spurge family have no true petals or sepals.

The seed capsules are seldom more than 1⁄8 inch (3 mm) long and have three rounded lobes. The seeds are smooth, gray, and mottled with brown.

The structure of the flower of seaside spurge is not visible without a magnifying lens, but the plant is easy to identify in the Northeast because it is the only spurge that grows on the beaches there. In the South, however, a similar species, southern seaside spurge (*Chamaesyce bombensis* [Jacq.] Dugand, or *Euphorbia ammanioides* Kunth, according to some authorities), also grows on the beaches from Virginia south to Texas. It has fruits that are about 1⁄16 inch (2 mm) long and smaller leaves than *Chamaesyce polygonifolia*.

Tread-softly, *Cnidoscolus stimulosus*

Tread-softly, Bull-nettle

Cnidoscolus stimulosus (Michx.) Englem. & Gray
Spurge Family, Euphorbiaceae

RANGE: Virginia south to Florida and west along the Gulf coast to Alabama and Mississippi.
HABITAT: Stable dunes, sandy open woods, and fields in the coastal plain and piedmont.

This stinging nettle is a herbaceous perennial that is monoecious; the male and female flowers are on the same plant but are separate from one another. The plants may be erect or sprawling and usually range in height from 4 to 20 inches (10–50 cm), although plants twice this tall have been reported. This species has a deep root, an adaptation to living in the dry soils where it thrives. Like many other members of the spurge family, tread-softly has milky sap.

The leaves are alternate and are lobed or dissected. The inflorescence is a terminal cluster of brilliantly incandescent white tubular flowers that are divided into five lobes. It is the sepals that form the showy white flowers since the plant lacks true petals.

Although *Cnidoscolus* flowers are reportedly fragrant, you may not want to get close enough to sample their aroma. The entire plant—stem, leaves, and flowers—is covered with stinging hairs that give the flowers an incandescent glow, even in the shade, but when broken release a substance that will cause extremely painful welts on the skin if touched by any part of the plant. Plants of tread-softly should always be examined at a safe distance, and anyone unfortunate enough to come into contact with a plant should consult a physician since some people have severe reactions to it.

Tread-softly is often called stinging nettle, although it is not related to the true stinging nettle (*Urtica dioica* L.). Its scientific name, *Cnidoscolus*, comes from the Greek words *cnide*, meaning "nettle," and *scolops*, meaning "prickle" or "sting"; *stimulosus* also refers to the stinging nature of this species.

Silver-leaf Croton

Croton punctatus Jacq.
Spurge Family, Euphorbiaceae

RANGE: Southeast Virginia south to Florida and west to Texas; also south to Venezuela.
HABITAT: Ocean beaches and dunes.

Silver-leaf croton is easily recognized because it is one of the few plants that flourish on ocean beaches and dunes, and it does not look like any other plant that grows there. It is a rounded bush that may reach over 3⅓ feet (1 m) in diameter and may be annual or partially perennial. If the plant is perennial, the branches of the previous year are killed by frost, and new branches grow from the crown of the original plant.

Like other plants that live in adverse environments, silver-leaf croton has developed protective anatomical features that enable it to withstand the impact of severe abrasion by sand, wind, and waves encountered on ocean beaches and nearby dunes.

The entire plant, except for the upper surface of the leaves, is covered with a thick layer of star-shaped silver hairs, each of which has a red elevated dot in the center. This hairy surface makes the plant look gray rather than green. The upper surface of the leaves is covered with star-shaped silver hairs without red dots. The leaves are alternate and oval. They are ⅜–2⅜ inches (1–6 cm) long and ⅜–1½ inches (1–4 cm) wide. They have fairly long petioles and taper to a point; some leaves have acute points, whereas others have more rounded points.

Silver-leaf croton, *Croton punctatus*

Silver-leaf croton is monoecious, having both male and female flowers on the same plant but not necessarily in the same place. The flowers are so inconspicuous that they are rarely noticed. They bloom from May to November on short spikes at the tips of some of the branches. The female flowers, each with 3 pistils, are at the bottom; the male flowers, each with 12–15 stamens, are at the top. The resulting fruit is a three-lobed capsule with the texture of a green snap bean, and the seeds within are gray mottled with darker gray.

Another species of croton, tooth-leaved croton or hogweed (*Croton glandulosus* L. var. *septentrionalis* Muell.-Arg.), is common on dunes, along roadsides, in fields, and in open woodlands from Virginia south to Florida and west to Texas. It is an annual that grows up to 2 feet (60 cm) tall and develops a taproot that has a spicy fragrance. The leaves are oblong to lance-shaped and up to 3½ inches (9 cm) long and 1½ inches (4 cm) wide, with margins that are wavy and irregularly toothed. The petioles of the leaves are often as long as 1½ inches (4 cm), and each petiole has one or two large glands at the top. The seeds are grayish-tan mottled with black.

In spite of their caustic sap, many species of croton have been used in Native American medicine. The crotons have value for wildlife since the seeds are relished by doves and quail and eaten by a variety of songbirds and small mammals.

Poison ivy, *Toxicodendron radicans*

Poison Ivy

Toxicodendron radicans (L.) Kuntze
Cashew Family, Anacardiaceae

RANGE: Southern Nova Scotia south to Florida and Central America and west to Michigan, Minnesota, Nebraska, Oklahoma, and Texas.
HABITAT: Landward edges of salt marshes, dunes, open woods, swamps, meadows, disturbed areas, waste places, and roadsides.

This is one plant that everyone should be able to identify! "Leaflets three—let it be" is a phrase children learn to help them spot poison ivy and its close cousin, poison oak. Poison ivy is a woody plant that grows as a trailing or climbing vine, using aerial roots to help it climb; occasionally it even takes the form of a shrub, especially on dunes. People have been known to mistakenly pick the fruit of poison ivy on beach dunes, believing it to be northern bayberry (*Myrica pensylvanica*) fruit; the results were not pleasant!

Poison ivy has alternate compound leaves with three oval or elliptical leaflets that are usually a deep green and often shiny but occasionally velvety with fine hairs. The leaflets have long pointed tips. Sometimes they have a few teeth or are irregularly lobed, often varying considerably from one plant to another. The terminal (middle) leaflet has a long leaf stalk, and the two lateral leaflets are short-stalked or sessile.

The greenish-white flowers of poison ivy are arranged in loose, branched clusters that grow from the axils of the leaves. As the grayish-white fruit develops, the inflorescence elongates, and when the fruit is ripe, the fruit stalks hang below the leaves. Poison ivy turns yellow, orange, or a vibrant red in the late summer or early fall, advertising its ripe fruit with its brilliant foliage (botanists call this a "foliar fruit flag"). Many species of birds, from songbirds to woodpeckers to gamebirds, eat the fruit of poison ivy, especially during the winter when other food sources are scarce.

Poison ivy contains urushiol, an oil that causes an allergic reaction (usually a severe itching and painful rash) in many people. All parts of the plant—leaves, stems, roots, flowers, and fruits—except for the pollen contain this oil. Although the oil is not volatile (i.e., it does not spread through the air), it can be picked up by touching clothing or pets that have rubbed against the plant. The oil can also cling to ash particles when the plant is burned and cause death if inhaled. Sensitivity to poison ivy may change within a person's lifetime, so it is a good idea to avoid the assumption that you are "immune" to the plant.

Poison ivy thrives in a variety of habitats and is especially common along disturbed edges of roads and fields. Poison oak (*Toxicodendron pubescens* P. Mill.) grows in sandy soils and pine woodlands as far north as southern New Jersey, south to Florida, and west to Oklahoma and Texas. It lacks aerial roots, taking the form of a shrub with few branches up to 3⅓ feet (1 m) in height. Its leaves are also divided into three leaflets that are rounded or blunt at the tip and often possess lobes that make them reminiscent of oak leaves. The leaf stalk is covered with fine hairs, as are both the upper and lower surfaces of the leaflets. Like poison ivy, the plant's parts contain urushiol and may cause an allergic reaction.

Poison ivy, poison oak, and poison sumac (*Toxicodendron vernix*) were once included in the genus *Rhus*, but current nomenclature lists them in the genus *Toxicodendron*, which means "poison tree."

Poison sumac, *Toxicodendron vernix*

Poison Sumac

Toxicodendron vernix (L.) Kuntze
Cashew Family, Anacardiaceae

RANGE: Southern Maine and Nova Scotia south to Florida and west to southwestern Ontario, Minnesota, and Texas.
HABITAT: Swamps, bogs, pocosins, and wet woods.

Unlike its familiar cousins poison ivy (*Toxicodendron radicans*) and poison oak (*Toxicodendron pubescens*), poison sumac is rarely encountered, and few people can identify it readily. It is a small, straggly tree or shrub of wooded swamps, usually found in shade and seldom growing more than 10–15 feet (3–4.5 m) tall. It may sometimes have multiple stems that grow from the base but often has a single stem with a few branches, the leaves clustered at the top of the plant. The bark is smooth and gray and studded with lenticels that allow the flow of oxygen into the plant, an adaptation to the very wet soils in which it grows.

Poison sumac has pinnate compound leaves with 7–13 leaflets each. The leaves grow in an alternate pattern. The entire leaf may be 1–2 feet (30–60 cm) in length, and the petiole is often red, especially on the upper surface. The oblong or elliptical leaflets have smooth edges, pointed tips, wedge-shaped bases, and reddish midribs; the leaflets are usually attached to the main petiole by a short stalk.

The flowers of poison sumac, like those of poison ivy and poison oak, are small, inconspicuous, and greenish or yellowish-white and form loose clusters. The fruits are a dull white and hang below the leaves in a long open cluster, often with reddish stems. The foliage of poison sumac turns a brilliant red-orange or coral early in the season and is easily noticed (and, unfortunately, sometimes cut for fall arrangements). Like the other members of the genus *Toxicodendron*, all parts of this species contain the oil urushiol and may cause a severe allergic dermatitis; no one should assume a lifetime of immunity from the effects of this oil.

In swamps, poison sumac is most likely to be confused with ash (*Fraxinus* spp.), but ash trees have opposite compound leaves and branches. The other common sumacs in this book's range have alternate compound leaves like those of poison sumac but do not tend to grow in wet habitats. These sumacs of drier sites, such as staghorn sumac (*Rhus hirta* [L.] Sudworth), smooth sumac (*Rhus glabra* L.), and shining sumac (*Rhus copallinum* L.), all have erect, pointed clusters of red fruit that develop above the leaves. These species also may form large colonies, unlike poison sumac, which is usually found as an individual plant.

Black Ti-ti, Leatherwood

Cyrilla racemiflora L.
Cyrilla Family, Cyrillaceae

RANGE: Southeastern Virginia south to Florida and west to Texas; also in the West Indies and Central and South America.
HABITAT: Sandy swamps, pocosins, streambanks, pond shores, and wet woods on the coastal plain.

Black ti-ti is a very handsome wetland plant. Taking the form of a shrub or small tree that can grow as tall as 33 feet (10 m) or more, it has a short trunk, a wide branching pattern, and elongated showy clusters of white flowers.

Cyrilla is evergreen except in the northern portions of its range or during very cold winters, when it will lose most of its leaves. The leaves are simple, alternate, elliptical, ⅜–4 inches (1–10 cm) long and up to 1 inch (2.5 cm) wide, and without teeth, although the margins are sometimes wavy. They are glossy and leathery, are paler underneath, and tend to be clustered near the ends of the twigs. The

Black ti-ti, *Cyrilla racemiflora*

petioles may be up to ¼ inch (7 mm) long. In the autumn, the leaves turn orange or red, and in the winter, those that remain on the plant may be a deep purplish-green.

The star-shaped flowers appear from May to July on arching, slender racemes that develop below the leaf clusters. The racemes may be as much as 6 inches (15 cm) long, with the flowers at the base of the racemes blooming first. Each white flower is attached to the raceme with a short stalk and has a single pistil, five petals, five sepals, and five stamens that are slightly shorter than the petals. Black ti-ti often produces a large number of flowering racemes and is a beautiful sight when in full bloom. The bees find the fragrant flowers attractive as well; since it produces large quantities of nectar, *Cyrilla* is considered an excellent honey plant.

The fruits are small dry capsules about ⅛ inch (3 mm) long. Initially yellow, they eventually turn brown or gray and may remain on the plant until the following year's blooming season.

Cyrilla is sometimes planted as an ornamental. It is surprisingly hardy in colder climates out of its natural range and more tolerant to drier soils than might be expected of a wetland species. It is valued especially for its attractive flowers, brilliant fall foliage, and resistance to disease and pests.

Buckwheat-tree or ti-ti tree (*Cliftonia monophylla* [Lam.] Britt. *ex* Sarg.) is another southern member of the cyrilla family, found growing in habitats similar to those of black ti-ti on the coastal plain from Georgia south to northern Florida and west to Louisiana. It may grow as tall as 30 feet (9 m) and, like black ti-ti, has alternate, leathery, evergreen leaves. Its leaves, however, are usually sessile, may be up to 4 inches (10 cm) long and ¾ inch (2 cm) wide, and are dotted with tiny glands. The stout flower clusters rise above the leaves at the ends of the twigs and are usually no more than 3½ inches (9 cm) long. In bud, the white flowers are often tinged with pink; when open, they have 5–8 blunt-tipped petals and 10 stamens. Similar to the flowers of *Cyrilla*, the fragrant flowers are an excellent source of nectar for bees.

The fruit is about 5/16 inch (8 mm) long and has two to four wings, looking much like fruit of members of the buckwheat family, which is why this species has been called buckwheat-tree. The fruits are yellow when ripe, turn brownish with age, and may persist in clusters until the following growing season.

The cyrilla family is named in honor of an Italian professor of medicine, Domenico Cirillo (1734–1799).

American Holly

Ilex opaca Ait.
Holly Family, Aquifoliaceae

RANGE: Eastern Massachusetts south to Florida and west to Missouri and Texas.
HABITAT: Sandy soils and moist woodlands.

With its distinctive prickly evergreen leaves and scarlet berries, American holly is one of North America's most beautiful native trees. It grows 30–50 feet (9–15 m) tall and at times may reach 80–100 feet (25–30 m) in the South. The trunk is usually 1–3 feet (30–90 cm) in diameter but may occasionally reach 4 feet (1.5 m). The bark is thin, light gray, and either smooth or warty and rough.

The crown is usually shaped like a slender cone that is slightly wider at the bottom, with the branches at right angles to the trunk. If the tree is growing in full sun, the foliage is dense, but if it is in the shade, it will be more open and have fewer branches.

The leaves are elliptical or oblong and usually 2–4 inches (5–10 cm) long. They have thick undulate margins with a sharp spine at the tip and usually several spines along the margins, although some

American holly, *Ilex opaca*

plants may have leaves without spines or with only the single spine at the leaf tip.

The leaves are thick, leathery, a dull deep green with conspicuous veins and midribs, and often paler green on the undersides. They remain on the tree for three years and are shed in the spring of the fourth year.

American holly is dioecious, meaning "living in two houses," since the male and female flowers are found on separate plants. Occasionally, however, a tree with both male and female flowers will be found.

Holly flowers are greenish-white and ¼ inch (7 mm) wide, with four oval petals united at the base, a calyx with four pointed sepals, and a short pedicel. The flowers appear with the new leaves in the spring. The female flowers, which produce the berries, tend to be borne singly or in clusters of 2–3 on the stems below the new leaves and the male flowers in clusters of 3–12 in the axils of the new leaves. American holly blooms from April to June from south to north.

The berries are round, fleshy, and ¼–½ inch (7–12 mm) in diameter, and when ripe, they are usually bright scarlet, although an occasional tree will produce yellow fruit. Holly berries are somewhat toxic and should be kept away from children. Birds and other wildlife do eat the fruit, but not until after it has been subjected to severe frost.

The wood of American holly is fine-grained, white, and dense. It is prized for marquetry and inlay in fine cabinetwork and is also used in wood carving and to make musical instruments.

In the U.S. Department of Agriculture's *Plant Hardiness Zone Map* (1990), American holly is placed in Zone 6, where the average low temperature is −10 to 0°F. The map indicates that American holly grows well in a narrow strip of land along the New England coast, from coastal Massachusetts to southern Rhode Island. Above this line, it does not survive. Farther south, it grows inland as well as along the coast.

A number of other *Ilex* species grow in this book's range. The deciduous shrub winterberry (*Ilex verticillata* [L.] Gray) is often found on damp upland borders of salt marshes in the northern part of this book's range, although it is generally a more inland plant in the South. Like American holly, its bright red berries persist into the winter, only to be gobbled up by birds and small mammals after several hard frosts. Another red-fruited deciduous species, possum-haw (*Ilex decidua* Walt.), grows in coastal plain swamps and wet woodlands from Maryland south to Florida and west to Texas. The black-fruited inkberry (*Ilex glabra* [L.] Gray), which has smooth evergreen leaves, is an important shrub of coastal plain wetlands in the Middle Atlantic states and grows from Nova Scotia south to Florida and west to Louisiana.

Several evergreen hollies grow in maritime forests and damp coastal plain habitats in the South. Yaupon (*Ilex vomitoria* Ait.) is a shrub or small tree with short, leathery, elliptical leaves that have small rounded teeth along their margins. The shiny red fruits may form dense clusters along the gray twigs and persist into the winter. Native Americans have used yaupon leaves, which contain caffeine, to induce vomiting and purging of the body for ritual cleansing, hence the name *Ilex vomitoria*.

Dahoon or cassena (*Ilex cassine* L.) is a small evergreen tree growing in wet soils (and sometimes brackish areas) from North Carolina south to Florida and west to Texas. Its leaves may be up to 4 inches (10 cm) long and are either entire or have teeth that are tipped with short bristles. Like the other hollies, it is popular in holiday decorations and is a valuable winter food source for many birds and mammals. Myrtle-leaf holly (*Ilex myrtifolia* Walt., treated as a subspecies of *Ilex cassine* by some authorities) is similar but has shorter, narrower leaves and a slightly larger fruit.

Red buckeye, *Aesculus pavia*

Red Buckeye

Aesculus pavia L.
Horse-chestnut Family, Hippocastanaceae

RANGE: Coastal plain from North Carolina south to Florida and west to central Texas; inland to Kentucky, Illinois, and Missouri.
HABITAT: Understory of moist, rich woodlands and edges of swamps and streams.

When red buckeye or firecracker-plant blooms in the spring, the woodlands seem lit with torches of red flowers. The beauty of the flowers and the handsome dark green foliage has not been overlooked by the horticultural trade, and red buckeye is a popular ornamental, especially in the southeastern United States.

Red buckeye is a deciduous shrub or small tree that grows 3⅓–33 feet (1–10 m) tall, although most often in this book's range it is a shrub no more than about 12–15 feet (3.5–4.5 m) tall. Like other members of the horse-chestnut family, it has opposite, palmately compound leaves that are borne on long petioles and elongated terminal clusters of flowers that may be perfect or either male or female.

Each red buckeye leaf has five (or sometimes seven) oblong leaflets that are broadest at or just above the middle, wedge-shaped at the base, and tapered to a pointed tip. The leaflets may be as much as 6 inches (15 cm) long and 2⅜ inches (6 cm) wide and are irregularly saw-toothed along the margins. The leaves are thin in texture with prominent veins, deep glossy green on the upper surface, and sometimes covered with very fine hairs on the lower surface.

The flower clusters may be as much as 8–10 inches (20–25 cm) long and bear numerous flowers that are up to 1½ inches (4 cm) long, with a tubular, deep scarlet calyx at the base. The calyx has five blunt, shallow lobes and is densely covered with fine hairs, giving it a velvety look. Each flower has four red petals that are unequal in size, broadest at the rounded tips, and narrowed to elongated claws. The two narrow upper petals flare upward, often revealing bright yellow on the undersides, and the two wider lateral petals enfold the stamens and pistil, which project beyond the tips of the lateral petals. There are tiny stalked glands along the margins of the petals.

Red buckeye has been listed as one of the most important nectar sources for hummingbirds in the eastern United States. Bees and other insects also pollinate the buckeyes, although buckeye nectar and pollen have been shown to be toxic to honeybees, causing deformities when fed to the brood.

The fruit of red buckeye is a smooth round capsule 1³⁄16–2⅜ inches (3–6 cm) across. When ripe, it splits into two or three segments and contains one to three shiny brown seeds that are poisonous. In spite of their toxicity, *Aesculus* seeds have been used in traditional Native American medicine, as well as for food. Native Americans have also used the leaves and ground fruits to stun fish in pools, making them easy to catch. The fruits of other members of this family, including horse-chestnut (*Aesculus hippocastanum* L.), a European species that is widely planted in the United States, are also poisonous, but fortunately the reputedly bitter flavor prevents most people from consuming enough to be harmful.

A similar species, painted buckeye (*Aesculus sylvatica* Bartr.), may be found in a few coastal plain counties in North Carolina but is primarily a plant of piedmont woodlands and streambanks, growing from southern Virginia south to Alabama and northern Florida. Its flowers are a dull yellow or yellow-red, and the margins of the petals have fine hairs rather than glands.

Some authorities now include the horse-chestnut family in the soapberry family (Sapindaceae) since the two families have many common characteristics.

Swamp rose-mallow,
Hibiscus moscheutos

Swamp Rose-mallow

Hibiscus moscheutos L. ssp. *moscheutos*
Mallow Family, Malvaceae

RANGE: Massachusetts and New York south to Florida and west to Wisconsin, Ohio, Missouri, and Texas; also in California.
HABITAT: Freshwater, brackish, and saline marshes and shallow ponds.

There are three forms of swamp rose-mallow. The most common and widely distributed type has creamy-white flowers with a wide, dark red band at the base of each petal extending about one-quarter of the length of the petal. This form is found infrequently in New England, but south of New England to the Gulf of Mexico, it is common. Plants with pink flowers and red bands at the petal bases grow in the same range as the cream-colored plants.

Plants with rose-pink or pure white flowers with no red bands at the base of the petals are restricted to coastal southern New England

and a site in North Carolina. Some authorities consider this a separate variety, *Hibiscus moscheutos* L. ssp. *palustris* (L.) Clausen, or even a separate species, *Hibiscus palustris* L., but the system used here includes the solid pink form within the subspecies *moscheutos*.

The plants with red bands tend to grow as separate clumps with four or five stems in each clump, often singly or as a few scattered clumps but not in solid stands like the pink-flowered plants in New England. In Rhode Island, before the advent of major coastal development, solid stands of pink swamp rose-mallow bordered the western shore of Narragansett Bay and Block Island Sound in a series of shallow brackish ponds from East Greenwich to the Connecticut border, and stands also existed on Conanicut Island and the east side of Narragansett Bay.

Swamp rose-mallow plants are perennial and grow 3⅓–6½ feet (1–2 m) tall. The flowers, which are borne in the axils of the upper leaves, are often 7 inches (18 cm) wide and beautiful shades of pale to deep rose-pink. The petals are finely striated, not smooth. As is typical in members of the mallow family, the stamens are united into a column that projects from the base of the petals. The yellow anthers are arranged along the sides of the column, which terminates with five round stigmas. The very showy flowers of plants in the genus *Hibiscus* are pollinated by insects and hummingbirds.

The flowers have no fragrance, but the whole plant, especially when slightly bruised, has a musty odor. The flowers, which bloom from July to October, are followed by round seedpods that taper to a point in the center. Several seeds may be found within each of the fruit segments.

The leaves are dark green, smooth on the upper surface, and covered with fine hairs on the lower surface. The leaves vary widely in shape. Some are lance- or egg-shaped, whereas others have three lobes. They are rounded or heart-shaped at the base, toothed along the margins, and tapered to a point at the tip.

The stems of swamp rose-mallow are thick and rough and appear to be woody but are actually herbaceous. In most areas, the stems are killed by frost and replaced by new stems in the spring, but in southern Florida, the stems do not die back.

The mallow family contains many prized ornamental species, including rose-of-Sharon (*Hibiscus syriacus* L.), which is cultivated as far north as Canada, and China rose (*Hibiscus rosa-sinensis* L.), a tropical Asian species frequently grown outdoors in warm climates and in indoor gardens and greenhouses in cold climates. Okra (*Abelmoschus esculentus* [L.] Moench) is a well-known edible member of the mallow family, and several plants in this family are grown for fiber, including cotton (*Gossypium* spp.) and China jute (*Abutilon theophrasti* Medik.). China jute has naturalized in North America and grows in disturbed sites and waste places throughout this book's range, where it is commonly known as pie marker or velvet leaf.

Seashore Mallow

Kosteletzkya virginica (L.) K. Presl *ex* Gray
Mallow Family, Malvaceae

RANGE: Long Island south to Florida and the West Indies and west to Texas.
HABITAT: Brackish marshes and ditches.

This member of the mallow family is a perennial and, in many respects, resembles swamp rose-mallow (*Hibiscus moscheutos*). The smaller flowers of the seashore mallow, however, and the lone seed in each fruit segment readily distinguish the two species. The genus is named in honor of nineteenth-century European botanist Vincenz Franz Kosteletzky (1801–1887).

Seashore mallow grows as single plants with several stems that are covered with fine, short, star-shaped hairs and a mass of tough, fibrous roots. It does not grow in colonies. The stems are usually 4–6 feet (1.2–1.8 m) tall and have several flowers among the leaves at the upper end of each stalk.

The leaves range in length from 1 to 6 inches (2.5–15 cm) and are gray-green. The lower ones are somewhat heart-shaped, rounded, or angular at the base and may have coarse teeth. The upper leaves are much more slender and may have pointed basal lobes.

The flowers are 2–3 inches (5–8 cm) in diameter, each with five rounded petals that taper toward the base. The flowers are usually rose-pink but may also be white or lavender. The pistil and stamens emerge from the center of the flower in a 2-inch (5 cm) curved column. The five stigmas are at the end of the column, and the anthers are pressed tightly around the pistil. When the flowers bloom from July to October, each one lasts only a day.

The fruit is about ⅜ inch (1 cm) across and covered with coarse

Seashore mallow,
Kosteletzkya virginica

hairs. It has five segments, and a single seed develops within each segment.

Another member of the mallow family, marsh mallow (*Althaea officinalis* L.), is a native of Europe that has naturalized in salt and brackish marshes from Massachusetts south to Virginia. It is an erect, branching perennial that grows 1½–4 feet (45–120 cm) tall. The pale pink, five-petaled flowers are smaller than those of seashore mallow, 1–1½ inches (2.5–4 cm) across, and borne in clusters growing from the axils of the upper leaves. The velvety leaves are coarsely toothed and vary in shape but frequently have three lobes. The style is divided into 15 or more branches, and the fruit has as many segments as there are style branches (unlike the fruit of seashore mallow, which has five segments). As in seashore mallow, each segment contains only one seed.

Marsh mallow roots, which contain mucilage, were once used to make candy, although modern marshmallow candy contains no ingredients from *Althaea*. Marsh mallow leaves and roots are still eaten in some parts of the world, especially in times of famine, and the plant has had many medicinal uses as well. The scientific name *Althaea* derives from the Greek word *althaino*, "to heal," and refers to the soothing properties of the mucilaginous substance extracted from the roots and leaves.

Loblolly Bay

Gordonia lasianthus (L.) Ellis
Tea Family, Theaceae

RANGE: Coastal plain from North Carolina south to Florida and west to Louisiana.
HABITAT: Moist forests, pocosins, and shallow swamps.

Depending on the moisture and fertility of the soil in which it grows, loblolly bay may be either an evergreen tree or a shrub. At favorable sites, it may reach the height of 82 feet (25 m), but in drier, infertile soil, it will remain a shrub.

The leaves are simple, elliptical, leathery, and evergreen. Both surfaces of the leaf are smooth, the upper dark, glossy green and the lower pale green; the edges are bluntly toothed. The tips of the leaves may be pointed or rounded, with the blade 3–6 inches (8–15 cm) long and 1 3/16–2 inches (3–5 cm) wide.

The flower buds are borne in clusters on long reddish stalks that emerge from the axils of the leaves. The flowers are fragrant and open one at a time in each cluster of buds. They have five fringed or wavy-edged petals and are usually 2–4 inches (5–10 cm) wide. The backs of the petals are covered with silky hairs, which explains why this species was given the descriptive name *lasianthus*, meaning "woolly-flowered." The snow-white petals surrounding the masses of creamy to bright yellow stamens with the pistil in the center make a very showy contrast against the dark, glossy foliage. They bloom throughout the summer.

The geographical limits of native plants of *Gordonia lasianthus* are well documented within the coastal zone. The species may be difficult to grow as an ornamental, but when planted in moist soil in full sun, it grows well into the piedmont and Middle Atlantic regions. *Gordonia* is named in honor of James Gordon, the nurseryman who introduced the ginkgo tree (*Ginkgo biloba* L.) into cultivation.

Loblolly bay,
Gordonia lasianthus

The common name loblolly apparently derives from two words meaning "cooking porridge" and "a thick soup." In the southern United States, loblolly has come to mean a mudhole or swampy place, so it is an appropriate name for plants such as loblolly bay and loblolly pine (*Pinus taeda*), which grow in moist habitats.

Except as an ornamental, loblolly bay has never had much economic value. In the past, the bark was used for tanning leather, and the wood is still used occasionally in cabinetmaking. Deer browse on the plant, and many observers (especially photographers seeking the "perfect shot") have noted that insects frequently chew on the leaves. Since members of the tea family are known to contain alkaloids and saponins, it is possible that consuming *Gordonia* leaves gives insects a bad taste, which helps protect them from predation, much as eating milkweed makes monarch butterflies less palatable.

Beach heather, *Hudsonia tomentosa*

Beach Heather

Hudsonia tomentosa Nutt.
Rockrose Family, Cistaceae

RANGE: Labrador south to North Carolina.
HABITAT: Coastal sand dunes and beaches.

The gray-green mats of beach heather or beach heath are often the predominant vegetation on windblown sand in coastal areas where few other plants can become established. Because it grows in such poor soils, it is also sometimes called poverty-grass, although it is not a grass but a member of the rockrose family.

The low-growing plants are woody perennials. They seldom exceed 3–4 inches (7.5–10 cm) in height and grow in mats that vary in diameter from a few inches to several feet. The branches are covered with closely overlapping, persistent, gray-green, hairy, scalelike alternate leaves. Physically, the plants look as if they should be members of the heath family, but close examination of the flowers will show the characteristics of the rockrose family.

The flowers are less than ¼ inch (7 mm) in diameter, with 5 sulphur-yellow petals and up to 30 projecting stamens. Even though the flowers are small, they are borne in such masses that at times the leaves are completely hidden. The flowers have no pedicel (stalk) and are attached directly to the stem. They bloom in May and June.

Although the common name of *Hudsonia tomentosa* is beach heather, it is more likely to be found growing on the lee side of dunes or in interdune areas than on the beach itself. This plant is well adapted to this harsh, dry habitat. It develops an extensive network of threadlike roots that gather whatever moisture may be available. It also traps the blowing sand on dunes and thus helps to form and stabilize coastal dunes.

Beach Pinweed

Lechea maritima Leggett *ex* B.S.P. var. *maritima*
Rockrose Family, Cistaceae

RANGE: New Brunswick south to Virginia.
HABITAT: Sand beaches, dunes, and flats near the coast, as well as sandy soils inland at a few New England sites.

Plants that grow in exposed habitats, such as deserts, sand dunes, and beaches, have developed adaptations that help prevent dehydration and protect them from intense solar radiation. These plants may be fleshy, such as seabeach sandwort (*Honckenya peploides*); grow very low to the ground to avoid drying winds, such as seaside spurge (*Chamaesyce polygonifolia*); or be covered with hairs, such as dusty miller (*Artemisia stelleriana*). Beach pinweed is no exception: the entire plant, both leaves and stems, is covered with short, dense, grayish hairs.

Beach pinweed is usually a perennial but is occasionally biennial and produces only foliage the first year. It grows from a perennial underground base that produces one or more new stems annually. The stems tend to be thick and have a large number of branches that may be up to 16 inches (40 cm) long and are either erect or prostrate.

The plants also have basal shoots that are covered with closely packed, whorled leaves. These basal branches, which may be either erect or prostrate, live through the winter and produce flowers the following summer. The thick, dark green leaves on the flowering stalks are elliptical, grow to ½ inch (12 mm) in length, and are less than ¼ inch (7 mm) wide.

Both flowers and fruits are tiny but conspicuous because they grow in large masses. The flowers are borne in late summer in clusters of three or four in the axils of the leaves and are rarely seen

Beach pinweed,
Lechea maritima

in bloom since they are open only in the early morning. The flowers are extremely small, are dark red, and have three petals that are shorter than the five sepals, which are in two layers, two outer sepals and three inner ones that overlap one another and surround the fruit capsule. The flowers are much less noticeable than the fruits, which are most visible in early autumn when the branches are covered with dense masses of chocolate-brown seedpods.

Beach pinweed often grows in association with tall wormwood (*Artemisia campestris* ssp. *caudata*). Several other species of pinweed may be found growing in coastal plain habitats in this book's range; they are differentiated by the technical characteristics of the flowers and fruits and often by the degree of hairiness on the leaves and stems.

The genus *Lechea* is named in honor of Swedish botanist Johan Leche (1704–1764).

Lance-leaved violet, *Viola lanceolata*

Lance-leaved Violet

Viola lanceolata L.
Violet Family, Violaceae

RANGE: Southern Quebec and New England south to Florida and west to Ontario, Minnesota, Oklahoma, and Texas.
HABITAT: Damp sand, clay, or peaty soils in sun or light shade.

The lance-leaved violet is common and easily recognized by the shape of its leaves, which gives it its common name. The leaves tend to be long, slender, and lance-shaped, with relatively long petioles; they are usually about three times as long as they are wide.

The plants may vary considerably in size. New plants growing on moist, south-facing slopes, which bloom early in the spring and have only a single flower and one pair of leaves, may reach only 1 inch (2.5 cm) in height. Older plants may have eight or more white flowers and pairs of leaves, bloom in the summer, and grow to 4 inches (10 cm) high.

The plants may grow singly or in colonies, and both leaves and flowers tend to stand erect, so the plants can be easily recognized when growing among other plants.

Another white violet, the primrose-leaved violet (*Viola primulifolia* L.), may also be found in this book's range. It grows in moist open meadows and along streambanks, generally in damp, sandy soils and sometimes in light shade. It is found from New Brunswick south to Florida and west to Indiana, Oklahoma, and Texas but is more common in the eastern portion of its range.

Like most species of white violets, the flowers of the primrose-leaved violet have no particular distinguishing features, but they are easily recognized by the leaves, which lack the heart shape typical of most violets. Instead, the leaf has an oblong or elliptical shape and tapers abruptly where the blade meets the petiole, giving it an almost paddlelike shape. From this point, a "wing" extends partway down each side. The leaf tends to be 1½–2½ times as long as it is wide. The leaf of this species more closely resembles a primrose leaf than a violet leaf, which is the reason for its common name.

The plants produce stolons and tend to grow in clusters rather than as single plants. Plants in bloom are usually no more than 2–4 inches (5–10 cm) in height; depending on the location, they may flower from early March to July.

Over 85 species of *Viola* exist in North America; as a group, they are among the most treasured of spring flowers. They are well designed for insect pollination, with bright-colored flowers in varying shades of yellow, lavender, blue, purple, and white. Bees, flies, bee flies, moths, and butterflies are among the pollinators of violets.

Violets have five petals of unequal size. The two upper petals point upward, the two lateral petals extend on each side, and the lower petal points downward and often has a beard of hairs (sometimes the lateral petals are bearded as well). Dark lines on the petals guide insects toward the nectar at the base of the flower. In some species, the back portion of the lower petal forms a spurlike appendage that contains nectar. It is not unusual to find an insect piercing the spur to gather the nectar (or to see the hole the insect has left) rather than going in the "front door" and helping to pollinate the flower.

In addition to the showy flowers, many species of violets produce cleistogamous (meaning "hidden gametes") flowers. These flowers do not have petals and never open; they look like small buds tucked underneath the foliage. They self-pollinate, so the seeds they produce are identical to the parent plant (unlike seeds from the showy cross-pollinated flowers, which have characteristics of both parent plants). Gardeners who are unaware of these hidden flowers often wonder how violets manage to produce so many offspring!

The fruit capsule of violets may open suddenly, scattering seeds as far away as 6 feet (1.8 m) from the parent plant. Ants have also been observed dispersing violet seeds. They are attracted to an appendage on the seeds that contains oil, and research has shown that violet seeds that have been handled by ants produce healthier seedlings than those that lack such contact.

A variety of songbirds, gamebirds, and small mammals eat violet seeds, and the rhizomes are especially relished by the wild turkey.

Eastern Prickly Pear

Opuntia humifusa (Raf.) Raf.
Cactus Family, Cactaceae

RANGE: Eastern Massachusetts south to Florida and west to southern Ontario, Minnesota, and eastern Texas and rarely to Montana.
HABITAT: Coastal dunes, nonsaline dry sands, rocks, roadsides, and sandy fields.

When most people think of New England, they think of lobster or snow, not cactus, but the northeasternmost limits of the eastern prickly pear reach to Cape Cod.

Eastern prickly pear plants may grow erect to 16 inches (40 cm) tall or spread flat on the ground in mats as wide as 3⅓ feet (1 m). Each plant is composed of thick, flattened oval pads that are actually joints of the stem; they may produce a few simple scalelike leaves that are soon shed. The pads of *Opuntia humifusa* are firmly attached to one another and difficult to separate, unlike the pads of some other species of prickly pear, which separate easily. They are a medium shade of green, with smooth, dull surfaces except when the plants are very young, at which time the developing pads are shiny and dark greenish-red. These pads are excellent water-storage devices for the cacti, which usually grow in warm, dry habitats.

At regular intervals of ⅜–1½ inches (1–2.5 cm) across the flat surfaces of the pads are small nodes called areoles. Each areole contains a tuft of numerous reddish-brown bristles known as glochids. Some areoles may also have one or rarely two sharp-pointed, light brown to whitish round spines up to 1³⁄₁₆ inches (3 cm) long. These spines are as sharp as a needle, although they are large enough to be seen and avoided. The glochids look less dangerous but also should not be touched because their barbed edges can lacerate flesh. The wounds from glochids can be extremely painful.

Eastern prickly pear, *Opuntia humifusa*

Blooming in May and June (and sporadically later in the summer), the flowers are a bright yellow, may have a red center, and are up to 3 inches (7.5 cm) in diameter. The fruit is dark red or purple and also has nodes with glochids.

The prickly structure of prickly pear is an adaptation that protects it from being eaten by moisture-seeking animals. The spines also appear to aid in seed dispersal, for the spiny fruits may catch on mammals' fur or birds' feathers and be transported to a new location. In spite of the dangers, however, species of *Opuntia* are an important source of food for wildlife, especially in the arid West.

Many references list this species as *Opuntia compressa* J. F. Macbr. *Opuntia* is a name that the "father of botany," Theophrastus (371–287 B.C.), gave to a group of plants, but certainly not the plants of this genus since all of the *Opuntia* have their origin in the New World. The name *humifusa* means "spreading on the ground," a very accurate description of the growth habit of this plant.

Another species of *Opuntia* in southeastern coastal areas is *Opuntia pusilla* (Haw.) Nutt. (or *Opuntia drummondii* Graham in some references). It grows on sand dunes and in maritime forests and sometimes forms mats. Reaching no more than 8 inches (20 cm) in height, the pads are up to 2 inches (5 cm) long and ¾ inch (2 cm) wide and are easily detached from one another (which probably helps this species disperse its fruit). Each node has glochids as well as two to four spines that may be up to 1 3/16 inches (3 cm) long. Because *Opuntia pusilla* grows so low to the ground, it is often partly covered by shifting sands and not noticed until it is stepped on with bare feet or the spines pierce the soles of shoes. Small wonder that its common name is devil-joint!

Barbary fig (*Opuntia monacantha* [Willd.] Haw., or *Opuntia vulgaris* P. Mill. in some references) is also sometimes called prickly pear. A tropical species that has naturalized in the South, it has been observed growing on the upper portions of tidal salt marshes and in disturbed sites inland. Unlike the prostrate growth habit of eastern prickly pear, Barbary fig grows to 5 feet (1.5 m) tall in this book's range (it can reach 20 feet [6 m] in tropical climates) and is always erect. This species has been cultivated in many parts of the world because it is a host to the insect that yields the valuable red dye, cochineal. The dried, ground-up bodies of these mealybugs (*Dactylopius coccus*) are used to make cochineal. Use of this dye goes back at least as far as the ancient Aztecs in Mexico, and the dye is still used to make cosmetics and to color food, beverages, and medicine.

Showy Evening-primrose

Oenothera speciosa Nutt.
Evening-primrose Family, Onagraceae

RANGE: Native from Kansas and Missouri south to Texas and northeastern Mexico; escaped from cultivation (and perhaps from natural populations) and naturalized from Louisiana east to Florida and north to Illinois and Virginia.
HABITAT: Dry open areas such as fields, pastures, waste places, and roadsides.

Whether seen from a distance as a mass of pink blossoms carpeting a dusty roadside or viewed closely enough to see the delicate patterning on the petals, a patch of showy evening-primrose in full bloom is a lovely sight. Although it is not native to the eastern United States, showy evening-primrose is a popular ornamental and is often used in highway wildflower-seed mixes. In the southeastern United States, it appears to have spread from cultivated sites and to have naturalized fairly widely, and there is now some concern that it may become an invasive pest.

Oenothera speciosa is a perennial plant that is usually no more

Showy evening-primrose, *Oenothera speciosa*

than 1–2 feet (30–60 cm) in height. Growing from creeping underground roots, this plant has stems and branches that are covered with fine hairs that tend to press upward against the stems. Its linear or lance-shaped leaves are as much as 3½ inches (9 cm) long and usually slightly toothed along the upper margins, with the lower halves of the leaves more sharply toothed or deeply cut into irregular lobes.

The flower buds form in the axils of the upper leaves and initially are nodding. When the four-petaled flowers open, they may be 3 inches (7.5 cm) across, although they are often smaller later in the blooming season, which may be from March to August, depending on the location. The flowers range in color from deep to pale pink to white.

Whatever the color, the broad petals have a pattern of fine lines that lead to their bright yellow bases and the nectar glands that attract the insects that pollinate this plant. Each flower has eight large stamens and a white style that extends beyond the stamens and ends in four slender stigma lobes that form a cross shape. The narrow sepals may be as long as an inch (2.5 cm) and point sharply downward when the flower reaches full bloom.

Oenothera speciosa is one of many species of evening-primrose that may be found in this book's range. Common evening-primrose (*Oenothera biennis* L.) is the species most likely to be encountered in coastal habitats in the northern part of the range (it grows from Canada south to Florida and west to Arizona). It is a large, coarse, mostly biennial plant of fields and waste places (and in the Northeast, sand dunes and cobble beaches), reaching as much as 6½ feet (2 m) in height, with stiff, often-branched flower stalks that bear large (1–2 inches [2.5–5 cm] in diameter) yellow flowers. Like the flowers of showy evening-primrose, the flowers of common evening-primrose have eight stamens, a cross-shaped stigma, and reflexed sepals. The fruit is an elongated capsule about four times longer than it is wide that usually persists into the winter. The lance-shaped, slightly toothed leaves are 4–8 inches (10–20 cm) long and frequently wavy along the margins. Often mottled with purple, the main stalk of the plant is usually somewhat hairy. The flowers of this species open at dusk and close by noon the following day, so they are pollinated primarily by insects, such as moths, that are active at night.

Seaside evening-primrose (*Oenothera humifusa* Nutt.) grows on beaches and sand dunes from New Jersey south to Florida and west to Louisiana. A perennial with a sprawling growth habit, it has branches that may be up to 32 inches (80 cm) long. The oblong leaves are often crowded together and are as much as 1½ inches (4 cm) long and 5⁄16 inch (8 mm) wide; they may be entire, be wavy along the margins, or have a few shallow teeth. The yellow night-blooming flowers are about ¾ inch (2 cm) in diameter. The whole plant is densely covered with fine hairs, including the cylindrical seed capsules.

Other species of evening-primrose that may be found in this book's range include beach evening-primrose (*Oenothera drummondii* Hook.), sundrops (*Oenothera fruticosa* L.), and cut-leaved evening-primrose (*Oenothera laciniata* Hill).

Beach Pennywort

Hydrocotyle bonariensis Comm. *ex* Lam.
Parsley Family, Apiaceae

RANGE: North Carolina south to Florida and west to Texas; also in South America and South Africa.
HABITAT: Open sandy areas such as dunes, dune swales, roadside ditches, and moist edges, including saline and brackish shores.

The glossy round leaves of beach pennywort are a common sight in southern coastal regions, often covering large areas along damp

Beach pennywort, *Hydrocotyle bonariensis*

sandy roadsides. In parts of Florida, it is known as dollar-weed since the round leaves resemble silver dollars.

Hydrocotyle bonariensis is a low-growing perennial plant with slender creeping stems that root at the nodes. The smooth, thick leaves grow from these nodes and are a deep, glossy green, with the petiole attached to the center of the leaf on the lower surface. The main veins radiate out from this central point of attachment. The margins of the leaf are shallowly toothed and somewhat wavy; an indentation along one edge prevents the leaf from being perfectly circular. The leaves are typically 2–4 inches (5–10 cm) across.

The inconspicuous five-petaled flowers are white to greenish-yellow and grow in many-branched umbels that are 1–3 inches (2.5–7.5 cm) in diameter. The flowering stems are at least as tall as the petioles (which are usually about 4–10 inches [10–25 cm] tall in this book's area). They bloom from April until frost, and flowers and fruit are frequently found simultaneously on a plant.

Several other species of *Hydrocotyle* may be found in freshwater wetland habitats in this book's range.

Swamp azalea, *Rhododendron viscosum*

Swamp Azalea, Swamp Honeysuckle

Rhododendron viscosum (L.) Torr.
Heath Family, Ericaceae

RANGE: Southern Maine south to Florida and west to Ohio and southeastern Texas.
HABITAT: Bogs, swamps, pocosins, wet woods, and the edges of ponds and streams.

In late spring to midsummer, the dark edges of swamps and bogs are illuminated by the bright white flowers of the swamp azalea. Blooming later than other coastal plain azaleas, the swamp azalea is often called swamp honeysuckle because it has a strong, sweet fragrance like that of the true honeysuckles and because of the flowers' superficial resemblance to honeysuckles, which are in the Caprifoliaceae.

Swamp azalea is an irregularly branched wetland shrub, usually less than 10 feet (3 m) tall. It may occur as individual plants or in colonies. The leaves are entire, ovate, and alternate. They are 1–2⅜ inches (2.5–6 cm) long, are usually broadest across the upper third of the leaf, and may be rounded at the tip or come to an abrupt point. The leaves are shiny, bright green on the upper surface, and green or pale on the underside. The surface of the young twigs often has coarse hairs, and the margins of the leaves and the underside of the midrib may have short, stiff hairs.

The showy white or occasionally pink flowers bloom after the leaves emerge. Each flower has fused petals that form a long slender tube that flares into five broad lobes; the flowers may be as much as 1½ inches (4 cm) across. Extending beyond the flower lobes are five long up-curving stamens and one even longer up-curving pistil with a broad pink stigma.

Both the inside and the outside of the flower are covered with fine hairs; in addition, the outside of the tube and undersides of the flower lobes are densely covered with stalked pink-purple glands. These glands are sticky to touch, which is why swamp azalea is sometimes called clammy azalea. The descriptive name, *viscosum*, means "sticky."

Swamp azalea flowers are beautifully designed for insect pollination. Their fragrance draws insects in search of nectar, and the shape of the flower and projecting stamens and pistils ensures that insects laden with pollen from other plants will first brush against the sticky stigma, depositing that pollen load, and then pick up another load by brushing against the azalea's anthers. The insects get the nectar and the flower is cross-pollinated, yet another example of nature's amazing engineering.

Hammock sweet azalea is a southern form of *Rhododendron viscosum*, although some authorities treat it as a completely different species, *Rhododendron serrulatum* (Small) Millais. It grows in swamps and damp sandy woodlands from southeastern Virginia south to Florida and west to Louisiana and may reach a height of 23 feet (7 m). Its leaves have very fine teeth on the margins, the leaves and flowers tend to be somewhat larger than those of swamp azalea, and the inside of the flower is mostly without hairs.

Several other deciduous azaleas may be found in coastal habitats in the South. Dwarf azalea (*Rhododendron atlanticum* [Ashe] Rehd.) grows in pine barrens, savannas, and sandy soils from southern New Jersey south to Alabama. Blooming in April and May, this low-growing colonial species rarely reaches more than 4 feet (1.2 m) in height. The fragrant flowers are purple to pink (or sometimes white) and usually appear before the leaves emerge or just as they are unfolding. As in swamp azalea, the outside of the flower tube and lobes are covered with tiny glands.

Woolly or wild azalea (*Rhododendron canescens* [Michx.] Sweet) is another pink-flowered azalea and is found in moist woods from Delaware south to Florida and west to Texas. It is a sparingly branched shrub up to 10 feet (3 m) tall that is usually found as a single plant rather than in colonies and blooms in very early spring. The flower tube is about twice as long as the lobes, and the margins of the lobes are wavy, giving this flower a very elegant look.

Highbush Blueberry

Vaccinium corymbosum L.
Heath Family, Ericaceae

RANGE: Nova Scotia and Maine south to Florida and west to Michigan, Illinois, Oklahoma, and eastern Texas.
HABITAT: Bogs, swamps, open forests, and landward edges of freshwater and brackish marshes.

Highbush blueberry is a slow-growing, multistemmed shrub that increases in both size and number of stems as it ages. It grows best in sites with adequate light and moisture and limited competition from faster-growing species. Under favorable conditions, the bushes are long-lived and may reach 13 feet (4 m) in height and width. Highbush blueberry is found in bogs, swamps, old fields, pastures, and sometimes open woodlands. Upland areas where highbush blueberry grows are usually near a pond or wetland, suggesting the existence of a high water table.

In southern New England, in the past when agriculture was less intensive and cattle grazed among the bushes on open land, highbush blueberry was common. The cattle did not eat the leaves, presumably because they were either unpalatable or poisonous (*Vaccinium* has not been reported as poisonous, but several other members of the heath family are toxic to cattle, and highbush blueberry may be as well). As land use intensified, pine trees were planted for timber and the number of developments increased; consequently, highbush blueberry has become less common in upland areas.

Highbush blueberry has some tolerance for salt but not at the high concentration of sea water. Vigorous old plants are often found along the banks of estuaries, on the edges of salt marshes,

Highbush blueberry, *Vaccinium corymbosum*

around coastal salt ponds, or on islands in salt ponds. In these places, the branches may hang down over the water, making the berries easy to pick from a boat.

The leaves of highbush blueberry, like those of other members of the heath family, are simple, alternate, and oval in shape, with smooth margins and short petioles. The leaves are slightly rounded at the base and taper abruptly to a small tip at the upper end. They are usually 1 3/16–3 inches (3–7.5 cm) long and 5/8–1 1/2 inches (1.5–4 cm) wide. Both surfaces are smooth except for the fine hairs on the veins on the underside (some more hairy varieties are treated as distinct species by some authors).

In autumn, the leaves of highbush blueberry turn several shades of bright red or orange, making the plants valuable as ornamentals in addition to being prized for their delicious fruit.

The flowers are snow-white, bell-shaped, and borne in dense clusters. The bells taper slightly toward the lower end, where they are encircled by a tiny ruffle. The flowers are usually 3/16–3/8 inch (5–10 mm) long and are not fragrant. Flowering time varies from February to June, depending on the location.

The lobes of the calyx are broadly triangular and, like the berries, are covered with a waxy bloom. The lobes persist, eventually forming the crown on the ripe berry. The globular berries, which range in color from blue to nearly black, are sweet and juicy and have a delicious flavor when ripe. They ripen from July to September and vary in diameter from 3⁄16 to ½ inch (5–12 mm).

The fruit of *Vaccinium corymbosum* is the blueberry commonly sold to be used fresh. Over the years, plant breeders have developed plants that produced large crops of extralarge berries, but many of these had little flavor. The newer varieties of cultivated berries, however, not only are large but also have the flavor of the wild berries. Like the wild berries, cultivated blueberries are in the market from July to September.

American Cranberry

Vaccinium macrocarpon Ait.
Heath Family, Ericaceae

RANGE: Newfoundland south to North Carolina and west to Manitoba, Ohio, and Illinois.
HABITAT: Sunny freshwater and brackish bogs, wet meadows, and swamps near ponds.

American cranberry is a trailing, somewhat tangled evergreen shrub with extremely thin, wiry, branching stems. The leaves are small elongated ovals, dark green on top, paler underneath, and seldom more than ⅝ inch (16 mm) long. They are rounded at the tip, are attached directly to the stem with no petiole, are leathery in texture, and have an upper surface that is either flat or somewhat rounded.

The flowers are produced either singly or in small clusters from the axils of the lower leaves and hang down on slender wirelike stalks. They vary in color from white to pale pink and are less than ½ inch (12 mm) wide. The flowers are basically bell-shaped but are deeply cut into four segments that resemble petals. The petals are sharply turned back, revealing the pistil and stamens below them. The flowers bloom from June to August.

The fruits ripen in the fall. They are globular, glossy, and rarely more than ⅝ inch (16 mm) in diameter. The fruits vary in color from solid bright red to mottled red and white to white with a red cheek.

Small cranberry (*Vaccinium oxycoccos* L.) grows in similar habitats. A circumboreal species, it may be found growing south to New Jersey and inland to Ohio, Indiana, and Minnesota. The leaves

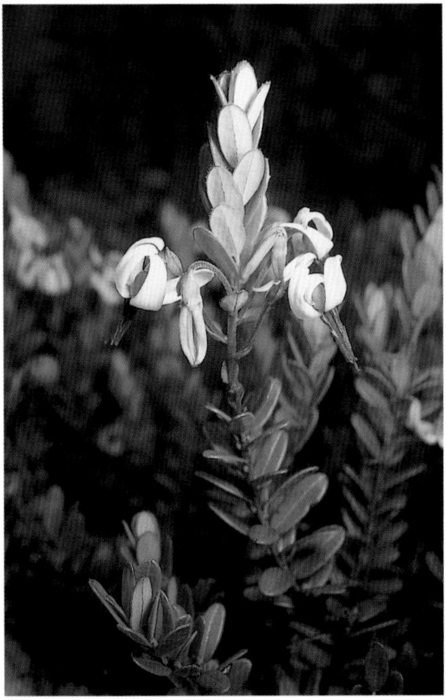

American cranberry,
Vaccinium macrocarpon

may be flat, but more often the margins are strongly rolled under. As the name implies, the fruit of this species is smaller than that of American cranberry, usually less than ½ inch (12 mm) in diameter.

Native Americans ate wild cranberries fresh, dried them for winter use, and introduced them to the early settlers. This is probably the reason cranberries are considered to be a traditional dish at Thanksgiving.

Cranberries are now popular enough to be grown as a commercial crop on bogs constructed for that purpose. They are cultivated extensively on Cape Cod and in New Jersey, Oregon, Washington, Wisconsin, and other areas where growing conditions are suitable. To harvest the berries commercially without bruising them, the bogs are flooded, then special machines strip the fruit from the vines. The berries are gently removed from the water, graded, and packed.

Although plant breeders have tried to develop more productive cranberry plants, most of the plants being grown are selections from wild plants that have larger and more brightly colored fruits rather than plants developed in breeding programs.

Scarlet Pimpernel

Anagallis arvensis L.
Primrose Family, Primulaceae

RANGE: Cosmopolitan; found as a weed in the temperate zone throughout the world.
HABITAT: Rocky shores on the New England coast; fields, lawns, disturbed areas, and dry sandy soils from New Jersey south; sometimes found along salted highways.

Scarlet pimpernel was originally a native of Eurasia but is now naturalized in almost all of the temperate regions of the world. In the South, it may be considered a weed, but in New England, it grows along the shore in the crevices of granite cliffs swept by salt spray, where people who encounter it treasure its beauty and tenacity. It is not surprising, therefore, that its scientific name, *Anagallis*, is probably derived from the ancient Greek words *ana*, meaning "again" and *agallein*, "to delight in." It blooms from March to September, depending on the location.

The plants are sprawling annuals, 4–12 inches (10–30 cm) in diameter, with branches that often root at the nodes. The leaves are sessile, somewhat succulent, oval in shape, pointed at the upper end, and black-spotted on the underside. They clasp the stem in pairs and are usually less than ¾ inch (2 cm) long. The deep coral (or in the South, sometimes deep blue) flowers are solitary, suspended on slender stalks from the axils of the leaves. The flowers are actually tubular, but the rounded lobes are so deeply cut that the flowers appear to have five separate petals. The slender green sepals are usually as long as or slightly shorter than the lobes of the flowers.

Scarlet pimpernel can be grown in the garden if it is well weeded. It cannot survive competition with most garden weeds, but garden weeds cannot tolerate the salt spray on the rocky cliffs where scarlet pimpernel can thrive. In England, one of the common names for scarlet pimpernel is poor man's weather-glass because the flowers close quickly at the approach of bad weather and open again when the storm passes and the sun comes out. This plant was made famous by the Baroness Orczy in her book *The Scarlet Pimpernel*

Scarlet pimpernel, *Anagallis arvensis*

(1902), in which the hero, an aristocrat helping friends flee the terror of the French Revolution, uses the elusive scarlet pimpernel as his symbol.

In the past, scarlet pimpernel was widely used as a medicine that was reputed to cure almost any ailment and also as a cosmetic. We know now that it produces two kinds of toxic organic chemical compounds—glucosides and saponins—both of which can be poisonous to cattle and sheep if sufficient amounts of the plant are consumed; calves and lambs are apparently more sensitive than adult animals.

Sea Lavender, Marsh Rosemary

Limonium carolinianum (Walt.) Britt.
Leadwort Family, Plumbaginaceae

RANGE: Labrador south to Florida and west to Texas and northeastern Mexico.
HABITAT: Coastal salt marshes, rocky shores, edges of salt flats, and salt thickets at the upper edges of salt marshes.

Sea lavender is a component of the high salt marsh and generally grows in association with salt hay grass (*Spartina patens*). Although the plant grows more vigorously where it is inundated daily by the

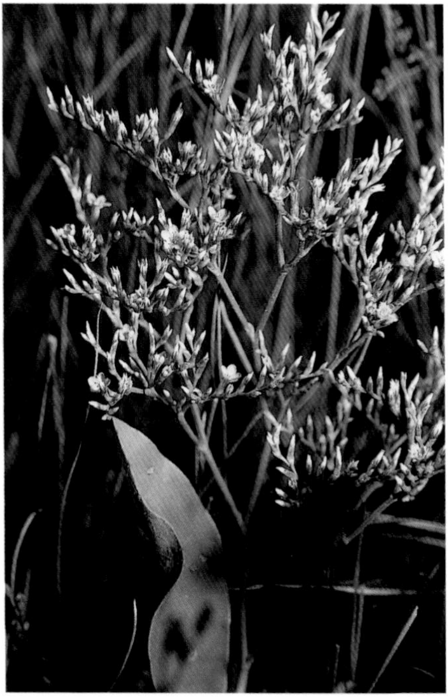

Sea lavender,
Limonium carolinianum

changing tides, the dwarfed remnants of older populations may be found around salt pannes or at the upper levels of marshes where sand is encroaching from adjacent dunes.

Sea lavender is a perennial with a coarse, thick root that produces new plants annually. The leaves are basal and 3–6 inches (7.5–15 cm) long. They are lanceolate, dark green, and leathery and may be flat or cupped, with the edges raised above the center. The long, slender, reddish petioles of the leaves are often longer than the leaf blades. The leaves tend to be evergreen and can usually be found during the winter, disintegrating only shortly before the new spring leaves appear.

In contrast with the dark leathery leaves, the flower stalks are thin, delicate, and pale green, with panicles of flowers borne on lacy one-sided branches. These flowering stems are usually less than 2 feet (60 cm) tall with large masses of dainty pale lavender flowers. The tubular five-petaled flowers are rarely more than ⅛ inch (3 mm) in diameter, but when they bloom in late summer, they are so numerous that they color parts of the marsh a pale misty lavender. The small size of the flowers makes the nectar of sea lavender available to a variety of insects, including bee flies, which are among the pollinators of sea lavender.

The flowers retain their shape and color when dried, making them popular for dried bouquets. In recent years, people have harvested sea lavender in large quantities from salt marshes for winter bouquets, often pulling out entire plants by the roots. To prevent its being harvested to near extinction, as has happened with American ginseng (*Panax quinquefolius* L.) and many native trilliums, orchids, and cacti, several states have passed legislation protecting sea lavender.

Some authorities formerly listed *Limonium nashii* Small as a separate species of sea lavender, but the system used here includes *Limonium nashii* within *Limonium carolinianum* since recent studies have shown that *Limonium nashii* is not morphologically distinct.

Small Saltmarsh Pink, Sea Pink

Sabatia stellaris Pursh
Gentian Family, Gentianaceae

RANGE: Massachusetts south to Florida and west to Louisiana; also in Mexico.
HABITAT: Tidal salt and brackish marshes and interdune swales; also in freshwater sites in Florida and Mexico.

A colony of saltmarsh pink gives the impression of hundreds of small pink stars scattered through the grass. The flowers are a delicate wild-rose pink and ½–1½ inches (1.2–4 cm) in diameter. They usually have 5 somewhat pointed petals, although flowers with 4, 6, or even 7 petals are not uncommon. A few plants with white flowers may be found in large colonies of saltmarsh pink, but pink is the predominant color. At the base of each petal is a jagged yellow blotch about one-fifth as long as the petal. Around each yellow blotch is a zigzag line of red; these lines converge to repeat the star shape of the petals.

Saltmarsh pink is an annual or biennial at its northernmost limits in southern New England and an annual farther south. The plants die after they have bloomed and the seeds have matured. Saltmarsh pink reproduces only from seed, and if the growing con-

Small saltmarsh pink,
Sabatia stellaris

ditions in a given area are not favorable for the growth of seedlings, it will not survive there for any length of time. Like other members of the gentian family, saltmarsh pink is extremely sensitive to competition at the seedling stage, and as other species (such as phragmites) with more vigorous seedlings colonize an area, saltmarsh pink disappears rather rapidly.

It has a single taproot and a single stem that may or may not be branched. Some plants produce a flower when they are no more than 1–2 inches (2.5–5 cm) tall. Others branch freely and may reach as much as 2 feet (60 cm) in height in the southern part of the range. Branching is alternate along the stem, and the stems are round to square in cross section. The flowers are rather widely spaced among the branches on the stalks. Five somewhat leafy sepals spread beneath the petals (but are shorter than the petals), and after the petals fall, they leave a starflower pattern around the globular seed capsules.

The leaves are opposite, narrowly elliptical, and usually ½–1½ inches (1.2–4 cm) long. They are smooth rather than hairy and are delicate and easily bruised.

The flowering period is from mid-June to early October, with the peak of bloom in July and August. Since saltmarsh pink has a long blooming season, buds, flowers, and seed capsules are frequently seen simultaneously on a plant.

Perennial saltmarsh pink (*Sabatia dodecandra* [L.] B.S.P.) may also be found growing in this book's range from southern Connecticut and Long Island south to Florida and west to Texas. In Connecticut and New York, it grows in salt and brackish marshes, but from North Carolina south, it is more likely to be found in wet pinelands, savannas, and acid bogs. It is much larger than *Sabatia stellaris*, has short rhizomes, and reaches up to 3⅓ feet (1 m) in height. It has as many as 8–12 petals, and the whole flower may be as much as 2½ inches (6.5 cm) wide. The flowers are a deep rose-pink with a yellow center outlined in red. As in *Sabatia stellaris*, the branches of the inflorescence are alternate.

Plymouth gentian (*Sabatia kennedyana* Fern.) is a rare plant that grows in coastal plain marshes and along the edges of freshwater ponds and streams in southern Nova Scotia, southeastern Massachusetts, southern Rhode Island, southeastern North Carolina, and northeastern South Carolina. It is similar to *Sabatia dodecandra* and is considered a variety of this species by some authorities, but the leaves of Plymouth gentian are narrower, many of the branches of the inflorescence are opposite, and the calyx lobes lack conspicuous veins.

The genus *Sabatia* is named in honor of Liberto Sabbati, an Italian botanist in the eighteenth century.

Little Floating-heart

Nymphoides cordata (Ell.) Fern.
Buckbean Family, Menyanthaceae

RANGE: Eastern Canada south to New England, New York, and New Jersey and west to Ontario; rarely to Florida and Louisiana.
HABITAT: Freshwater ponds and other quiet waters primarily on the coastal plain.

The delicate white flowers and small leaves of the little floating-heart herald the arrival of full summer in the Northeast. Often

Little floating-heart, *Nymphoides cordata*

growing among white water-lily (*Nymphaea odorata*), spatterdock (*Nuphar lutea*), and water-shield (*Brasenia schreberi* J. F. Gmel.), they form part of a carpet of beauty across the summer pond.

These perennial plants may grow in water up to 10 feet (3 m) deep and develop from rhizomes rooted in the bottom of quiet ponds and swamps. The leaves float on the surface of the water, attached to the rhizomes by long slender stems.

The smooth leaves are heart-shaped, with a V-shaped opening where the narrow petiole (less than 1⁄32 inch [1 mm] thick) joins the leaf blade. The blades are ½–2¾ inches (1.2–7 cm) long (generally only about 2 inches [5 cm]) and ½–1½ inches (1.2–4 cm) wide. They are a deep reddish-purple on the undersurface and green on the upper surface mottled with purple. The margins of the leaves usually have a few shallow teeth.

The flower buds form underwater, just below the leaf blade or as much as 1½ inches (4 cm) below it. They all radiate out from the same part of the underwater stem, each flower developing a long stalk that eventually holds it just above the surface of the water. The small flowers (¼–½ inch [7–12 mm] in diameter) have five white petals, each with a yellow gland at its base, and five sepals that are smooth on the undersurface.

As the flowers mature and the seeds begin to develop, elongated roots emerge from the underwater stem at the point where the flower stalks are connected. These tuberous roots may be as long as 1 inch (2.5 cm) and are about 1⁄16 inch (2 mm) thick. Presumably they give floating-heart an alternative method of reproducing and spreading.

Big floating-heart (*Nymphoides aquatica* [J. F. Gmel.] Kuntze) is the species of floating-heart most likely to be encountered on the coastal plain from New Jersey south to Texas and is sometimes found in slightly brackish waters as well as tidal fresh waters. It is a larger, coarser plant, with stems up to 3⁄16 inch (5 mm) thick and leaves that may be 1½–8 inches (4–20 cm) long. The veins on the undersurface of the leaves are very prominent, unlike those of little floating-heart, and the upper surface of the leaves is completely green without purple mottling. The petioles and undersides of the leaves and sepals are bumpy with purple glands.

The flowers of big floating-heart develop as much as 3 inches (7.5 cm) below the leaf blade and may be over ¾ inch (2 cm) across. This species seldom produces the spurlike roots seen in little floating-heart.

A third species of floating-heart appears to be spreading in this book's range. Yellow floating-heart (*Nymphoides peltata* [Gmel.] Kuntze) is a native of Europe that has naturalized in this area. It has opposite leaves that are as much as 6 inches (15 cm) long and 6 inches (15 cm) wide and are usually unequal in size and bright yellow flowers with fringed edges. Hopefully this plant will not become yet another infamous species on the ever-growing list of invasive introduced plants that are diminishing native biodiversity.

Many authorities have included the genus *Nymphoides* in the gentian family, Gentianaceae, but recent research seems to warrant its placement in the buckbean family.

Butterfly-weed, Pleurisy-root

Asclepias tuberosa L.
Milkweed Family, Asclepiadaceae

RANGE: Southern New Hampshire south to Florida and west to Minnesota, South Dakota, Arizona, and Mexico.
HABITAT: Woodland edges and dry open meadows and roadsides, especially in sandy soils.

The bright orange flowers of butterfly-weed light up prairies, fields, and roadsides from May (in the South) to August (in the North).

Butterfly-weed, *Asclepias tuberosa*

Woe betide unwary people who try to pick them in southern areas, however, for they will likely find that the habitat where butterfly-weed thrives is also home to those obnoxious mites, chiggers—hence another common name for this plant, chigger-weed.

Butterfly-weed is the only milkweed with mostly alternate leaves and a nonmilky sap. A perennial that grows from a stout rhizome, it may bear a single stalk or be highly branched. Butterfly-weed is much leafier than other milkweeds; the leaves on the main stalks are alternate, but those on the branches are sometimes opposite one another. The whole plant is covered with rough hairs and tends to be erect or grow at an angle; it is usually 1–2½ feet (30–75 cm) in height.

The narrow lance-shaped leaves are a deep lustrous green, attached directly (or with a very short petiole) to the stalk, and often curly along the margins. The flowers range in color from yellow to orange-red and are pollinated by insects, especially butterflies, bees, wasps, and their relatives. The seeds develop in long narrow pods. As in other milkweeds, each seed is attached to a tuft of silky hairs that serves the purpose of catching the wind in order to disperse the seed.

The genus *Asclepias* is named in honor of the Roman god of medicine and healing, Aesculapius. Among many other uses, Native Americans have used butterfly-weed to treat respiratory ailments, which is why it is also known as pleurisy-root. Many milkweeds contain cardiac glycosides, toxic compounds that affect the heart muscles (digitalis, extracted from common foxglove [*Digitalis purpurea* L.], is one of the better-known cardiac glycosides). Butterflies that feed on milkweed, such as the monarch, may contain such high concentrations of poisonous chemicals in their tissues that birds become sick after eating them and eventually learn to avoid eating the parts of the butterfly that are least palatable.

Because it attracts butterflies, butterfly-weed is popular with gardeners. It can be cultivated in ordinary garden soil in full sun to light shade and grows best in dry soils.

A number of species of milkweed grow in coastal areas in this book's range. Swamp milkweed (*Asclepias incarnata* L.) has rose-pink flowers and can sometimes be found on the upper edges of New England salt marshes, where there is some freshwater inflow; south of New England, it is less common and found more frequently away from the coast. Few-flowered milkweed (*Asclepias lanceolata* Walt.) grows in swamps and brackish marshes from New Jersey south to Florida and west to Texas; it has orange-red to purplish-red flowers and very narrow leaves.

Other coastal plain species of milkweed, most of them southern, include blunt-leaved milkweed (*Asclepias amplexicaulis* Sm.), purple milkweed (*Asclepias humistrata* Walt.), long-leaf milkweed (*Asclepias longifolia* Michx.), pedicillate milkweed (*Asclepias pedicellata* Walt.), smoothseed milkweed (*Asclepias perennis* Walt.), and red milkweed (*Asclepias rubra* L.).

Beach or Fiddle-leaf Morning-glory

Ipomoea imperati (Vahl) Griseb.
Morning-glory Family, Convolvulaceae

RANGE: North Carolina south to Florida and west along the Gulf coast to Texas.
HABITAT: Sandy coastal beaches and dunes.

Beach morning-glory is a leafy, trailing, vigorous, perennial vine that roots at the nodes. It has numerous rich dark green, fleshy, three- to seven-lobed leaves. The upper lobe is ordinarily much larger than the lower ones, giving the leaf a shape resembling that of a fiddle and providing the source of one of its common names, fiddle-leaf morning-glory. The tip of the leaf is often notched.

The flowers are snowy-white with a yellow center and bloom

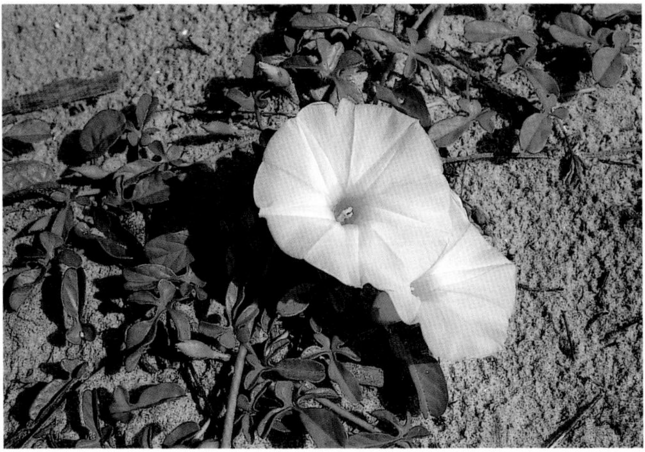

Beach morning-glory, *Ipomoea imperati*

from June to October. They are trumpet-shaped, up to 2 inches (5 cm) long, and as wide as they are long. Both the pistil and the stamens are confined within the tube of the flower.

The showy flowers of the morning-glories are pollinated by insects and hummingbirds. Usually the flowers are open only for a few hours one day and then wilt. If not animal-pollinated, the wilted flowers sometimes self-pollinate.

Field guides variously describe this species (listed as *Ipomoea stolonifera* [Cirillo] J. F. Gmel. by some authors) as infrequent or common. This suggests that the frequency or absence of this species might be related to an environmental factor, such as salt in the sand where it grows. The vigorous growth and large number of plants observed on narrow beaches on the ocean side of the Sea Islands off the coast of Georgia and on dunes close to the ocean suggest that beach morning-glory may require a higher level of salt (sodium) than many of the other plants that grow in these areas.

The edible sweet potato (*Ipomoea batatas* [L.] Lam.) is a member of the morning-glory family and is eaten by people around the world. Morning-glory seeds are consumed by some birds and small mammals but are not considered a very important food source for wildlife.

Many other members of the morning-glory family may be found in coastal plain habitats in this book's range.

Railroad-vine, *Ipomoea pes-caprae*

Railroad-vine, Goat-foot Morning-glory

Ipomoea pes-caprae (L.) R. Br.
Morning-glory Family, Convolvulaceae

RANGE: Coastal Georgia south to Florida and west to Texas; more common in the West Indies and Tropics.
HABITAT: Sand beaches and dunes associated with sea oats (*Uniola paniculata*).

Railroad-vine is well named. It is a sprawling perennial vine that spreads by thick, smooth, angular stems that may be over 100 feet (30 m) long. The vines cling to the ground, rooting at the nodes and growing in almost straight lines like railroad tracks, regardless of the contours of the land over which they travel.

The leaves are alternate, smooth, bright green, and fleshy. They vary in size and may be oval, round, or kidney-shaped. Each leaf is folded along the midrib, is notched at the tip, and ranges in length and diameter from 1³⁄₁₆ to 4 inches (3–10 cm).

The flowers have the tubular shape of most morning-glories. They are 2–3 inches (5–7.5 cm) wide at the open end and 2–2¾ inches (5–7 cm) long. The color of the flowers is an exceptionally brilliant shade of rose-pink with a rich purple throat. Several flowers are usually produced on stalks in the axils of the leaves and bloom one at a time, each flower lasting only a day. They are at their best about an hour after sunrise and fade by 10:00 A.M. At its northern limit in the southern states, railroad-vine blooms from May to September. In the Tropics, it blooms year-round.

Railroad-vine is more common and vigorous in tropical areas like Borneo and Singapore, as well as in the American Tropics. It has an exceptionally strong root system and is extremely valuable on tropical beaches because it stabilizes the sand and prevents erosion.

The name *pes-caprae*, which means "goat foot," was given to this particular species of *Ipomoea* because the shape of the leaves resembles goat feet. This is reflected in the common name goatfoot morning-glory used for this plant in the Tropics. The generic name *Ipomoea* comes from the Greek word meaning "resembling a worm," no doubt referring to the twining habit of these plants.

Some people use the synonym *Ipomoea brasiliensis* (L.) Sweet for this species.

American Germander, Wood Sage

Teucrium canadense L. var. *canadense*
Mint Family, Lamiaceae

RANGE: Maine south to Florida and Cuba and west to Texas.
HABITAT: Freshwater and brackish marshes and moist uplands.

American germander is a perennial that may grow 1–5 feet (0.3–1.5 m) tall, has a square stem like most members of the mint family, and may or may not have a few branches toward the top of the stalk. It has long slender stolons and tends to grow in colonies rather than as single plants. The leaves are opposite, usually 2–4¾ inches (5–12 cm) long, firm in texture, and only slightly aromatic when crushed, unlike many mint family members. They vary in shape from oblong to long and slender but tend to be narrow in proportion to length and taper to an acute tip. The upper surface of the leaves is rough and furrowed. The lower surface, calyx, and stems are covered with a thick layer of curled and twisted hairs.

The flowers are an irregular tubular shape, about ⅝ inch (16 mm) long, and pinkish-lavender in color. The tube of the flower is split across the center to the calyx on either side, forming an upper lip that juts so far forward that it does not resemble a lip. The lower lip is a single lobe.

The flowers are borne at the upper ends of the stems in dense

American germander, *Teucrium canadense*

spikes composed of two to five flowers crowded together at each node, although some plants have only one flower at each node. They bloom from June to August.

Teucrium canadense is a widely variable species that is divided into several varieties; the variety described here is the one that grows along the Atlantic coast. It is much more hairy than any of the varieties that grow inland.

American germander requires sun and is often found growing in freshwater or brackish areas around common reed (*Phragmites australis*), another plant that can tolerate low levels of salt but not the high concentration of pure sea water.

Teucrium is often confused with hedge-nettle (*Stachys palustris* L.), but the two genera can be distinguished by the lower lip of the flowers: the lip of *Stachys* has two lobes, whereas *Teucrium* has a single lobe.

A more aromatic European species of germander, cut-leaved germander (*Teucrium botrys* L.), has escaped from cultivation and become naturalized in some abundance in parts of New England and the Midwest. It is easily distinguished from the native species because the native species has entire leaves, whereas the leaves of the European species are dissected into several linear segments.

In earlier times, both the native and the introduced species of germander were used to make an herbal tonic, and before hops (*Humulus lupulus* L.) came into common use, germander was used to flavor ale.

Seaside Gerardia

Agalinis maritima (Raf.) Raf.
Figwort Family, Scrophulariaceae

RANGE: Nova Scotia south to Florida and the West Indies and west to Texas and Mexico.
HABITAT: Salt and brackish marshes and dune swales.

The gerardias are members of the same family of plants as the snapdragons. They are especially interesting because most of them are partial parasites that obtain some of their food (fats, carbohydrates, and proteins) through special structures called haustoria that are attached to the roots of other kinds of plants. Many members of this family are used as ornamental plants, including foxgloves (*Digitalis* spp.), slipper-flowers (*Calceolaria* spp.), beardtongues (*Penstemon* spp.), and snapdragons (*Antirrhinum* spp.).

Three annual species of gerardia add color to the grassy expanse of tidal salt marshes: seaside gerardia, purple gerardia (*Agalinis purpurea* [L.] Pennell), and fascicled gerardia (*Agalinis fasciculata* [Ell.] Raf.). Seaside gerardia grows best in marshes that are inundated regularly by tidal water and in sites where a well-defined layer of organic matter has developed. Purple gerardia and fascicled gerardia are essentially inland plants, although they may invade the upper borders of tidal brackish marshes, particularly where the substrate is sandy rather than organic. They are encountered more frequently than seaside gerardia, which is uncommon throughout its range.

Seaside gerardia ranges in height from 4 to 16 inches (10–40 cm), with the tallest plants found in the southern part of its range. The plants, which are succulent and have smooth, slender, fleshy leaves, are sparingly branched. The leaves are usually opposite but may be alternate at the ends of the branches.

Seaside gerardia, *Agalinis maritima*

The flowers vary in color from rosy-lavender to bright pink. They are tubular and have five lobes that tend to roll back slightly. When the lobes of the corolla are fully expanded, the flowers are ⅜–¾ inch (1–2 cm) in length and ½ inch (1.2 cm) across. In spite of their small size, the flowers are jewel-like in both color and texture. The two upper lobes are covered and edged with long silky hairs. The throat is striped with white and yellow, and spots of bright pink scattered across the stripes contrast with the bright yellow of the stamens. The calyx is fleshy with blunt lobes, and the spaces between the lobes are rectangular, a distinctive feature of this species that can be seen even when the flowers are wilted.

The flowers are seldom seen in full bloom. They bloom from May to August (depending on the location) and open fully only on sunny days from mid-morning until noon. By 2:00 P.M., sunny or cloudy, the flowers begin to fade and very soon drop from the plants.

Pollination is apparently accomplished by small wasplike insects when the flowers reach the appropriate stage, even on overcast or foggy days when the lobes never expand and the wasps must force themselves into the tubular part and then out again. The crop of seeds produced in the globe-shaped capsules is usually abundant.

Purple gerardia is not fleshy and is much larger and showier, sometimes reaching a height of 4 feet (1.2 m). The leaves are thin, and the flowers are much brighter, rose-purple in color, and more than twice as large, ranging from ¾ inch to 1½ inches (2–4 cm) in length. The flowers also have yellow and white stripes in the throat, but the lobes of the calyx are pointed and the spaces between the lobes are V-shaped or U-shaped. Purple gerardia grows on the margins of ponds, in interdune swales, and in damp woodlands and meadows from Nova Scotia south to Florida and the West Indies and west to Minnesota, South Dakota, Texas, and Mexico. A similar but smaller species, small-flowered gerardia (*Agalinis paupercula* [Gray] Britt.), grows from New Brunswick south to Long Island and inland to Iowa; some authorities include this species within *Agalinis purpurea*.

Fascicled gerardia may be found in similar habitats from southern Maryland south to Florida and west to Texas. It may grow as tall as 3⅓ feet (1 m) and, unlike seaside gerardia and purple gerardia, has stems and leaves that are rough to touch. Clusters of small leaves may grow from the axils of the longer leaves. The calyx lobes and sinuses are similar to those of purple gerardia. Several other species of *Agalinis* may also be found in coastal plain habitats in this book's range.

Atlantic Mudwort

Limosella australis R. Br.
Figwort Family, Scrophulariaceae

RANGE: Along the Atlantic coast from Newfoundland and Quebec south to North Carolina (where it is very rare); also in South America.
HABITAT: Mudflats and muddy or sandy ponds and streams in areas between low and high tide levels in waters more brackish than salty.

Atlantic mudwort is a small member of the figwort family, a large family that includes snapdragons (*Antirrhinum* spp.), mulleins (*Verbascum* spp.), and turtleheads (*Chelone* spp.). Mudwort grows in mud in brackish ponds and estuaries along the coast. Linnaeus, the botanist who named this plant, gave it the diminutive *limus*, the Latin name for mud, saying that it "had been called from its native mud."

Mudwort is an annual with creeping stems that root at the nodes

Atlantic mudwort, *Limosella australis*

and form sodlike mats in mud or wet sand. Its fleshy, cylindrical leaves grow from these nodes in tufts of 5–10 leaves. The leaves have blunt tips and no petioles, are usually ¾–2 inches (2–5 cm) long, and are uniform in width from the base to the upper end.

The flowers grow singly on separate stalks that are shorter than the leaves. They are usually white but may be tinged with pink and bloom from June to October. They are only about ⅛ inch (3 mm) long and are bell-shaped, with five rounded lobes emerging from a bell-shaped green calyx that also has five lobes. The seed capsule is globular and contains a large number of seeds.

This plant is described as rare, but it is so small and inconspicuous that it may be overlooked in many places where it grows.

Some authorities list this species as *Limosella subulata* Ives. Another species, northern mudwort (*Limosella aquatica* L.), is found locally in Newfoundland and southeast Labrador, across Canada to the West Coast, and south to Minnesota, New Mexico, Arizona, and California. This species, which grows in freshwater and brackish sands, is also found throughout Europe.

Purple bladderwort,
Utricularia purpurea

Purple Bladderwort

Utricularia purpurea Walt.
Bladderwort Family, Lentibulariaceae

RANGE: Coastal Nova Scotia, New Brunswick, Quebec, and New England south to Florida and west to Louisiana; also inland and in the West Indies.
HABITAT: Quiet freshwater ponds and sluggish streams.

Carnivorous plants grow in water or in wet soils that are so acidic that certain elements essential for plant growth are not available. Over the centuries, some plants have developed processes for obtaining these essential nutrients from animals living in the same environment. Familiar carnivorous plants include pitcher-plants (*Sarracenia* spp.), sundews (*Drosera* spp.), Venus fly-trap (*Dionaea muscipula* Ellis), and a number of bladderworts. Purple bladderwort is one of the most familiar carnivorous bladderworts.

Purple bladderwort is a free-floating, immersed aquatic plant that has slender stems up to 3 1⁄3 feet (1 m) long with whorls of leaves or leaflike structures (authorities differ as to whether they are leaf or stem tissue) arranged at intervals. The ends of some of the leaves bear very small (1⁄32 inch [1 mm]) traps that catch the insects and other small aquatic invertebrates that supply the required nutrients.

The traps are somewhat globular with a round door at one end; empty, they have slightly negative water pressure inside. Stalked glands on the outside surface of the door attract the prey—mostly tiny crustaceans, small aquatic insects, and various larvae; a set of bristles around the door serves as the trigger mechanism that opens and closes it. When an animal brushes against the trigger, the animal and water are sucked inside, the door closes, and the water pressure becomes the same inside as it is outside.

On the inside, enzymes from glandular hairs in the bladder digest the trapped animal. After the desired nutrients are extracted, the door opens, the remains are washed out, and the trap is ready for the next victim.

In a normal year, a stand of purple bladderwort usually has only a few plants that flower. Every six or seven years, however, conditions for flowering may become especially favorable, and every body of water will be covered with a solid sheet of the highly visible pink-purple flowers. The flowers are on stalks (scapes) 1 3⁄16–6 inches (3–15 cm) long and are pale pinkish-lavender, lipped with two lobes on the upper lip and three on the lower lip. The lower lip has a yellow spot at the base. The flowering may continue for at least a month from May to September, depending on the location.

Bladderwort propagates from seed or from vegetative winter buds that develop in September, fall to the bottom of the pond, and remain there until they germinate in the spring of the following year.

Floating Bladderwort

Utricularia radiata Small
Bladderwort Family, Lentibulariaceae

RANGE: Maine south to Florida and west to Texas.
HABITAT: Freshwater pools and ponds in the coastal plain (rarely inland).

Many species of yellow-flowered bladderworts may be found in this book's range. Floating bladderwort (listed by some authorities as

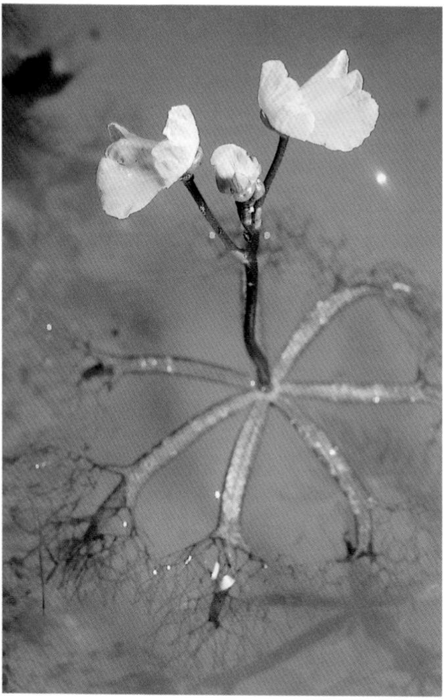

Floating bladderwort, *Utricularia radiata*

Utricularia inflata Walt. var. *minor* Chapman) and its close relative inflated bladderwort (*Utricularia inflata* Walt.) have inflated stems at the base of the flowering stalk. These stems form a whorl that holds the flower stalks above the surface of the water. Below the water's surface are other leaves and stems, finely dissected, that contain the bladders that trap tiny aquatic organisms.

Floating bladderwort has four to seven inflated stems or floats. The flowering stalk (scape) that rises above each whorl of floats may have one to five flowers (occasionally as many as seven), and each flower stalk has a tiny bract, sometimes lobed and at least as wide as it is long, at its base. The floats are ⅜–1½ inches (1–4 cm) long.

Inflated bladderwort grows from Delaware south to Florida and west to Texas and was recently discovered at sites in southern New York and southeastern Massachusetts. It is a larger plant overall, with 3–8 (usually 5) floats and as many as 6–14 (sometimes up to 17) flowers on a single scape. The floats are 1³⁄₁₆–3⅛ inches (3–8 cm) long. The bract at the base of each flower's stem is longer than it is wide and is never lobed.

Other yellow-flowered bladderworts in this book's range lack the whorled floats and are identified by technical characteristics such as the shape of the flower parts, the winter buds, the leaf divisions, and the seed shapes. Whereas some species, like those described here, are free-floating, other bladderworts may be rooted in wet sands or peat.

The generic name *Utricularia* comes from the Latin word *utriculus*, meaning "little bladder."

Seaside Plantain

Plantago maritima L. var. *juncoides* (Lam.) Gray
Plantain Family, Plantaginaceae

RANGE: Circumboreal, as far south on the Atlantic coast as New Jersey.
HABITAT: Coastal rocky shores, salt marshes, and beaches.

Plantago maritima is a complex of several variable forms that grow in the Northern Hemisphere along the Atlantic and Pacific coasts of North America, on the southern tip of South America, and along the northern coast of the Mediterranean Sea. The variety described here is the one most likely to be encountered in this book's range.

Seaside plantain may grow as scattered clumps or as small plants growing together so closely that they resemble a stand of fleshy grass. It is a deeply rooted perennial with one to many crowns and numerous slender, brittle, fleshy leaves. The leaves arise directly from the crown and are usually erect, although on some exposed sites on rocks, they may be spreading.

Under favorable growing conditions, the leaves are ¼–½ inch (7–12 mm) wide and up to 6 inches (15 cm) long (or even longer in the northern parts of the plant's range), tapering to a slender tip. The veins are inconspicuous, and the surface is a dull, pale gray-green, with a suggestion of a waxy bloom.

The flower stalks (scapes) also arise from the crown and may extend several inches above the leaves. The nondescript flowers grow in crowded spikes on the upper portion of the stalk. The flowers are not showy and contain only the parts essential for seed production. Most conspicuous are the fleshy sepals that surround the seeds and

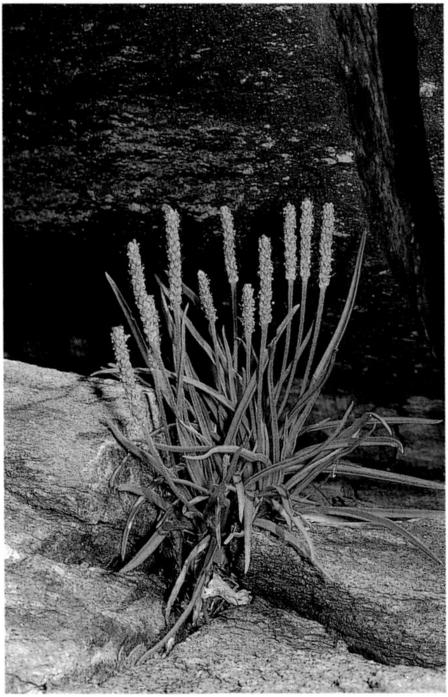

Seaside plantain,
Plantago maritima

the bright yellow anthers on long filaments. Rings of flowers reach the blooming stage in succession from the base to the top of the spike. The flowers may bloom from early June to September, and it is not unusual to find young flower stalks and seeds on the same plant throughout the summer. The plant is primarily wind-pollinated, but insects have been observed gathering pollen from plantains, so it is possible that they, too, play a role in pollination.

Seaside plantain is adapted to a wide range of conditions. It can be found growing in crevices of rocks washed by salt spray, in association with the delicate scarlet pimpernel (*Anagallis arvensis*), or in tidal salt marshes. It is sometimes the last remnant of salt-marsh vegetation when a dune is encroaching on a marsh. In salt marshes, seaside plantain usually grows at the higher levels of the marsh mixed with salt hay grass (*Spartina patens*) and sea lavender (*Limonium carolinianum*) rather than in the lower areas occupied by smooth cordgrass (*Spartina alterniflora*). It is tolerant of a wide range of substrates, from sandy to those with clay or a high percentage of organic matter, but it seems to be more abundant under waterlogged conditions than in well-aerated sites. It is often found bordering salt pannes or shallow depressions.

Older people in Rhode Island remember collecting seaside plantain—which they called goose-tongue—to cook as a vegetable, but in southern New England, it is now too scarce to gather. In Wales, seaside plantain has been cultivated as fodder for sheep.

Buttonbush

Cephalanthus occidentalis L.
Madder Family, Rubiaceae

RANGE: Nova Scotia, New Brunswick, Quebec, and New England south to Florida and west to Minnesota, Texas, Arizona, and California; also in Mexico and the West Indies.
HABITAT: Freshwater marshes, swamps, and edges of streams, lakes, and ponds.

This common wetland shrub is striking when in bloom, loaded with round, creamy-white flower heads and attracting many different kinds of bees, wasps, and butterflies seeking its nectar.

The spherical flower head of buttonbush is ¾–1½ inches (2–4 cm) across and is made up of densely packed tubular flowers. The individual flowers are about 5⁄16 inch (8 mm) long, end in four petals, and have a long style protruding from the opening of the tube. The stigma at the end of each style is often bright yellow from the pollen deposited by visiting insects.

The dark, glossy green leaves are entire, 3–6 inches (7.5–15 cm) long, and opposite one another or in whorls of three or four. Each leaf is rounded at the base (or sometimes wedge-shaped) and comes to a sharp point at the tip; the major veins are quite prominent. The leaves may be smooth, or in the more southern form, the twigs and lower surfaces of the leaves may bear fine hairs.

The whole plant usually grows as a shrub that may reach 10 feet (3 m) in height, although 6 feet (1.8 m) is more common in this book's range (in the southernmost portion of its range, it may take the form of a tree as tall as 40 feet [12 m]). It blooms from June to August, depending on the location, and produces fruit in the late summer and early fall. In the early spring, it can appear dead since it tends to leaf out later than most native shrubs. Thanks to the pres-

Buttonbush, *Cephalanthus occidentalis*

ence of lenticels on its bark, which aid in oxygen exchange, it is more tolerant of high water levels than are most shrubs.

Buttonbush plants may grow in wet areas around freshwater ponds, or they may grow in standing water, forming solid stands as large as several acres. Apparently, the stems are short-lived because colonies of buttonbush usually have a large proportion of dead stems.

The madder family, to which buttonbush belongs, is one of great economic importance throughout the world. Beautiful ornamental plants, such as those in the genera *Gardenia* and *Ixora*, are in this family, as is coffee (*Coffea arabica* L.) and several important dye plants, such as madder (*Galium* spp.). Important pharmaceutical plants, such as the plants that produce ipecac and quinine (at one time an important medicine in treating malaria), belong to the Rubiaceae. Buttonbush itself has been used by Native Americans in a manner similar to the use of quinine.

Buttonbush plants are browsed by deer, muskrat, and beaver, and the seeds are eaten by a variety of ducks and marshbirds. Buttonbush is also used as a nesting and roosting site by many birds, providing excellent cover for wood ducks, and is a primary food for the caterpillars of several butterflies and moths.

The generic name *Cephalanthus* comes from the Greek words *cephale*, meaning "head," and *anthos*, meaning "flower." The name *occidentalis* alludes to the fact that this plant is from the Western Hemisphere. The common name buttonbush refers to the round, brown fruit heads resembling buttons that form in late summer and often remain on the shrub through the winter. Other descriptive common names for this species include honey-ball, pin-ball, little snowball, and globe-flower.

Coral Honeysuckle, Trumpet Honeysuckle

Lonicera sempervirens L.
Honeysuckle Family, Caprifoliaceae

RANGE: Connecticut south to Florida and west to Iowa, Oklahoma, and Texas; escaped from cultivation in other areas, especially north of Connecticut.
HABITAT: Edges of woodlands and thickets and along fencerows; thrives in full sun and good soil.

Coral honeysuckle has been a popular ornamental vine since the United States was settled by the Europeans. Brides often brought a plant from home to their new house when they married, so that now this vine can be found even in seemingly wilderness areas where no home remains, a reminder of new beginnings and the ceaseless march of time.

Coral honeysuckle is a woody vine that climbs to about 16 feet (5 m). The stems are smooth, and the leaves are partially evergreen, depending on the climate. The opposite leaves vary in shape from elliptical to oval, are broader at the lower end, and tend to be green above and whitened beneath. At the flowering tips of the stems, the last two pairs of leaves are usually joined to make a single oval leaf 1³⁄16–2¾ inches (3–7 cm) long and slightly less than 1¾ inches (4.5 cm) wide.

The flowers develop in whorls at the tips of the branches. The narrow, trumpet-shaped blossoms are 1³⁄16–3 inches (3–7.5 cm) long, a brilliant scarlet or sometimes bright yellow on the outside, and often yellow on the inside. The flowers have five lobes that are much shorter than the tube of the trumpet, and the stamens and style do not extend beyond the mouth of the trumpet. The flowers bloom from March (in southern areas) to autumn, making this plant particularly desirable as an ornamental. The fruit is a red berry about ¼ inch (7 mm) across.

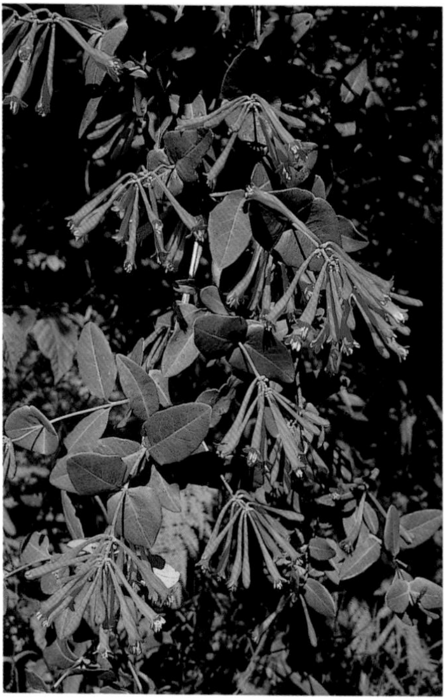

Coral honeysuckle,
Lonicera sempervirens

Coral honeysuckle is pollinated by insects and hummingbirds and has been ranked as one of the most important hummingbird plants in the eastern United States, along with other native North American species such as wild columbine (*Aquilegia canadensis* L.), jewelweed (*Impatiens capensis* Meerb.), red buckeye (*Aesculus pavia*), cardinal flower (*Lobelia cardinalis* L.), and trumpet creeper (*Campsis radicans* [L.] Seem. *ex* Bureau). Unlike insects, hummingbirds have color vision and are especially attracted to yellow, red, and orange flowers.

Several introduced species of honeysuckle have become increasingly common in this book's range. These honeysuckles were brought to North America as ornamental plants and have been used widely during the past century for landscaping, controlling erosion, and attracting wildlife. They adapted well to the climate and soils and became naturalized, spreading beyond the original planting sites. The indiscriminate introduction of such species has come to be seen as a serious environmental error, affecting biodiversity and the functioning of ecosystems as well as human activities such as agriculture, commercial fishing, and recreation.

The best-known invasive honeysuckle is Japanese honeysuckle (*Lonicera japonica* Thunb.), introduced from eastern Asia in the early 1800s as a prized ornamental vine. For most people, this plant needs little description. Its fragrant white to yellow flowers and black fruit are familiar throughout the South, and it appears to be spreading rapidly in the Northeast as well. It is now considered one of the most invasive species in the United States, able to grow from mountain forests to coastal thickets. A fast grower, it climbs over native species and can literally crush plants with the weight of its vines.

Morrow honeysuckle (*Lonicera morrowii* Gray) is another invasive Asian honeysuckle that has spread across southern Canada and the northern United States and seems to be extending southward. It is a shrub with soft hairy leaves, cream-colored flowers that fade to yellow, and dark red fruit. This shrub has been observed taking over habitats from the edges of rich upland woods and farm fields to the margins of salt marshes.

Tartarian honeysuckle (*Lonicera tatarica* L.) is another Eurasian bush honeysuckle that sometimes spreads from cultivation in this book's range and is a dominant shrub on some barrier beaches in the northeastern United States. Its leaves are usually smooth, and it has white to pink flowers. The fruit is red or occasionally yellow. Morrow honeysuckle and tartarian honeysuckle hybridize to produce bella honeysuckle (*Lonicera* × *bella* Zabel), which has been reported as far south as North Carolina. It has pink flowers that fade to yellow.

Arrowwood

Viburnum dentatum L.
Honeysuckle Family, Caprifoliaceae

RANGE: New Brunswick south to Florida and west to Ontario, Michigan, Ohio, and Texas; escaped from cultivation in other areas.
HABITAT: Sunny open areas, thickets, borders of woodlands, and swamps in moist to dry soils.

Arrowwood is a deciduous shrub with simple, opposite, toothed leaves and flat-topped clusters of white flowers that bloom from

Arrowwood, *Viburnum dentatum* var. *venosum*

early spring to summer, depending on the location. Each inflorescence is a cyme, with five to seven branches and flowers packed so closely together that the clusters usually appear to be nearly circular. The individual flowers are five-lobed and have five protruding stamens and a single short pistil. They are pollinated by insects and hummingbirds. The fruits that develop after pollination turn a deep blue-black. The bitter fruit is eaten by a variety of birds and mammals.

Viburnum dentatum is a variable species that has been treated in many different ways by taxonomists. One alternate name for northern arrowwood, *Viburnum recognitum* Fern., reflects the confusion, since *recognitum* means "restudied." According to the system used here, three varieties of *Viburnum dentatum* are in this book's range.

Common arrowwood (*Viburnum dentatum* L. var. *dentatum*) grows along the coastal plain from New Jersey south to Florida and west to Texas in moist to dry sandy thickets and the edges of woods. It is a shrub that rarely grows over 10 feet (3 m) tall, although it sometimes reaches up to 16½ feet (5 m) in height. The coarsely toothed leaves are up to 4¾ inches (12 cm) long and 4 inches wide (10 cm), are ovate to lance-shaped, and tend to be thin in texture, with hairs on the petioles and sometimes on the undersurface. Occasionally the fruits are pubescent.

Northern arrowwood (*Viburnum dentatum* L. var. *lucidum* Ait., or *Viburnum recognitum* Fern., according to some authorities) grows in swamps, moist woods, and damp thickets from New Brunswick south to North Carolina (and in the mountains to Georgia) and west to Ohio. It usually grows about 5 feet (1.5 m) tall but may reach up to 10–12 feet (3–3.7 m), with multiple stems that are usually no more than 2 inches (5 cm) thick and numerous lateral branches that grow upward. Unlike southern arrowwood, it tends to form thickets rather than grow as isolated bushes.

The dull leaves are usually round to oblong-ovate and are about 2½ inches (6.5 cm) long and broad in proportion to the length, with prominent veins on the underside. The base is rounded or heart-shaped, and the smooth petioles are about 1³⁄₁₆ inches (3 cm) long. The edges of the leaves have coarse, acutely pointed teeth. The upper and lower surfaces of the leaves may be smooth, or there may be hairs in the axils of the veins on the underside of the leaves.

Southern arrowwood (*Viburnum dentatum* L. var. *venosum* [Britt.] Gleason) grows from southeastern Massachusetts and Rhode Island south to New Jersey in moist to dry sandy soils in sunny areas or borders of thickets within sight of or adjacent to salt water. It is a shrub 3⅓–8 feet (1–2.4 m) tall (although in some situations, it may be much taller), usually rounded in shape with leafy branches all the way to the ground and smooth gray bark. Young branches may be either densely or slightly pubescent. The shiny leaves are large, 1–5 inches (2.5–13 cm) long and 2–5 inches (5–13 cm) wide, and are orbicular to round, ovate-oblong, or almost heart-shaped at the base. The edges have coarse teeth, with as many as 22 teeth on each side and one at the tip. In exposed areas, the blades of the leaves are thick, firm, and corrugated and have prominent veins on the underside. In more protected sites, they are thinner and more delicate and may be sparsely pubescent on the upper surface and smooth on the undersurface. The petioles are ¼–¾ inch (7–20 mm) long and are covered with branching hairs.

In the 1970s in Rhode Island and southeastern Massachusetts, most of the land adjacent to the ocean was cultivated, and southern arrowwood was limited to a few undisturbed areas near the ocean, such as on Block Island and Conanicut Island. By contrast, northern arrowwood was essentially a weed, moving in quickly to form thickets in inland open spaces. Today, with almost no agriculture near the ocean, southern arrowwood is growing vigorously on abandoned farmland near the ocean.

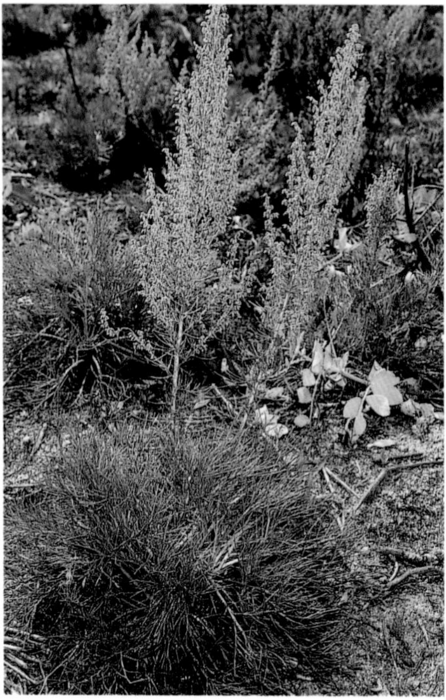

Tall wormwood,
Artemisia campestris

Tall Wormwood

Artemisia campestris L. ssp. *caudata* (Michx.) Hall & Clements
Aster Family, Asteraceae

RANGE: Southern Maine south to Florida and west to Texas and Arizona.
HABITAT: Coastal dunes and other areas with loose sand, including thin sandy soils in rocky or sandy woodlands.

Tall wormwood is one of the few native artemisias that grow on the East Coast. Most of the others, such as dusty miller (*Artemisia stelleriana*), are species that have been introduced from Asia or Europe and have become naturalized.

Tall wormwood is primarily a biennial but is occasionally a short-lived perennial. It has a taproot but lacks rhizomes and reproduces only from seed. In the first year of growth, the biennial plants are composed of dense rosettes of intricately cut lacy leaves. They are dark green and have long petioles. Each leaf has two or three ranks of finely cut flat, linear segments that resemble those of cosmos (*Cosmos* spp.), a cultivated garden flower that is also a member of the aster family. The rosettes of the first-year plants are 7–12 inches (18–30 cm) in diameter and 7–9 inches (18–23 cm) tall.

During the second year, the shape of the plant changes completely. The low-lying biennial rosettes produce seven or more tall, ascending stems that may vary in height from 12 to 60 inches (30–150 cm), depending on the location, with the tallest plants in the southern portion of its range. The perennial plants produce only one to three flowering stalks.

The lower part of the stem is thickly covered with leaves that resemble the rosette leaves but are much smaller and less intricately cut. Both stem and rosette leaves on the biennial plants are brown and dry by the time the flowers bloom in July to October, depending on the location. On the perennial plants, however, the rosette and stem leaves remain bright green at flowering time.

The upper two-thirds of the stem is covered with dense lateral branches that usually have three or four ranks of lateral branches that are also ascending. The result is a dense inflorescence that tapers at both ends. All of the branches are covered with masses of tiny oval green flowers that resemble nodding green beads. The flower heads are covered with flat green scales and have a fringe of cream-colored, pistillate, fertile ray flowers around the edge; the inner disk flowers are sterile.

The flowers are succeeded by small brown seeds that hang from tiny parachutes of cream-colored hairs and float away on the wind to new locations.

Tall wormwood is another beach plant that should be granted legal protection to save it from extinction. The sandy beaches where it grows best are the kinds of beaches people use most frequently, so the plant is becoming increasingly uncommon.

The common name wormwood is given to several species of *Artemisia* and refers to their use in traditional medicine to expel internal parasites. *Artemisia* has been used for numerous other medicinal purposes by the Chinese, Europeans, and Native Americans.

Some authorities have called this plant *Artemisia caudata* Michx., but the system used here lists it as a variety of *Artemisia campestris*, a complex group of plants.

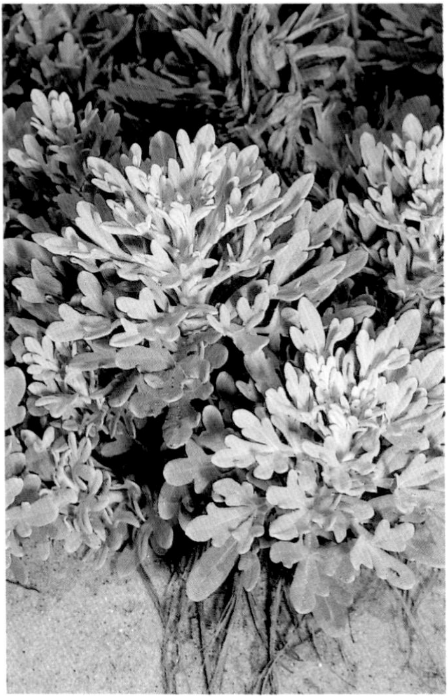

Dusty miller,
Artemisia stelleriana

Dusty Miller, Beach Wormwood

Artemisia stelleriana Bess.
Aster Family, Asteraceae

RANGE: Northeastern Asia and Alaska; introduced and naturalized from Nova Scotia and Quebec south to Virginia and occasionally west to the shores of the Great Lakes and Washington.
HABITAT: Dunes, beaches, and sandy soils.

Dusty miller is native to northeastern Asia and has also been found in Alaska. It was introduced as an ornamental from Japan around 1880 and has since escaped and become naturalized, especially on beaches and sandy soils near the ocean.

Dusty miller is a perennial that, unlike some other members of the aster family such as goldenrod and daisies, has inconspicuous flowers and showy leaves. The leaves are 1–4 inches (2.5–10 cm) long (including the petiole) and are divided into two or three blunt lobes with rounded tips. They are covered with a dense layer of tangled white hairs that give the plants a silvery color. The leaves grow in rosettes around sprawling stems that root as they grow and, at intervals, send up shoots 8–12 inches (20–30 cm) tall. They form mats that eventually may be several yards in diameter but more often are a foot (30 cm) or less across.

The flower stalks emerge from old leafy offshoots and, depending on the size of the plant, vary from 8 to 30 inches (20–75 cm) in height. The flowers are hemispherical and somewhat bell-shaped and are usually ¼ inch (7 mm) long and ⅜ inch (1 cm) wide. A dense tangle of long white hairs covers the outside of the bell, and the only color is the pale yellow of the tiny disk flowers at the end. The flowers grow in clusters of two or three along the flower stalks and are interspersed with small leaves that increase in size toward the bottom. The inconspicuous flowers are pollinated by the wind and bloom from May to September. The hairy bell that contains the seeds remains on the plant into autumn.

Although dusty miller grows better in sandy soils than in garden loam, it was introduced as an ornamental when carpet bedding was in vogue. In this style of gardening, sometimes seen in city parks today, low-growing plants formed elaborate designs and were sheared regularly to maintain the sharp edges of the pattern. The designs were often arabesques and curlicues similar to those in oriental rugs, geometric shapes, or even mottoes. Plants with red, gray, yellow, or variegated foliage were eagerly sought after.

The foliage of dusty miller has an unpleasant pungent odor when bruised. In this respect, it is similar to other species of *Artemisia* that are often grown in herb gardens. These include mugwort (*Artemisia vulgaris* L.), southernwood (*Artemisia abrotanum* L.), wormwood (*Artemisia absinthium* L.), and tarragon (*Artemisia dracunculus* L.). Tarragon is originally from Asia, but the other species are European.

New York aster, *Aster novi-belgii*

New York Aster

Aster novi-belgii L.
Aster Family, Asteraceae

RANGE: Newfoundland south to Georgia, primarily on the coastal plain.
HABITAT: Moist habitats, from borders of salt, brackish, and freshwater marshes to pine barrens and savannas.

The aster family contains more than 20,000 species and is one of the largest families of flowering plants. The genus *Aster* alone has over 250 species, with more than 110 species occurring in North America north of Mexico. Many of these species are difficult to identify, and to further confound matters, asters tend to hybridize with one another.

As a group, asters have daisylike flower heads with fertile pistillate ray flowers and fertile perfect (both male and female) disk flowers. The ray flowers are white, pink, purple, or bluish but never yellow, and the disk flowers may be yellow, red, or purplish. At the base of the flower head is a series of overlapping bracts called phyllaries. Most species of *Aster* are perennial, and they all have simple, alternate leaves. The small size of the flowers makes the pollen and nectar available to a wide variety of insects, which has probably been one of the major reasons for the evolutionary success of this genus and the aster family as a whole.

Asters bloom from midsummer to autumn, unlike the similar fleabanes (*Erigeron* spp.), which tend to bloom from spring to summer (although some of the weedier fleabanes bloom into the fall). Characteristics that distinguish asters include the color and number of the ray flowers, the structure of the phyllaries (involucral bracts), and leaf attributes.

New York aster is one of the most handsome coastal plain asters. It is a perennial that grows 1–4 feet (30–120 cm) tall, with flower heads that are 1–1½ inches (2.5–4 cm) across arranged in a broadly branched panicle. The ray flowers, which number from 20 to 50, are pale to deep lavender (or occasionally white or pink), and the disk flowers are yellow fading to deep wine-red. The lance-shaped leaves are sessile or slightly clasping and smooth except for the rough margins. They may be entire or sharply toothed and are 1½–7 inches (4–18 cm) long and up to 1 inch (2.5 cm) wide. The phyllaries are elongated and tend to arch outward at the tips.

For pure showiness in the fall, few plants can match New England aster (*Aster novae-angliae* L.), which in the northern portion of its range may be found within sight and sound of the ocean. It grows in moist open fields, thickets, and woodland edges from New Brunswick south to Alabama and west to Alberta, Wyoming, North Dakota, and New Mexico. In the southern portion of this book's range, it is strictly a mountain plant.

A perennial, New England aster may reach over 7 feet (2.1 m) in height, with flower heads that are up to 2 inches (5 cm) across. Each flower head has 45–100 ray flowers that vary in color from deep purple to deep rose; the disk flowers are yellow, fading to red. The rough, lance-shaped leaves of New England aster are strongly clasping, and the stem is covered with stiff hairs. The phyllaries are slender and spreading.

Other lavender asters with fairly large flower heads growing in this book's range include eastern silvery aster (*Aster concolor* L.) and purple-stemmed aster (*Aster puniceus* L.). *Aster concolor*, which is also called wand aster, grows in dry sandy habitats from Massachusetts south to Florida and west to Louisiana. It is very rare in the northern portion of its range. It grows 1–3 feet (30–90 cm) tall on a slender stem, with the flower heads growing directly from the central stem and rarely forming side branches. The flower heads are approximately ¾ inch (2 cm) across and have 8–16 violet rays. The elliptical leaves are sessile or slightly clasping, up to 2 inches (5 cm) long, and covered with silky hairs, as are the narrow phyllaries.

Aster puniceus, also known as swamp aster, is a highly variable species that grows in swamps and moist places, including dune swales, from Newfoundland south to Florida and west to Saskatchewan and Nebraska. It can grow to 8 feet (2.4 m) tall and usually has stout reddish-purple stems with bristly hairs. The lanceolate leaves clasp the stem and are usually rough and hairy. The flowers are 1–1½ inches (2.5–4 cm) across, with 30–60 lilac (or sometimes white or pink) rays. The slender phyllaries are spreading. Some authorities consider southern swamp aster (*Aster elliottii* Torr. & Gray) to be a separate species, but the system used here includes it under *Aster puniceus*.

Annual Saltmarsh Aster

Aster subulatus Michx.
Aster Family, Asteraceae

RANGE: New Brunswick and southeastern Maine south to Florida, west to California, and occasionally inland to Michigan and Nebraska; also in tropical America.
HABITAT: Salt, brackish, and freshwater marshes and moist low areas, including coastal thickets, disturbed areas, and lawns.

Annual saltmarsh aster grows from a short taproot and sometimes forms large bushy plants on the edges of coastal marshes. Although the flower heads are smaller than those of the perennial saltmarsh aster (*Aster tenuifolius*), only ¼–½ inch (7–12 mm) across, the entire plant may grow as tall as 3½ feet (1.1 m) (occasionally to 6 feet [1.8 m]) and may be profusely branched.

The alternate, sessile leaves are smooth, somewhat fleshy, and up to 8 inches (20 cm) long and ⅜ inch (1 cm) wide. They are linear or very narrowly lanceolate in shape, broadest at the upper and central sections of the leaf, narrow at the base, and pointed at the tip.

The flowers bloom from July to November, depending on the location. The flower heads may have no visible rays or as many as 20 very short rays up to ⅛ inch (3 mm) long. The rays are pale

Annual saltmarsh aster,
Aster subulatus

blue or purple and roll inward toward the center of the flower after it is pollinated. After pollination, the disks darken from yellow to purplish-red.

The base of the flower head is narrow with erect, elongated green phyllaries that are tinged with purple at the tips. When the fruit forms, it is attached to fine white pappus hairs that enable the seeds to be carried to new sites by the wind.

Several other small-flowered asters grow in coastal plain habitats in this book's range. Heath-aster or squarrose white aster (*Aster ericoides* L.) grows in open dry habitats from Maine south to Delaware and northern Virginia and west to Manitoba, Arkansas, Texas, and Arizona. It is a perennial that grows 1–3 feet (30–90 cm) tall and may be erect or arching. The linear sessile leaves are no more than 2⅜ inches (6 cm) long and ¼ inch (7 mm) wide, with the longest leaves on the lower portion of the stem. The leaves are rough along the margins and on the undersides, and the stems are covered with hairs. The flowering branches are densely covered with numerous short, stiff leaves no longer than ⅜–½ inch (10–12 mm), and there may be tufts of tiny leaves in the axils of the longer leaves. Although the flower heads are usually less than ½ inch (12 mm) across, they may be so crowded on the stems that the whole plant seems to be a snowy mass of flowers. Each flower head has 8–20 ray flowers that are usually white but may be pale blue or pink, and the disk flowers are yellow, fading to purple after pollination. The phyllaries are broad, green, and spreading, with sharp awl-like tips and numerous tiny hairs on the undersides.

Calico or starved aster (*Aster lateriflorus* [L.] Britt., which includes *Aster vimineus* Lam.), small white aster (*Aster fragilis* Willd.), and several other species of small white asters may be found growing in this book's range.

Perennial Saltmarsh Aster

Aster tenuifolius L.
Aster Family, Asteraceae

RANGE: Massachusetts south to Florida and west to southeastern Texas.
HABITAT: Salt and brackish marshes and flats, as well as coastal thickets and dredge-spoil disposal areas.

From late summer to fall, the flowers of perennial saltmarsh aster look like little daisies scattered across the salt marsh. The entire flower head is usually ½ inch (12 mm) across but may be as much as 1 inch (2.5 cm) in diameter. The ray flowers, which number from 15 to 25, are tinged with pink when the buds open, are pure white when in full bloom, and turn pink or lavender as the flowers fade. Each ray has three toothlike segments at the tip and curls up toward the disk after pollination. The disk flowers are initially yellow but darken to rosy-pink. The pappus hairs attached to the seed are tan.

The leaves and stems are gray-green and smooth and waxy to touch. The leaves are slightly fleshy, are narrow in proportion to length, and taper to a slender point. The smooth edges of the leaves and the edges and tips of the green phyllaries surrounding the flower buds are lined with dark purple. The leaves are widely spaced along the slender single (or slightly branched), often zigzagging stem, and they range in length from 1½ to 6 inches (4–15 cm).

The stems develop from the terminal buds on the tips of the

Perennial saltmarsh aster,
Aster tenuifolius

underground runners or stolons from the previous year. In the northern portion of this book's range, the stems may be 6–28 inches (15–70 cm) in length, but farther south they may be as much as 4 feet (1.2 m) long.

In northern salt marshes, this aster usually grows in mixed stands with sea lavender (*Limonium carolinianum*), salt hay grass (*Spartina patens*), and saltgrass (*Distichlis spicata*) where marshes are inundated by midsummer tides and are regularly flooded by the high tides of late August and September. These high tides tend to flatten saltmarsh plants unless they have rigid stems, and by the time perennial saltmarsh aster is in bloom from late August to September, the stems have been inundated and flattened by the high tides. Short plants tend to remain erect, but taller plants lie along the ground with ascending tips. The plant often looks much shorter than it is until the stem is traced to its point of origin among the tangle of grasses.

Several other species of asters with similarly sized flowers grow in coastal plain habitats in this book's range, including long-stalked aster (*Aster dumosus* L.) and awl-aster (*Aster pilosus* Willd.). Long-stalked or bushy aster is a perennial aster that grows in dry to moist open habitats, especially in sandy soils of the coastal plain, from southern Maine south to Florida and west to Michigan, Arkansas, and eastern Texas. It is a widely branching plant that may stand erect or arching and grows 1–$3\frac{1}{3}$ feet (30–100 cm) tall. The leaves are sessile, linear to lance-shaped, and usually entire, although there may be a few scattered teeth on the larger stem leaves. The leaves on the main portion of the stem are up to $4\frac{3}{8}$ inches (11 cm) long, but the numerous leaves on the long flowering stalks are tiny. The tips of the leaves tend to be blunt. The flower heads are $\frac{1}{2}$–$\frac{3}{4}$ inch (12–20 mm) across, with 13–30 rays that may be white, bluish, or lavender. The phyllaries tend to be narrow and straight, not recurved.

Awl-aster (also known as frost aster) grows in open habitats from Nova Scotia and Maine south to northern Florida and west to Minnesota, Kansas, and Louisiana. It is a variable species that has been separated into several varieties. Usually it is a stiffly branched, erect or arching plant that grows to 5 feet (1.5 m) tall, but in sites with direct exposure to ocean winds and salt spray, it may be prostrate and grow no more than 8–12 inches (20–30 cm) long. The stem and leaves may be densely covered with spreading hairs or may be smooth. The leaves are lance-shaped to elliptical, may be toothed or entire, and come to a sharp point at the tip. The lower leaves have petioles and are up to 4 inches (10 cm) long, but the upper leaves are sessile and much shorter. The flower heads are up to $\frac{3}{4}$ inch (2 cm) across, with 16–40 rays that are usually white but may be pale pink. Often all of the flowers will appear to grow on one side of the flowering branch. The involucre is spreading at the base but narrows in the center to give it an urnlike shape. The phyllaries come to a very sharp tip (hence the name awl-aster) and are in-rolled on their margins; often they spread outward.

Groundsel tree, *Baccharis halimifolia*, fruits

Groundsel Tree, Sea Myrtle

Baccharis halimifolia L.
Aster Family, Asteraceae

RANGE: Massachusetts south to Florida and west to Arkansas and Texas; also in the West Indies.
HABITAT: Upper edges of irregularly flooded tidal freshwater and brackish marshes, freshwater swamps, coastal hammocks and thickets, edges of beaches, and inland on roadsides and in old fields and disturbed areas.

In autumn, a stand of groundsel tree may form a frothy white border along the upper edge of a salt marsh. After seeing a shimmering stand of groundsel tree in the fall, one can understand how the plant gained another common name, silverling.

Groundsel tree is a graceful rounded shrub that may reach 10–13 feet (3–4 m) in height. The alternate leaves are thick, smooth, and somewhat fleshy. They are up to 2½ inches (6.5 cm) long, are broader at the base, and taper slightly to the tip. Usually they have coarse teeth, but the smaller leaves at the upper ends of the twigs may have no teeth. Both sides of the leaves are the same shade of green.

The plants are dioecious, with the male and female flowers on different plants. Both male and female flowers are borne in clusters

Groundsel tree,
Baccharis halimifolia,
male flowers

on long stalks at the ends of the flowering branches. The corolla of the female plant is very slender, threadlike, and inconspicuous. The larger, five-lobed male flowers are arranged in a tight disk and are also inconspicuous. In fruit, however, in the fall, the male plants are covered with clusters of small white (fading to tan) disk-shaped flower heads, and the much more conspicuous female plants are covered with fruits that resemble small brushes, with long snow-white bristles and a green base divided by a zigzag border of brilliant purple.

In New England, more groundsel tree is present in coastal habitats now than was evident 25 years ago. Usage of the land has changed during the past decades, and much less cultivation and grazing takes place along the edges of salt marshes. This decline in agriculture has probably enabled groundsel tree to return to its typical coastal habitats. Groundsel tree has also moved inland, spreading along the interstate highways as they were built and heavily salted during the winter.

Groundsel tree is advertised as a choice plant for landscaping, both around homes and along highways, especially in areas with poor soils and soils exposed to limited amounts of salt. Because of its cultivation and use along highways, groundsel tree has spread well into the piedmont zone in several southern states.

Baccharis halimifolia has also become naturalized in Australia, and since 1900, it has spread along the coastal plain of New South Wales and Queensland, growing in disturbed areas as well as swamps dominated by the native paperbark tea tree (*Melaleuca quinquenervia* [Cav.] Blake). *Melaleuca* in turn has invaded large tracts of Florida swamps, where groundsel tree may be found growing along with it.

Studies have shown that a single *Baccharis* plant can produce over 1 million seeds, and these seeds are easily spread by wind and water. *Baccharis* species are often plant pioneers in disturbed soils throughout the world, moving in quickly after lava flows, floods, fires, drought, and other disturbances.

Two other species of *Baccharis* may be found in coastal habitats in this book's range. Narrow-leaved groundsel tree or false willow (*Baccharis angustifolia* Michx.) grows at the edges of salt and brackish marshes, in dune swales, and in disturbed areas from North Carolina south to Florida and west along the Gulf coast. It is a shrub that may grow as tall as 6½ feet (2 m). The thick, alternate, sessile leaves are shiny green and very narrow, no more than 3/16 inch (5 mm) wide, and usually less than 2 inches (5 cm) long. Most of the leaves are entire, although leaves on the lower portion of the plant may have a few scattered teeth. The dioecious flowers are in heads that may be solitary or in clusters and sessile or on short stalks.

Baccharis glomeruliflora Pers., also called groundsel tree, grows in damp low areas, ditches, and dune swales from southern North Carolina to Florida. It is a small shrub that grows up to 6½ feet (2 m) tall. Its dull green leaves tend to be broadest near the top and taper to a wedge at the base; there are usually a few teeth near the top. The leaves may be sessile or have a short petiole. The dioecious flowers are borne in sessile clusters scattered along the flowering branches.

Sea ox-eye,
Borrichia frutescens

Sea Ox-eye, Sea Daisy

Borrichia frutescens (L.) DC.
Aster Family, Asteraceae

RANGE: Virginia south to Georgia, Florida, and the West Indies and west along the Gulf coast to Texas and Mexico.
HABITAT: Coastal shores, salt flats, and the margins and upper edges of brackish and salt marshes; inland (in Texas and Mexico) in areas of poor drainage and where salt accumulates.

Sea ox-eye is a shrub that often forms dense colonies in wet coastal sands. From a distance, the plants appear gray; close inspection shows that the stems and leaves (especially when young) are covered with short, grayish-white, downy hairs. Although this low-growing, often sparingly branched shrub may be as tall as 4 feet (1.2 m), it more typically reaches about 2½ feet (75 cm) in height.

The leaves are opposite and attach directly to the stalk without a petiole (a few may have a very short petiole). They vary in shape, some wide at the top and tapering sharply to the base and others much longer in proportion to width with almost straight sides. Some leaves are entire and others have teeth along the sides, but all have a sharp point at the tip. The leaves tend to be thick and somewhat succulent.

The flower heads are borne singly on stiff, straight stems. Each flower head has 12–30 bright yellow ray flowers, each ray about ⅜ inch (1 cm) long. The central portion of the flower head, made up of numerous tall yellow disk flowers, may be as much as ¾ inch (2 cm) in diameter. Both the ray flowers and the disk flowers are fertile.

The bracts at the base of the flower heads have spiny tips, making the fruiting head very prickly. In addition to growing from seeds, the plant can reproduce by rhizomes.

In parts of Mexico and the Caribbean, *Borrichia* has had several medicinal uses, including use as an antidote for poisoning caused by eating certain kinds of fish.

Shaggy Golden Aster

Chrysopsis mariana (L.) Ell.
Aster Family, Asteraceae

RANGE: Block Island, Rhode Island, and Long Island south to Florida and west to Texas.
HABITAT: Sunny, sandy soils along the coast, pine barrens and woodlands, and thin woods inland.

The northern limit of shaggy golden aster is a sunny meadow high above the Atlantic Ocean on Block Island, Rhode Island; from this vantage point, Long Island is a misty blue line on the southwestern horizon. The plants on Block Island probably originated from seeds blown from Long Island.

Shaggy golden aster is a fibrous-rooted perennial with one or more thick erect stems that are densely covered with shaggy, silky hair when young and smooth when mature. Northern plants are rarely more than 8 inches (20 cm) tall, but those at the southern end of the range may reach 32 inches (80 cm), and the stems and leaves are proportionately larger.

The plants have both basal and stem leaves. The basal leaves are about twice as long as they are wide and have fine teeth along

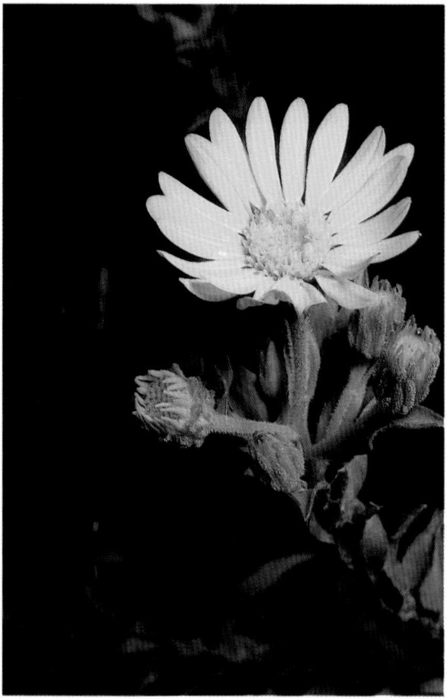

Shaggy golden aster, *Chrysopsis mariana*

the edges and petioles. Including the petioles, the leaves are rarely more than 1 inch (2.5 cm) long. The stem leaves are conspicuously smaller, with smooth edges and no petioles. Both surfaces of the basal and stem leaves are smooth, and the veins are netted.

The flowers are bright yellow and have the typical pattern of aster flowers—a flat round center covered with small disk flowers surrounded by a circle of slender ray flowers. The entire head has 13–21 ray flowers and is usually no more than ¾ inch (2 cm) in diameter. The blooming season usually extends from late June to October, depending on the location.

The distribution of shaggy golden aster is a good example of the influence of ocean temperature on the presence or absence of certain plants along the shore. Although shaggy golden aster has been reported growing in Connecticut, no records have confirmed its presence there. The land mass of Connecticut is apparently a sufficient distance from the ocean to reduce the average low temperature enough to prevent shaggy golden aster from growing there; this also explains the absence of shaggy golden aster in places in Rhode Island other than Block Island.

An alternate scientific name for shaggy golden aster is *Heterotheca mariana* (L.) Shinners.

The *Chrysopsis-Heterotheca-Pityopsis* complex of plants has been classified in many different ways. A number of species in these genera grow in coastal plain habitats in this book's range, especially south of New Jersey.

Hightide Bush, Marsh Elder

Iva frutescens L.
Aster Family, Asteraceae

RANGE: Nova Scotia and Massachusetts south to Florida and west to Texas.
HABITAT: Uppermost levels of tidal salt marshes, brackish marshes, and drainage ditches.

In a tidal salt marsh on the day of the highest tide of the year, if there is no wind to affect the movement of the water, the tidal flow will slowly creep up the marsh to the uppermost edge until the soil around the base of the hightide bush is moistened. The water will remain still for a few minutes and then slowly recede.

This explains why this plant was given the common name hightide bush. It requires a wet saline environment to survive, but it must also be able to tolerate the dry periods when the tides are at the lowest point of the year and the only moisture comes from rain. Plants in this location must also be able to endure being covered with salt water for a week or more during storms when the tides are exceptionally high and the marshes do not drain on schedule.

Hightide bush is a branched woody shrub that may grow 2–12 feet (0.6–3.5 m) tall, but plants are more frequently in the 4- to 6-foot (1.2–1.8 m) range. The lower portions of the stems are smooth, but the upper parts are usually covered with short stiff hairs. Apparently the stems are short-lived since a few dead stems can generally be found among the younger living ones in any colony of hightide bush.

The leaves are hairy on both upper and lower surfaces and are opposite, except for a few small alternate leaves at the upper end of the flowering stem. They are somewhat fleshy, up to 4 inches

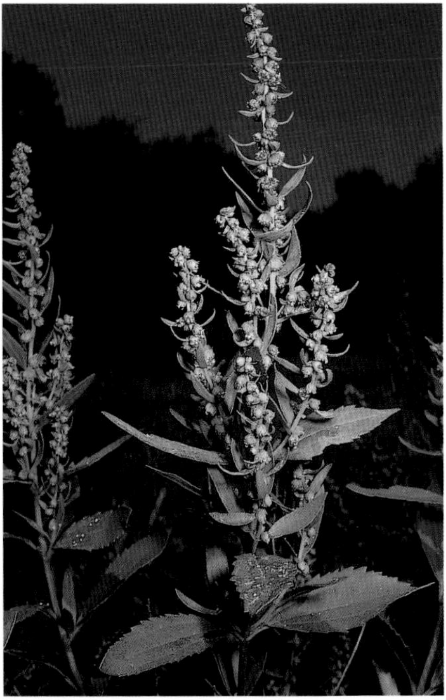

Hightide bush,
Iva frutescens ssp. *oraria*

(10 cm) long, and rather slender in proportion to width, usually less than four times as long as they are wide. They may taper at both ends or be wider at the lower end. The edges of the leaves have 8–17 teeth on the margins, the leaf tip is pointed, and the petioles are short.

In August, the flowers begin to bloom along the upper ends of the twigs. They are about 3⁄16 inch (5 mm) broad with a disk surrounded by small rounded green bracts. A few male flowers are scattered around the edges of the disk, and the center is filled with deep rose-pink tubular female flowers and dry, thin scales known as chaff.

When the fruits have ripened, they resemble small silky brushes. The seeds blow away suspended on fine white hairs.

Hightide bush might be confused with groundsel tree (*Baccharis halimifolia*), but groundsel tree grows above the marsh, whereas hightide bush grows in areas of the marsh that are inundated by tidal waters. In addition, the leaves of *Baccharis* are all alternate, whereas *Iva* has mostly opposite leaves. In this book's range, high-tide bush is divided into two subspecies: *Iva frutescens* L. ssp. *oraria* (Bartlett) R. C. Jackson, which grows from Virginia north, and *Iva frutescens* L. ssp. *frutescens*, which grows from Virginia south.

Dune marsh elder (*Iva imbricata* Walt.) may be found on coastal dunes from Virginia south to Florida and west to Louisiana, as well as in the Bahamas and Cuba. The branches form at the base of the plant and spread over the ground, with the top portions of the branches growing upward no more than 3⅓ feet (1 m). As in high-tide bush, the leaves are fleshy, but only the larger, lower leaves are opposite, and the whole plant is smooth. The leaves may be entire or have a few scattered teeth. The bracts at the base of the flower disks are imbricate, overlapping one another like shingles, which gives the plant its specific name, *Iva imbricata*.

Northern Blazing Star

Liatris scariosa (L.) Willd. var. *novae-angliae* Lunell
Aster Family, Asteraceae

RANGE: Coastal New England and New York.
HABITAT: Dry open areas and upper edges of cobble beaches and brackish marshes.

The blazing stars (*Liatris* spp.) are among the handsomest flora of this book's range. The erect, spikelike flower stalks grow as tall as 6½ feet (2 m), and the upper portions are covered with round heads of deep pink-purple flowers when the plant is in full bloom.

At least eight species of blazing star grow in coastal plain habitats in this book's range. They tend to grow in dry sandy or rocky soils, open woods, prairies, and exposed shores. They are perennial plants, and their leaves are alternate, entire, narrow or lance-shaped, and often attached directly to the stem without a petiole. The leaves are longest near the base of the flowering stem and become progressively shorter as they near the top of the plant. All have rounded flower heads densely covered with small, tubular, purple-pink (or occasionally white in some forms) flowers, with the styles projecting beyond the opening of the flower tubes.

Below each flower head are small leaves called phyllaries or involucral bracts; they overlap one another like roof shingles. Identification of the blazing stars is often based on the shape, size, and

Northern blazing star,
Liatris scariosa

margin characteristics of these phyllaries; in addition, the number of flowers per head and characteristics of the fruits are important diagnostic aids.

Northern or New England blazing star is usually 2–4 feet (60–120 cm) in height, with crowded stem leaves below the flowering portion of the stalk. The lower leaves may be as much as 14 inches (35 cm) long and ½–¾ inch (1.2–2 cm) wide; they may be smooth or have hairs on the midrib of the lower leaf surface. The flower heads are on stalks up to 2 inches (5 cm) long, and each head has up to 80 flowers on it. The phyllaries have dark red margins, rounded tips, and a fringe of tiny hairs. The upper ones tend to be pressed fairly tightly against the flower head, but the lower ones may spread.

Robust specimens of this species over 4 feet (1.2 m) tall, each with five or six stalks, have been observed in a brackish salt marsh, blooming along with thousands of sea pinks (*Sabatia stellaris*).

This species has been treated as *Liatris borealis* Nutt. by some authorities.

Other species of blazing star that may be found along the coastal plain in this book's range are *Liatris elegans* (Walt.) Michx., *Liatris gracilis* Pursh, *Liatris graminifolia* Willd., *Liatris spicata* (L.) Willd. var. *resinosa* (Nutt.) Gaiser, *Liatris squarrosa* (L.) Michx., *Liatris squarrulosa* Michx., and *Liatris tenuifolia* Nutt.

Several cultivated forms of blazing star are popular with gardeners. The blazing stars have also been used in Native American medicine. Another common name for some blazing stars is button-snakeroot, referring to the buttonlike flowers and the former use of the plant to treat snakebite.

Saltmarsh Fleabane

Pluchea odorata (L.) Cass. var. *succulenta* (Fern.) Cronq.
Aster Family, Asteraceae

RANGE: Southern Maine south to Florida and the Tropics and west to Texas; also occasionally inland in the north-central states.
HABITAT: Salt and brackish marshes and rarely freshwater marshes.

This member of the aster family is an annual in the northern portions of its range and an annual or a perennial in the southern areas. It can grow as tall as 5 feet (1.5 m) but rarely exceeds 2 feet (60 cm) in height at its northern limits.

Saltmarsh fleabane grows best in full sun but can survive for years under stands of common reed (*Phragmites australis*). It also grows better in soils rich in organic matter than in sandy areas.

The simple, alternate leaves are bright green, fleshy, and usually smooth on both surfaces, although the leaves of some plants are slightly downy. They are 1–6 inches (2.5–15 cm) long, half as wide, and taper at both ends. The same plant may have both smooth and toothed leaves, and the leaves may have short stalks or be attached directly to the stem. The stems are paler green than the leaves and are profusely branched. When crushed, the plant has an unpleasant odor but not as unpleasant as that of other *Pluchea* species that grow in the South and West, which are variously called stinking fleabane, camphorweed, and stinkweed.

The flowers are clustered in flat circles about ¼ inch (7 mm) in diameter. They resemble the disk flowers at the center of a daisy. The outer ring of flowers are pistillate (female), and the inner flow-

Saltmarsh fleabane, *Pluchea odorata*

ers of the disk are perfect, with both male and female parts. They are usually a purplish-rose color, but plants with white flowers have also been observed.

Each disk of flowers rests on a short-stemmed hemispherical base covered with short, narrow, pale-green bracts, which are blanketed with very short glandular hairs. The stems grow in clusters of 8–12 flowers and are in turn gathered into bunches on separate stems. The flower cluster on the main central stem of the plant is usually noticeably shorter than the lateral branches of the main stem. The whole plant tends to be more leafy below the clusters of flowers.

Saltmarsh fleabane flowers from July to October.

An older name for this species is *Pluchea purpurascens* (Sw.) DC. The genus is named in honor of eighteenth-century French naturalist Abbot Pluche.

Several other species of *Pluchea* may be found in coastal plain habitats south of New England. Camphorweed (*Pluchea camphorata* [L.] DC.) grows from Delaware south to Florida and west to Texas. It is very similar to saltmarsh fleabane, but its lateral branches are usually no longer than the central stem, and the floral bracts are not hairy (although they may be glandular). Camphorweed is most likely to be found in freshwater habitats.

Stinkweed (*Pluchea foetida* [L.] DC.) grows from southern New

Jersey south to Florida and west to Texas. The flowers of this perennial species are cream-colored, and the leaves have broad, clasping bases. Like camphorweed, it is found primarily in freshwater wetlands or wet open habitats mostly along the coastal plain but occasionally inland as well.

Marsh fleabane (*Pluchea rosea* Godfrey) is also a perennial with clasping, sessile leaves, but its flowers are a deep rose-pink. As in saltmarsh fleabane, the lateral branches are longer than the central stem. This species grows in wet woods, pond edges, and ditches from North Carolina south to Florida and west to Texas, as well as in the West Indies, where members of this genus have been used for a variety of medicinal purposes.

Long-leaved camphorweed (*Pluchea longifolia* Nash) is endemic to northern Florida, where it grows in tidal brackish and freshwater marshes and hammocks. Its flower heads are twice the size of those of saltmarsh fleabane, and its leaves are large and sharply and irregularly toothed.

Seaside Goldenrod

Solidago sempervirens L. var. *sempervirens*
Aster Family, Asteraceae

RANGE: Outer coastal plain from Newfoundland and Quebec south to Virginia; also inland along salted highways.
HABITAT: Margins of salt marshes and sand dunes and in brackish, loamy, sandy, or peaty soils close to salt water.

Seaside goldenrod is not only one of the handsomest goldenrods but also one of the showiest of the coastal plants. It is probably the most easily recognized goldenrod because of its large flowers and because it always grows near salt water (or where salt has been added to the soil). Whether the salt water is 20 miles inland on the banks of a river flushed by tides or in a salt marsh close to the ocean, seaside goldenrod is likely to be found nearby.

The plants may grow erect 1–6½ feet (0.3–2 m) tall. They may sprawl in almost flat mats, with the branches radiating from the perennial root like the spokes of a wheel, or they may grow at any angle between erect and prostrate. Sprawling plants tend to grow in open exposed places, and erect plants are usually mixed with other erect species.

Seaside goldenrod, *Solidago sempervirens*

The stems of seaside goldenrod tend to be rather thick, striped with parallel lines, and sometimes dark red. The leaves are thick, smooth, somewhat fleshy, and rich green on both surfaces. Often they have a line of dark red around the entire edge.

The basal leaves may be up to 16 inches (40 cm) long and taper at both ends. The base of the stem leaves often clasps the stem, almost completely encircling it. These stem leaves are somewhat shorter than the basal leaves, but in other respects, they are similar.

The flowers are borne in panicles at the tips of the stems and are the most distinctive feature of the plant, whether the plant has a single flowering panicle or a dozen. The panicles usually range from 4 to 12 inches (10–30 cm) long and are broad at the base and taper toward the tip, with most of the flowers in a panicle blooming at the same time.

Seaside goldenrod is the only goldenrod with flowers large enough that the structures can be seen without a magnifying lens. Each flower is like a small yellow daisy, ¼–½ inch (7–12 mm) in diameter; the individual ray flowers and disk flowers can be seen clearly. They bloom from late August to November, with the southern plants blooming later.

A variety of seaside goldenrod, *Solidago sempervirens* L. var. *mexicana* (L.) Fern., which has smaller heads and narrower leaves, grows from New Jersey south to Florida and west to Texas and

Mexico and is occasionally found as far north as southern New York and southeastern Massachusetts. A number of other species of goldenrod grow in coastal plain habitats in this book's range.

Seaside goldenrod has been shown to be a short-day plant, which means that flowering is initiated in the growing tips of the plants when the hours of daylight are reduced to a certain length, with corresponding long periods of darkness. This is true of many plants that bloom in the fall. Knowledge of this phenomenon has been used commercially to produce chrysanthemums on a year-round basis and to ensure that poinsettias bloom in time for Christmas.

Researchers conducted an experiment on seaside goldenrod in which plants were dug in late fall in Florida, North Carolina, and New York and then grown in a greenhouse in New York until they bloomed the following year. Each group of plants bloomed at the same time as the plants remaining at the original site. The plants from Florida did not bloom until November, whereas those from North Carolina and New York bloomed earlier. Clearly, initiation of flowering had occurred in the fall, before the plants were dug.

Common Cocklebur

Xanthium strumarium L. var. *canadense* (P. Mill.) Torr. & Gray
Aster Family, Asteraceae

RANGE: Cosmopolitan, probably originally from the New World.
HABITAT: Coastal beaches and dunes, freshwater shores, fields, disturbed areas, and waste places.

Common cocklebur, also known as sea burdock or clotbur, is a coarse plant of shores and waste places. Cocklebur is well named since almost every part of the plant is either prickly or rough. A widely branching annual with a taproot, the plant may reach up to 6½ feet (2 m) in length and may be erect or sprawl over the ground.

Cocklebur stems are spotted with purple blotches and covered with stiff hairs. The long-stalked, alternate leaves vary widely in shape but are usually broadest—and frequently heart-shaped—at the base, with three to five irregular lobes and smaller teeth along the margins. The leaves may be up to 6 inches (15 cm) in length and are covered with short hairs that give them a somewhat rough texture.

Male and female flowers grow separately on the same plant. The

Common cocklebur, *Xanthium strumarium*

inconspicuous male flowers grow in small heads at the end of the stems and drop off the plant shortly after pollination. The female flowers develop within burs in the leaf axils, each bur containing two green flowers. When mature, the egg-shaped, brownish burs are up to 1⅜ inches (3.5 cm) long and woody, are covered with hooked prickles, and contain two seeds. At the end of each bur is a pair of stout, inwardly curved beaks. The prickly burs attach to animals' fur (or people's clothing), which helps to disperse the seeds; the fruits are also able to float in water and may be spread in this way as well.

Farmers find cocklebur a troublesome weed. The burs can not only become entangled in sheeps' wool but also cut the mouths of grazing animals and damage their intestinal tracts. The young plants and seeds are toxic to livestock.

Cocklebur was formerly used to treat the disease scrofula; the descriptive name, *strumarium*, refers to the tumors or strumae that this disease causes. Native Americans had many medicinal uses for the plant.

Because there is so much variation within this species, the taxonomy of *Xanthium* has been treated in many different ways. According to the system used in this book, *Xanthium strumarium* var. *canadense* includes *Xanthium echinatum* Murr., *Xanthium italicum* Moretti, and *Xanthium pensylvanicum* Wallr.

Selected Coastal Natural Areas

Below are natural areas that include coastal ecosystems, arranged by state in the range of this book from north to south. These sites were chosen not only because they contain fine examples of coastal plant communities but also because they are easily accessible to the public. The Nature Conservancy, local Audubon Societies, the U.S. Fish and Wildlife Service, land trusts, state departments of environmental management, and similar groups are other excellent sources for locating local natural areas.

Massachusetts

Cape Cod National Seashore, Barnstable Co.
Demarest Lloyd State Park, Bristol Co.
Edgartown–Oak Bluffs State Beach Park, Martha's Vineyard, Dukes Co.
Felix Neck Wildlife Sanctuary, Martha's Vineyard, Dukes Co.
Halibut Point Reservation, Essex Co.
Horseneck Beach State Park, Bristol Co.
Martha's Vineyard State Forest, Dukes Co.
Monomoy National Wildlife Refuge, Barnstable Co.

Myles Standish State Forest, Plymouth Co.
Nantucket National Wildlife Refuge, Nantucket Co.
Nantucket State Forest, Nantucket Co.
Parker River National Wildlife Refuge, Barnstable Co.
Plum Island State Park, Essex Co.
R. C. Nickerson State Park, Barnstable Co.
Richard T. Crane Memorial Reservation, Essex Co.
Shawme Crowell State Forest, Barnstable Co.
Standish Monument State Reservation, Plymouth Co.
Wellfleet Bay Wildlife Sanctuary, Barnstable Co.

Rhode Island

Beavertail State Park, Conanicut Island, Newport Co.
Block Island National Wildlife Refuge, Washington Co.
Colt State Park, Bristol Co.
Emilie Ruecker Wildlife Refuge, Newport Co.
Marsh Meadows Wildlife Refuge, Newport Co.
Napatree Point, Washington Co.
Narragansett Bay National Estuarine Sanctuary, Prudence Island, Newport Co.
Ninigret National Wildlife Refuge, Washington Co.
Norman Bird Sanctuary, Newport Co.
Pettaquamscutt Cove National Wildlife Refuge, Washington Co.
Sachuest Point National Wildlife Refuge, Newport Co.
Sapowet Management Area, Newport Co.
Succotash Marsh Management Area, Washington Co.
Trustom Pond National Wildlife Refuge, Washington Co.

Connecticut

Barn Island Wildlife Management Area, New London Co.
Bluff Point State Park, New London Co.
Charles Wheeler Wildlife Area, New Haven Co.
Great Island Wildlife Area, New London Co.
Greenwich Point Park, Fairfield Co.
Haley Farm State Park, New London Co.
Hammonasett Beach State Park, Middlesex Co.
Harkness Memorial State Park, New London Co.
Milford Point Sanctuary, New Haven Co.

Quinnipiac River Marsh Wildlife Area, New Haven Co.
Rocky Neck State Park, New London Co.
Seldon Neck State Park, New London Co.
Sherwood Island State Park, Fairfield Co.
Silver Sands State Park, New Haven Co.

New York

Bear Mountain State Park, Rockland Co.
Captree State Park, Suffolk Co.
Caumsett State Park, Suffolk Co.
Fire Island National Seashore, Suffolk Co.
Gateway National Recreation Area, Kings Co., Queens Co., and Richmond Co.
Gilgo Beach State Park, Suffolk Co.
Governor Alfred E. Smith Sunken Meadow State Park, Suffolk Co.
Heckscher State Park, Suffolk Co.
Hither Hills State Park, Suffolk Co.
Hook Mountain State Park, Rockland Co.
J. F. K. Memorial Wildlife Sanctuary, Nassau Co.
Jamaica Bay Wildlife Refuge, Queens Co.
Jones Beach State Park, Nassau Co.
Montauk Point State Park, Suffolk Co.
Orient Beach State Park, Suffolk Co.
Oyster Bay National Wildlife Refuge, Nassau Co.
South Beach and Race Point, Fishers Island, Suffolk Co.
Wildwood State Park, Suffolk Co.

New Jersey

Barnegat National Wildlife Refuge, Ocean Co.
Brigantine National Wildlife Refuge, Atlantic Co.
Cape May National Wildlife Refuge, Cape May Co.
Cheesequake State Park, Middlesex Co.
Dennis Creek Wildlife Area, Cape May Co.
Dix Fish and Wildlife Management Area, Cumberland Co.
Fortescue Fish and Wildlife Management Area, Cumberland Co.
Gateway National Recreation Area, Sandy Hook Unit, Monmouth Co.
Great Bay Fish and Wildlife Management Area, Ocean Co.

Heislerville Fish and Wildlife Management Area, Atlantic Co.
Island Beach State Park, Ocean Co.
Killcohook National Wildlife Refuge, Salem Co.
Mad Horse Creek Wildlife Management Area, Salem Co.
Sandy Hook National Recreation Area, Monmouth Co.
Tuckahoe–Corbin City Fish and Wildlife Management Area, Atlantic Co.

Delaware

Augustine Wildlife Area, New Co.
Bombay Hook National Wildlife Refuge, Castle Co.
Cape Henlopen State Park, Sussex Co.
Delaware Seashore State Park, Sussex Co.
Fenwick Island State Park, Sussex Co.
Prime Hook National Wildlife Refuge, Sussex Co.

Maryland

Assateague Island National Seashore, Somerset Co.
Blackwater National Wildlife Refuge, Dorchester Co.
Calvert Cliffs State Park, Calvert Co.
Cedar Island Wildlife Management Area, Somerset Co.
Deal Island Wildlife Management Area, Somerset Co.
E. A. Vaughn Wildlife Management Area, Worcester Co.
Eastern Neck Island National Wildlife Refuge, Kent Co.
Elk Neck State Forest, Cecil Co.
Elk Neck State Park, Cecil Co.
Elk Neck Wildlife Management Area, Cecil Co.
Ellis Bay Wildlife Management Area, Wicomico Co.
Fairmount Wildlife Management Area, Somerset Co.
Fishing Bay Wildlife Management Area, Dorchester Co.
Isle of Wight Wildlife Management Area, Worcester Co.
Janes Island State Park, Somerset Co.
Martin National Wildlife Refuge, Somerset Co.
North Point State Park, Baltimore Co.
Pocomoke Sound Wildlife Management Area, Somerset Co.
Point Lookout State Park, St. Mary's Co.
Sandy Point State Park, Anne Arundel Co.

South Marsh Island Wildlife Management Area, Somerset Co.
St. Clement's Island State Park, St. Mary's Co.
Susquehanna National Wildlife Refuge, Harford Co. and Kent Co.
Taylors Island Wildlife Management Area, Dorchester Co.
Wye Island National Reservation Management Area, Queen Anne's Co. and Talbot Co.

Virginia

Assateague Island National Seashore, Accomack Co.
Back Bay National Wildlife Refuge, York Co.
Chincoteague National Wildlife Refuge, Accomack Co.
Eastern Shore of Virginia National Wildlife Refuge, Northampton Co.
False Cape State Park, York Co.
First Landing/Seashore State Park, York Co.
Fishermans Island National Wildlife Refuge, Northampton Co.
Great Dismal Swamp National Wildlife Refuge, York Co.
Mackay Island National Wildlife Refuge, York Co.
Mason Neck National Wildlife Refuge, Fairfax Co.
Plum Tree Island National Wildlife Refuge, York Co.
Seashore State Park, York Co.

North Carolina

Alligator River National Wildlife Refuge, Dare Co. and Tyrrell Co.
Buxton Woods, Dare Co.
Cape Hatteras National Seashore, Dare Co. and Hyde Co.
Cape Lookout National Seashore, Carteret Co.
Carolina Beach State Park, New Hanover Co.
Cedar Island National Wildlife Refuge, Carteret Co.
Croatan National Forest, Craven Co., Carteret Co., and Jones Co.
Currituck Banks, Currituck Co.
Currituck River National Wildlife Refuge, Currituck Co.
Goose Creek State Park, Beaufort Co.
Hammocks Beach State Park, Onslow Co.
Mackay Island National Wildlife Refuge, Currituck Co.
Pea Island National Wildlife Refuge, Dare Co.
Swanquarter National Wildlife Refuge, Hyde Co.
Theodore Roosevelt Natural Area State Park, Carteret Co.

South Carolina

Ace Basin National Wildlife Refuge, Colleton Co.
Cape Romain National Wildlife Refuge, Charleston Co.
Edisto Beach State Park, Charleston Co.
Francis Marion National Forest, Berkeley Co. and Charleston Co.
Hunting Island State Park, Beaufort Co.
Huntington Beach State Park, Georgetown Co.
Kiawah Island, Charleston Co.
Myrtle Beach State Park, Horry Co.
Pinckney Island National Wildlife Refuge, Chatham Co.
Santee Coastal Reserve, Charleston Co.
Savannah National Wildlife Refuge, Jasper Co.
St. Helena Sound Heritage Preserve, Colleton Co.

Georgia

Blackbeard Island National Wildlife Refuge, McIntosh Co.
Blackbeard Island Wilderness Area, McIntosh Co.
Crooked River State Park, Camden Co.
Cumberland Island National Seashore, Camden Co.
Cumberland Island Wilderness Area, Camden Co.
Harris Neck National Wildlife Refuge, McIntosh Co.
Jekyll Island State Park, Glynn Co.
Lewis Island Natural Area, McIntosh Co.
Ossabaw Island Heritage Preserve, Bryan Co.
Sapelo Island National Estuarine Sanctuary, McIntosh Co.
Savannah National Wildlife Refuge, Chatham Co.
Skidaway Island State Park, Chatham Co.
Tybee National Wildlife Refuge, Chatham Co.
Wassaw National Wildlife Refuge, Chatham Co.
Wolf Island National Wildlife Refuge and Wilderness Area, McIntosh Co.

Florida

Amelia Island, Nassau Co.
Anastasia State Park, St. Johns Co.
Canaveral National Seashore, Orange Co. and Volusia Co.
Faver-Dykes State Park, Flagler Co.

Flagler Beach State Park, Flagler Co.
Fort Clinch State Park, Nassau Co.
Gamble Rogers State Park, Flagler Co.
Guana River State Park, St. Johns Co.
Little Talbot Island State Park, Duval Co.
Merritt Island National Wildlife Refuge, Orange Co.
St. Johns National Wildlife Refuge, Orange Co.
Tomoka State Park, Volusia Co.
Washington Oaks Garden State Park, Flagler Co.

Glossary

Acute: Sharp-pointed (usually refers to the tip of a leaf).

Alkaloid: A varied group of alkaline, nitrogen-containing organic chemicals, many with active pharmacological properties (e.g., nicotine, morphine, quinine, caffeine, and cocaine).

Alternate: An arrangement in which a bud, leaf, or stem arises singly from a node and is not directly opposite another bud, leaf, or stem.

Annual: A plant that goes through its entire life cycle—germination, flowering, and seed production—in one year (see also *biennial* and *perennial*).

Anther: The portion of the stamen that bears the pollen.

Aquatic bed: A deepwater (deeper than 6½ feet [2 m]) or wetland habitat dominated by mosses, algae, or rooted, submerged, or floating herbaceous plants.

Areole: A small, distinctly bounded area of plant tissue; in members of the cactus family, a distinct area on the stem that bears spines, hairs, or glochids.

Awn: A long slender bristle.

Backdune: The portion of a dune that faces away from the winds and salt-laden waters coming from the ocean.

Bay: A partially enclosed inlet of the ocean (see also *estuary* and *lagoon*).

Biennial: A plant that goes through its entire life cycle—germination, flowering, and seed production—in two years (see also *annual* and *perennial*).

Bloom: A waxy coating, easily rubbed off, giving a surface a whitish cast.

Bog: A peatland with little freshwater input except from a high water table or rainfall; soils tend to be acidic (low pH) and low in oxygen and nutrients.

Brackish: Water that is less saline than ocean water but more saline than fresh water, with 0.5–30 parts per thousand salt.

Bract: A specialized leaf at the base of a flower or inflorescence.

Calyx: The sepals of a flower, collectively.

Chaff: Dry, thin scales or bracts.

Circumboreal: Distributed throughout the boreal regions around the North Pole in both Eurasia and North America.

Cleistogamous flower: A flower that is self-pollinated; the flower remains closed, and the seeds develop within the closed capsule.

Compound leaf: A leaf that is divided into two or more distinct leaflets.

Corolla: The petals of a flower, collectively.

Crown: The upper portion of a tree, including the leaves and branches; the persistent base of a perennial plant from which the roots and stems develop.

Cyme: A branched, usually somewhat flat-topped inflorescence in which the terminal flowers on each branch bloom first.

Decumbent: A growth pattern in which a plant has a prostrate or curved base and a tip that is erect or ascending.

Deepwater habitats: Permanently flooded aquatic habitats in which the water is usually at least 6½ feet (2 m) deep.

Dicotyledon: A group of flowering plants that have two cotyledons (seed leaves) in the seed (e.g., oaks, buttercups, mints, and asters).

Dioecious: Bearing male and female flowers or reproductive parts on separate plants.

Disk flowers: The central, tubular flowers found in members of the aster family (see also *ray flowers*).

Dune: A hill or ridge formed from windblown sand.

Ecosystem: A community of organisms (plants, animals, fungi, etc.) and the physical environment they inhabit. The organisms in an ecosystem interact with one another and with the physical environment to form a functioning unit for the flow of energy and the cycling of materials.

Endemic: Confined to a particular geographic region.

Entire: Having an unbroken margin of the leaf blade, without teeth, lobes, or cuts.

Epiphyte: A plant growing on another plant (not in soil) but without taking water or nutrients from the host plant.

Estuary: A partially enclosed coastal body of water in which fresh water from the land mixes with ocean water.

Fen: A peatland that usually has some groundwater inflow and thus generally has more nutrients and a higher pH than bogs.

Foredune: The portion of a dune that faces toward the winds and salt-laden waters coming from the ocean.

Fresh water: Water with less than 0.5 parts per thousand salt.

Frond: The leaf of a fern.

Fruitdot: A cluster of spore cases on a fern frond; also called a sorus.

Genus, *genera* (pl.): A taxonomic unit below a family and above a species in which all members of the unit share common characteristics (e.g., *Rosa*, *Rhododendron*, *Aster*).

Gland: A specialized portion of a plant—often on hairs or in depressions—that produces a sticky or greasy secretion.

Glochid: A tiny barbed bristle usually occurring in tufts in the cactus family.

Glycoside: An organic compound that breaks down to yield a sugar and one or more nonsugar compounds.

Habitat: The environment in which an organism lives.

Hammock: An elevated area in a wetland that supports a hardwood-plant community.

Haustorim: A specialized, often rootlike structure through which a parasitic plant connects to its host and extracts nutrients.

Imbricate: Overlapping in a shinglelike arrangement; e.g., the leaflike structures (see *bract*) at the base of many composites such as *Aster* spp. and *Liatris* spp. are imbricate.

Imperfect: A flower that has either male parts (staminate) or female parts (pistillate) but not both (see also *perfect*).

Inflorescence: The arrangement of flowers along an axis; a flower cluster.

Interdune: The area between sand dunes.

Invasive: A plant or animal that has naturalized in a region and is able to outcompete native species and alter ecosystem processes.

Involucre: A series of bracts at the base of a flower or inflorescence.

Lagoon: A body of water partially separated from the sea by an island, spit, reef, or sandbar.

Ligule: A hairy or leafy projection from the top of a leaf sheath found in members of the grass family and a few other families; the flat portion of the ray corolla in the aster family.

Monocotyledon: A group of flowering plants that have one cotyledon (seed leaf) in the seed (e.g., lilies, orchids, grasses, and sedges).

Monoecious: Bearing male and female flowers or reproductive parts separately on the same plant.

Native: Occurring naturally in a region, not introduced from another region.

Naturalized: Introduced from another region and spread beyond cultivated sites.

Node: The point on a stem from which a leaf develops.

Opposite: An arrangement in which a bud, leaf, or stem arises from a node directly across from another bud, leaf, or stem.

Panicle: An elongated, branching flower cluster.

Panne: A low area in a salt marsh where tidal water stands for days or weeks and salt accumulates in the soil.

Pappus: The specialized calyx, composed of hairs, awns, bristles, or scales, found at the top of the ovary and seeds in members of the aster family.

Pedicel: The stalk of a single flower in a flower cluster.

Peduncle: The stalk of an individual flower or flower cluster.

Perennial: A plant that lives longer than two years (see also *annual* and *biennial*).

Perfect: A flower that has both male parts (staminate) and female parts (pistillate) (see also *imperfect*).

Petal: A segment of a corolla, usually white or a color other than green.

Petiole: The stalk of a leaf.

Petiolule: The stalk of a leaflet in a compound leaf.

Phyllary: An involucral bract found in members of the aster family.

Pinna: A primary division of a leaf that is pinnately compound; also called a leaflet.

Pinnule: A division of a pinna or leaflet on a pinnately compound leaf; also called a subleaflet.

Pistil: The female organ of a flower, ordinarily composed of at least one stigma, style, and ovary.

Pistillate: Having one or more pistils but lacking stamens; also called female.

Pocosin: A freshwater swamp or boggy area on a plateau dominated by evergreen trees and shrubs with little if any open water; occurs mostly in coastal North Carolina.

Raceme: An elongated inflorescence with stalked flowers or small flower clusters arranged along an unbranched central axis.

Rachis: The main axis of a compound leaf.

Ray flowers: Flowers with a flattened corolla found in members of the aster family (see also *disk flowers*).

Rhizome: A horizontal underground stem; also called a rootstock.

Saline: Containing salt; "saline water" generally refers to ocean water, with at least 30 parts per thousand salt.

Saponin: A glycoside compound that foams when mixed with water.

Savanna: An open area usually dominated by grasses, with scattered trees and shrubs.

Scape: A leafless (sometimes with bracts) flowering stalk (peduncle) that grows directly from the root.

Sepal: A segment of the calyx, usually green or greenish.

Serrate: Having sharp, forward-pointing teeth along the margin of the leaf blade.

Sessile: Lacking a stalk.

Sorus, sori (pl.): A cluster of spore cases; also called a fruitdot; a term used with ferns and fern allies.

Spadix: A flower spike with the flowers crowded along a thick, fleshy axis (such as the "Jack" in Jack-in-the-pulpit).

Spathe: A large, usually solitary bract found at the base of or partially enclosing some flowers in the monocotyledons (such as the "pulpit" in Jack-in-the-pulpit).

Species: The most basic taxonomic group that is distinct from other groups and capable of interbreeding; the species name is a binomial (e.g., *Spartina patens*).

Spikelet: A term used primarily with sedges and grasses to indicate a basic flower structure composed of from one to many flowers and their associated bracts.

Stamen: The male organ of a flower, ordinarily composed of an anther and a filament.

Staminate: Having one or more stamens but lacking a pistil; also called male.

Stigma: The portion of the pistil that receives the pollen.

Stipe: A stalk; used most frequently to refer to the stalk of a fern between the frond and the rhizome.

Stipule: One or more usually small, leaflike appendages at or near the base of a petiole (such as in members of the willow, bean, and rose families).

Stolon: An elongated stem that creeps along the surface of the ground, or just below it, and produces a new plant at its tip; also called a runner.

Stomate: A tiny pore in plant tissue (usually the leaf) through which gases and water vapor are exchanged.

Style: The elongated portion of the pistil, usually slender, connecting the ovary to the stigma.

Swale: A low area behind a primary dune where the water table may be at or near the surface of the ground.

Tepal: A portion of a flower that cannot be clearly distinguished as either a petal or a sepal (such as in members of the iris family).

Terrestrial ecosystems: Ecosystems on land that are neither wetland nor aquatic systems (e.g., dunes, scrub thickets, and upland forests).

Tussock: A clump or tuft, as in some grasses and sedges.

Umbel: A flower cluster in which all of the flower stalks radiate out from the same level on the stem, resembling the ribs of an umbrella.

Wetland: A habitat intermediate between terrestrial and aquatic ecosystems in which the water table is usually above or near the surface, the water depth is no greater than 6½ feet (2 m), and the plant cover is dominated by hydrophytes (e.g., salt marshes, bogs, swamps, pocosins, fens, wet meadows, and vernal pools).

References

Anderson, Karl H., and Beryl R. Collins. 1994. *Plant Communities of New Jersey*. New Brunswick, N.J.: Rutgers University Press.

Bell, C. Ritchie, and Bryan J. Taylor. 1982. *Florida Wild Flowers and Roadside Plants*. Chapel Hill, N.C.: Laurel Hill Press.

Bellis, Vincent J. 1995. *Ecology of Maritime Forests of the Southern Atlantic Coast: A Community Profile*. Washington, D.C.: U.S. Department of Interior, National Biological Service, report no. 30.

Bertness, Mark D. 1999. *The Ecology of Atlantic Shorelines*. Sunderland, Mass.: Sinauer Associates.

Brown, Claud L., and L. Katherine Kirkman. 1990. *Trees of Georgia and Adjacent States*. Portland, Oreg.: Timber Press.

Bullard, Lacy F., ed. 1979. *Coastal Plants of Florida: A Key to Good Land Management*. [Tallahassee]: Division of Forestry, Florida Department of Agriculture and Consumer Services.

Carlton, Jedfrey M. 1975. *A Guide to Common Florida Salt Marsh and Mangrove Vegetation*. St. Petersburg: Florida Department of Natural Resources, Marine Research Publications, no. 6.

——. 1977. *A Survey of Selected Coastal Vegetation Communities of Florida*. St. Petersburg: Florida Department of Natural Resources, Marine Research Publications, no. 30.

Clewell, Andre F. 1985. *Guide to the Vascular Plants of the Florida Panhandle*. Tallahassee: Florida State University Press.

Cobb, Boughton. 1956. *A Field Guide to the Ferns*. Boston: Houghton Mifflin.

Collins, Beryl Robichaud, and Karl H. Anderson. 1994. *Plant Communities of New Jersey: A Study in Landscape Diversity*. New Brunswick, N.J.: Rutgers University Press.

Correll, Donovan Stewart, and M. C. Johnston. 1979. *Manual of the Vascular Plants of Texas*. Richardson: University of Texas at Dallas.

Cowardin, Lewis M., Virginia Carter, Francis C. Golet, and Edward T. LaRoe. 1979. *Classification of Wetlands and Deepwater Habitats of the United States*. Washington, D.C.: U.S. Department of the Interior, Fish and Wildlife Service, Biological Services Program FWS/OBS-79/31.

DiGregorio, Mario, and Jeff Wallner. 1989. *A Vanishing Heritage: Wildflowers of Cape Cod*. Missoula, Mont.: Mountain Press.

Douglas, Marjory S. 1947. *The Everglades: River of Grass*. New York: Rinehart.

Dowhan, Joseph J. 1979. *Preliminary Checklist of the Vascular Flora of Connecticut (Growing without Cultivation)*. Hartford: State Geological and Natural History Survey of Connecticut, report no. 8.

Duncan, Wilbur H., and Marion B. Duncan. 1987. *The Smithsonian Guide to Seaside Plants of the Gulf and Atlantic Coasts*. Washington, D.C.: Smithsonian Institution Press.

——. 1988. *Trees of the Southeastern United States*. Athens: University of Georgia Press.

Duncan, Wilbur H., and Leonard E. Foote. 1975. *Wildflowers of the Southeastern United States*. Athens: University of Georgia Press.

Dwelley, Marilyn J. 1980. *Trees and Shrubs of New England*. Camden, Maine: Down East Books.

Fernald, Merritt L. 1950. *Gray's Manual of Botany*. 8th ed. New York: American Book Company.

Flora of North America Editorial Committee, ed. 1993. *Pteridophytes and Gymnosperms*. Vol. 2 of *Flora of North America North of Mexico*. New York: Oxford University Press.

——. 1997. *Magnoliophyta: Magnoliidae and Hamamelidae*. Vol. 3 of *Flora of North America North of Mexico*. New York: Oxford University Press.

Foote, Leonard E., and Samuel B. Jones Jr. 1989. *Native Shrubs and Woody Vines of the Southeast: Landscaping Uses and Identification*. Portland, Oreg.: Timber Press.

Foster, Steven, and Roger Caras. 1994. *Venomous Animals and Poisonous Plants*. Boston: Houghton Mifflin.

Frankenberg, Dirk. 1997. *The Nature of North Carolina's Southern Coast: Barrier Islands, Coastal Waters, and Wetlands*. Chapel Hill: University of North Carolina Press.

Gleason, Henry A., and Arthur Cronquist. 1991. *Manual of Vascular Plants of Northeastern United States and Adjacent Canada*. 2d ed. Bronx: New York Botanical Garden.

Gould, Lisa L., Richard W. Enser, Richard L. Champlin, and Irene H. Stuckey. 1998. *Vascular Flora of Rhode Island: A List of Native and Naturalized Plants*. Kingston: Rhode Island Natural History Survey.

Gupton, Oscar W., and Fred C. Swope. 1982. *Wildflowers of Tidewater Virginia*. Charlottesville: University Press of Virginia.

Haines, Arthur, and Thomas F. Vining. 1998. *Flora of Maine*. Bar Harbor, Maine: V. F. Thomas.

Holmgren, Noel H. 1998. *The Illustrated Companion to Gleason and Cronquist's Manual: Illustrations of the Vascular Plants of Northeastern United States and Adjacent Canada*. Bronx: New York Botanical Garden.

Hotchkiss, Neil. 1972. *Common Marsh, Underwater, and Floating-Leaved Plants of the United States and Canada*. New York: Dover.

Jorgensen, Neil. 1978. *A Sierra Club Naturalist's Guide: Southern New England*. San Francisco: Sierra Club Books.

Justice, William S., and C. Ritchie Bell. 1968. *Wild Flowers of North Carolina*. Chapel Hill: University of North Carolina Press.

Kaplan, Eugene H. 1988. *A Field Guide to Southeastern and Caribbean Seashores: Cape Hatteras to the Gulf Coast, Florida, and the Caribbean*. Boston: Houghton Mifflin.

Kartesz, John T. 1994. *A Synonymized Checklist of the Vascular Flora of the United States, Canada, and Greenland*. 2d ed. Portland, Oreg.: Timber Press.

Little, Elbert L. 1980. *The Audubon Society Field Guide to North American Trees, Eastern Region*. New York: Alfred A. Knopf.

Magee, Dennis W. 1981. *Freshwater Wetlands: A Guide to Common Indicator Plants of the Northeast*. Amherst: University of Massachusetts Press.

Magee, Dennis W., and Harry E. Ahles. 1999. *Flora of the Northeast: A Manual of the Vascular Flora of New England and Adjacent New York*. Amherst: University of Massachusetts Press.

Mellinger, Marie B. 1984. *Atlas of the Vascular Flora of Georgia: A Georgia Botanical Society Project*. Milledgeville, Ga.: Studio Designs Printing.

Miller, Howard A., and Samuel H. Lamb. 1985. *Oaks of North America*. Happy Camp, Calif.: Naturegraph Publishers.

Mitchell, Richard S., and Gordon C. Tucker. 1997. *Revised Checklist of New York State Plants*. Albany: New York State Museum, bulletin no. 490.

Nelson, Gil. 1994. *The Trees of Florida*. Sarasota, Fla.: Pineapple Press.

Newcomb, Lawrence. 1977. *Newcomb's Wildflower Guide*. Boston: Little, Brown.

Nixon, S. W. 1982. *The Ecology of New England High Salt Marshes: A Community Profile*. Washington, D.C.: U.S. Fish and Wildlife Service.

Odum, Eugene P., and A. de la Cruz. 1967. "Particulate Organic Detritus in a Georgia Salt Marsh–Estuarine System." In *Estuaries*, edited by G. H. Lauff, 383–85. Washington, D.C.: American Association for the Advancement of Science, publication no. 83.

Perry, Bill. 1985. *A Sierra Club Naturalist's Guide: The Middle Atlantic Coast, Cape Hatteras to Cape Cod*. San Francisco: Sierra Club Books.

Peterson, Lee. 1978. *A Field Guide to Edible Wild Plants of Eastern and Central North America*. Boston: Houghton Mifflin.

Peterson, Roger Tory, and Margaret McKenny. 1968. *A Field Guide to Wildflowers of Northeastern and North-Central North America*. Boston: Houghton Mifflin.

Petrides, George A. 1988. *A Field Guide to Eastern Trees*. Boston: Houghton Mifflin.

Porcher, Richard D. 1995. *Wildflowers of the Carolina Lowcountry and Lower Pee Dee*. Columbia: University of South Carolina Press.
Radford, Albert E., Harry E. Ahles, and C. Ritchie Bell. 1968. *Manual of the Vascular Flora of the Carolinas*. Chapel Hill: University of North Carolina Press.
Richardson, C. J., ed. 1981. *Pocosin Wetlands: An Integrated Analysis of Coastal Plain Freshwater Bogs in North Carolina*. Stroudsburg, Pa.: Hutchison Ross.
Schneider, C. W., and R. B. Searles. 1991. *Seaweeds of the Southeastern United States, Cape Hatteras to Cape Canaveral*. Durham: Duke University Press.
Schoettle, H. E. Taylor. 1996. *A Guide to a Georgia Barrier Island*. St. Simons Island: Watermarks Publishing.
Silberhorn, Gene M. 1982. *Common Plants of the Mid-Atlantic Coast*. Baltimore: Johns Hopkins University Press.
Stuckey, Irene H. 1967. *Rhode Island Wildflowers*. Knoxville: University of Tennessee Press.
——. 1975–95. "Plants beside the Sea." *Maritimes* 19–38.
Taylor, Walter K. 1998. *Florida Wildflowers in Their Natural Communities*. Gainesville: University Press of Florida.
Teal, John M. 1981. *The Ecology of Regularly Flooded Salt Marshes in New England: A Community Profile*. Washington, D.C.: U.S. Fish and Wildlife Service.
Teal, John, and Mildred Teal. 1969. *Life and Death of the Salt Marsh*. Boston: Little, Brown.
Tiner, Ralph W. 1987. *A Field Guide to Coastal Wetland Plants of the Northeastern United States*. Amherst: University of Massachusetts Press.
——. 1993. *A Field Guide to Coastal Wetland Plants of the Southeastern United States*. Amherst: University of Massachusetts Press.
——. 1998. *In Search of Swampland: A Wetland Sourcebook and Field Guide*. New Brunswick, N.J.: Rutgers University Press.
U.S. Department of Agriculture. 1990. *Plant Hardiness Zone Map*. Washington, D.C.: U.S. Department of Agriculture Agricultural Research Service, miscellaneous publication no. 1475.
Villalard-Bohnsack, Martine. 1995. *Illustrated Key to the Seaweeds of New England*. Kingston: Rhode Island Natural History Survey.
Wells, B. W. 1932. *The Natural Gardens of North Carolina*. Chapel Hill: University of North Carolina Press.
Whitlatch, R. B. 1982. *The Ecology of New England Tidal Flats: A Community Profile*. Washington, D.C.: U.S. Fish and Wildlife Service.

Index

Abelmoschus esculentus, 190
Abutilon theophrasti, 190
Acer rubrum, 9
Acoraceae, 87–88
Acorus americanus, 11, 87–88
Acorus calamus, 88
Adam's needle, 101
Aesculus hippocastanum, 187
Aesculus pavia, 186–87, 237
Aesculus sylvatica, 187
Agalinis fasciculata, 225
Agalinis maritima, 96, 225–27
Agalinis paupercula, 227
Agalinis purpurea, 225, 227
Agavaceae, 101
Agave family, 101
Aizoaceae, 138
Aleurites spp., 174
Algae, 7
Althaea officinalis, 191
Amaranth, beach, 6
Amaranthus cannabinus, 10
Amaranthus pumilus, 6
Amelanchier canadensis, 9, 155–56
Amelanchier obovalis, 156
American beachgrass, 8, 44–45, 54, 56, 70, 170
American cranberry, 209–11
American dunegrass, 51
American ginseng, 214
American germander, 223–25
American holly, 9, 14, 117, 183–85
Ammophila arenaria, 45
Ammophila breviligulata, 8, 44–45, 54, 56, 70, 170
Amorpha fruticosa, 10, 166–67
Ampelopsis brevipedunculata, 13
Anacardiaceae, 178–81
Anagallis arvensis, 6, 211–12, 233
Andropogon gerardii, 15, 59
Andropogon glomeratus, 60
Andropogon gyrans, 60
Andropogon longiberbis, 60
Andropogon mohrii, 60
Andropogon scoparius, 59

Andropogon ternarius, 60
Andropogon virginicus, 60
Antirrhinum spp., 225, 227
Apiaceae, 203
Aquifoliaceae, 183
Aquilegia canadensis, 237
Araceae, 88, 89–92
Aralia spinosa, 14
Arctostaphylos uva-ursi, 9
Arecaceae, 82–86
Arenaria peploides, 141
Argentina anserina, 156–58
Arisaema triphyllum, 40, 88, 89, 91
Aronia spp., 13
Arrow arum, 11, 90–92
Arrow-grass, seaside, 10, 42–44, 96
Arrow-grass, slender, 44
Arrow-grass, southern, 11, 43
Arrow-grass family, 42
Arrowheads, 90, 91
Arrowwood, 238–40
Arrowwood, common, 239
Arrowwood, northern, 13, 239–40
Arrowwood, southern, 13, 240
Artemisia abrotanum, 244
Artemisia absinthium, 244
Artemisia campestris, 196, 241–42
Artemisia caudata, 242
Artemisia dracunculus, 244
Artemisia stelleriana, 4, 195, 241, 243–44
Artemisia vulgaris, 244
Arum, arrow, 11, 90–92
Arum, white, 92
Arum family, 89–92
Asclepiadaceae, 218
Asclepias amplexicaulis, 220
Asclepias humistrata, 220
Asclepias incarnata, 220
Asclepias lanceolata, 220
Asclepias longifolia, 220
Asclepias pedicillata, 220
Asclepias perennis, 220
Asclepias rubra, 220
Asclepias spp., 15, 219
Asclepias tuberosa, 218–20
Ash, 11, 181
Asian bittersweet, 13, 15, 164
Aster, annual saltmarsh, 10, 11, 247–49
Aster, awl-, 6, 251
Aster, bushy, 251
Aster, calico, 248
Aster, eastern silvery, 246
Aster, frost, 251
Aster, grass-leaved golden, 9
Aster, heath-, 248
Aster, long-stalked, 251
Aster, New England, 246
Aster, New York, 245–47
Aster, perennial saltmarsh, 10, 247, 249–51
Aster, purple-stemmed, 246–47
Aster, shaggy golden, 256–58
Aster, small white, 248
Aster, squarrose white aster, 248
Aster, starved, 248
Aster, swamp, 247
Aster, wand, 246
Asteraceae, 241–67
Aster concolor, 246
Aster dumosus, 251
Aster elliottii, 247
Aster ericoides, 248
Aster family, 15, 241–67
Aster fragilis, 248
Aster lateriflorus, 248
Aster novae-angliae, 246
Aster novi-belgii, 245–46
Aster pilosus, 6, 251
Aster puniceus, 246–47
Aster spp., 8
Aster subulatus, 10, 247–49
Aster tenuifolius, 10, 247, 249–51
Aster vimineus, 248
Atamasco lily, 105–6
Atlantic mudwort, 4, 227–28
Atlantic white cedar, 11
Atriplex arenaria, 124
Atriplex hastata, 125
Atriplex patula, 125
Atriplex pentandra, 8, 122–24
Atriplex prostrata, 11, 124–25

Atriplex spp., 10, 123, 124, 125, 135
Autumn olive, 13, 14, 15
Awl-aster, 6, 251
Awl-sedge, 71–73
Azalea, clammy, 206
Azalea, dwarf, 206
Azalea, hammock sweet, 206
Azalea, swamp, 13, 205–7
Azalea, wild, 207
Azalea, woolly, 207
Azaleas, 11

Baccharis angustifolia, 10, 254
Baccharis glomeruliflora, 11, 254
Baccharis halimifolia, 9, 252–54, 259
Bald cypress, 11, 35–37, 110
Bald cypress family, 35
Ball moss, 94
Bamboo vine, 12
Barbarea vulgaris, 152
Barbary fig, 201
Bassia, five-hook, 127
Bassia, hairy, 126–27
Bassia, hyssop-leaved, 127
Bassia hirsuta, 126–27
Bassia hyssopifolia, 127
Bassia spp., 123, 135
Bataceae, 135
Batis maritima, 10, 11, 135
Bay, loblolly, 12, 192–93
Bay, red, 12, 14
Bay, sweet, 13, 15, 147–48
Bayberry, northern, 3, 8, 13, 14, 113–16, 164, 178
Bayberry, southern, 14, 114–15
Bayberry family, 113
Beach amaranth, 5
Beach elder, 8
Beach evening-primrose, 9, 203
Beachgrass, American, 8, 44–45, 54, 56, 70, 170
Beachgrass, European, 45
Beach heather, 8, 9, 194–95
Beach morning-glory, 220–21
Beach pea, 8, 169–71
Beach pennywort, 8, 9, 203–4
Beach pinweed, 9, 195–96
Beach plum, 9, 158–61
Beach umbrella-sedge, 73–75
Beach wormwood, 243–44
Bean, castor-, 174
Bean, perennial wild, 172
Bean, trailing wild, 171–72
Bean, wild, 9
Bean family, 166–72
Bearberry, 9
Beardgrass, 59
Beardtongues, 225
Bear grass, 9, 101–3, 116
Bear oak, 116
Beech family, 116–21
Beets, 123
Bella honeysuckle, 238
Berchemia scandens, 11
Beta vulgaris, 123
Bittersweet, Asian, 13, 15, 164
Black cherry, wild, 9, 13, 14, 161–63
Black grass, 96–98
Black gum, 9, 11, 13, 14, 110
Black oak, 8, 120
Black rush, 10, 42, 47, 96–97, 98, 99, 128
Black ti-ti, 12, 181–83
Bladderwort, floating, 230–32
Bladderwort, inflated, 231
Bladderwort, purple, 229–30
Bladderwort family, 229–32
Bladderworts, 12
Blazing star, New England, 261
Blazing star, northern, 260–62
Bloodwort family, 107, 108
Blueberry, highbush, 11, 13, 207–9
Blue flag, common, 109
Blue flag, slender, 11, 108–10
Blue flag, southern, 109
Bluestem, big, 15, 59
Bluestem, little, 15, 59–60
Blue-stem palmetto, 82–83
Blunt-leaved milkweed, 220
Borrichia frutescens, 10, 255–56
Bracken, 26
Brasenia schreberi, 217
Brassicaceae, 150

Bromeliaceae, 92
Bromeliad family, 92
Broom, 59
Broomsedge, 60
Buckbean family, 216, 218
Buckeye, painted, 187
Buckeye, red, 186–87, 237
Buckeye family, 186
Buckthorns, 13
Buckwheat family, 121, 188
Buckwheat-tree, 182–83
Bull-nettle, 175
Bulrush, alkali-, 81
Bulrush, leafy, 79–81
Bulrush, river, 12, 81
Bulrush, saltmarsh, 80–81
Bulrushes, 10, 11, 78, 79–81
Bush honeysuckles, 13
Butterfly-weed, 218–20
Buttonbush, 234–36
Button-snakeroot, 262

Cabbage palm, 10, 11, 54, 83–85
Cactaceae, 199
Cactus, 9
Cactus, prickly-pear, 9
Cactus family, 199
Cakile edentula, 4, 132, 150–52
Cakile harperi, 151
Cakile lanceolata, 152
Cakile maritima, 152
Calamus, 87
Calceolaria spp., 225
Calla, wild, 12
Calla palustris, 12
Camphorweed, 262, 263
Camphorweed, long-leaved, 264
Campsis radicans, 237
Canada mayflower, 104–5
Candleberry, swamp, 13, 115
Caprifoliaceae, 205, 236–40
Cardinal flower, 237
Carex spp., 12, 71–73
Carex stipata, 71
Carolina laurelcherry, 14, 163
Caryophyllaceae, 139–43
Cashew family, 178–81
Cassava, 174
Cassena, 185
Cassia fasciculata, 169
Castor-bean, 174
Catbrier, 13, 14
Cattail, 11
Cattail, broad-leaved, 10, 11, 40–41
Cattail, narrow-leaved, 10, 11, 40–42, 109
Cattail, southern, 40–41
Cattail family, 40
Cedar, Atlantic white, 11
Cedar, eastern red, 8, 13, 38–40
Cedar, red, 14, 110
Cedar, salt-, 10
Cedar, southern red, 39–40
Celastrus orbiculata, 13, 164
Cenchrus carolinianus, 47
Cenchrus echinatus, 47
Cenchrus incertus, 47
Cenchrus longispinus, 8, 46
Cenchrus tribuloides, 8, 46–47
Cephalanthus occidentalis, 234–36
Chairmaker's rush, 76–78
Chamaecrista fasciculata, 168–69
Chamaecrista nictitans, 169
Chamaecyparis thyoides, 11
Chamaedaphne calyculata, 12
Chamaesyce bombensis, 174
Chamaesyce polygonifolia, 8, 173–74, 195
Chelone spp., 227
Chenopodiaceae, 122–38
Chenopodium, 122, 124
Chenopodium rubrum, 10
Cherry, choke-, 163
Cherry, wild black, 9, 13, 14, 161–63
Chestnut, horse-, 187
Chestnut oak, dwarf, 116–18
Chigger-weed, 219
Chinaberry tree, 14
China jute, 190
China rose, 189
Chinese tallow, 14
Chinquapin oak, dwarf, 116
Chokeberry, 13
Choke-cherry, 163

Chrysopsis mariana, 256–58
Chufa, 73, 75
Cinchona, 148
Cistaceae, 194–96
Cladium jamaicense, 99
Cladium mariscoides, 100
Cladium mariscus, 11, 99
Clethra alnifolia, 11
Cliftonia monophylla, 182
Climbing hempweed, 12
Clotbur, 266
Cnidoscolus stimulosus, 9, 175–76
Coastal dropseed, 49
Coastal plain serviceberry, 155–56
Coastal sandbur, 47
Coast blite, 10
Cocklebur, common, 8, 266–67
Coffea arabica, 235
Coffee, 235
Columbine, wild, 237
Conotrachelus nenuphar, 159
Convolvulaceae, 220–23
Coral honeysuckle, 236–38
Cordgrass, big, 10, 11, 63–64, 67
Cordgrass, freshwater, 10, 63, 67–68
Cordgrass, saltwater, 61
Cordgrass, smooth, 10, 47, 61–63, 64, 98, 130, 233
Corn, 13, 69
Cosmos spp., 242
Cotton, 190
Cottongrasses, 12
Cranberry, 12
Cranberry, American, 209–11
Cranberry, small, 209
Croton, silver-leaf, 6, 8, 9, 176–77
Croton, tooth-leaved, 177
Croton glandulosus, 177
Croton punctatus, 6, 176–77
Crown-of-thorns, 173
Cupressaceae, 38
Cymodocea filiformis, 7
Cyperaceae, 71–81, 100
Cyperus, 73–75
Cyperus esculentus, 73
Cyperus filicinus, 74
Cyperus papyrus, 73
Cyperus polystachyos, 73
Cypress, bald, 11, 35–37, 110
Cypress, pond, 15, 37
Cypress, summer, 123
Cypress family, 38
Cyrillaceae, 181
Cyrilla family, 181–83
Cyrilla racemiflora, 12, 181–83

Dactylopius coccus, 201
Dahoon, 185
Deschampsia spp., 8
Devil-joint, 201
Devil's walking-stick, 14
Dew-thread, 153
Dichromena, 76
Digitalis purpurea, 220
Digitalis spp., 225
Dionaea muscipula, 229
Distichlis spicata, 10, 42, 47–49, 65, 128, 135, 250
Dollar-weed, 204
Dropseed, coastal, 49
Drosera brevifolia, 154
Drosera capillaris, 154
Droseraceae, 153
Drosera filiformis, 153–54
Drosera intermedia, 154
Drosera rotundifolia, 154
Drosera spp., 12, 229
Dryopteris thelypteris, 28
Dunegrass, American, 51
Dune marsh elder, 260
Dune sandbur, 8, 46–47
Dune sandspur, 46
Dusty miller, 4, 8, 195, 241, 243–44

Earth almond, 75
Eastern prickly pear, 199–201
Eastern red cedar, 8, 13, 38–40
Eastern serviceberry, 155–56
Eastern silvery aster, 246
Eastern white pine, 30, 31–32
Eelgrass, 4, 7
Eichhornia crassipes, 94
Elaeagnus umbellata, 12

Elder, beach, 8
Elder, dune marsh, 260
Elder, marsh, 258
Elymus arenarius, 51
Elymus mollis, 51
Elymus virginicus, 49–51
Englemann's seagrass, 7
English oak, 120
Epidendrum conopseum, 110–12
Equisetaceae, 25
Equisetum arvense, 26
Equisetum hyemale, 25–26
Ericaceae, 205–10
Erigeron spp., 246
Eriophorum spp., 12
Euphorbia ammanioides, 174
Euphorbiaceae, 173–77
Euphorbia marginata, 174
Euphorbia polygonifolia, 173
Euphorbia pulcherrima, 173
Euphorbia splendens, 173
European beachgrass, 45
European water-lily, 146
Evening-primrose, beach, 9, 203
Evening-primrose, common, 202–3
Evening-primrose, cut-leaved, 203
Evening-primrose, seaside, 9, 203
Evening-primrose, showy, 15, 201–3
Evening-primrose family, 201
Everlasting pea, 170

Fabaceae, 166–72
Fagaceae, 116–21
False indigo, 10, 11, 166–67
False Solomon's seal, 103, 104
False willow, 10, 11, 254
Fern, marsh, 12, 27–28, 109
Fern, Massachusetts, 28
Fern, meadow, 27
Fern, New York, 28
Fern, resurrection, 29–30
Fern, Virginia chain-, 12
Fetterbush, 13
Fiddle-leaf morning-glory, 220
Field horsetail, 26
Fig marigold family, 138
Figwort family, 225–28
Firecracker-plant, 186
Fire-wheel, 9
Flag, blue, 11
Flag, common blue, 109
Flag, purple, 15, 109
Flag, slender blue, 108–10
Flag, southern blue, 109
Flatsedge, 73
Flatwood plum, 160
Fleabane, marsh, 264
Fleabane, saltmarsh, 10, 11, 262–64
Fleabane, stinking, 262
Fleabanes, 246
Floating bladderwort, 230–32
Floating-heart, big, 218
Floating-heart, little, 216–18
Floating-heart, yellow, 218
Foxglove, common, 220
Foxgloves, 225
Fragaria spp., 156
Fraxinus spp., 11, 181
Freshwater cordgrass, 10, 63, 67–68
Fringed gentian, 15
Fringed polygonella, 122

Gaillardia pulchella, 9
Galingale, 73
Galium spp., 235
Gama grass, 67–69
Gardenia, 235
Gentian, fringed, 15
Gentian, Plymouth, 216
Gentianaceae, 214, 218
Gentian family, 214, 218
Gentianopsis crinita, 15
Gerardia. See *Agalinis*
Gerardia, fascicled, 225, 227
Gerardia, purple, 225–27
Gerardia, seaside, 96, 225–27
Gerardia, small-flowered, 227
Germander, American, 223–25
Germander, cut-leaved, 224
Gingko biloba, 192
Gingko tree, 192
Ginseng, American, 214

Glasswort, annual, 62, 128, 129–31, 134
Glasswort, dwarf, 128–29
Glasswort, perennial, 9, 128, 133–35
Glassworts, 10
Glaucium flavum, 149–50
Globe-flower, 236
Goldcrest, 108
Golden aster, grass-leaved, 9
Golden aster, shaggy, 256–58
Golden club, 12, 89–90
Golden heather, 8
Goldenrod, 8
Goldenrod, gray, 3
Goldenrod, seaside, 8, 264–66
Goosefoot family, 122–38
Goose-tongue, 234
Gordonia lasianthus, 12, 192–93
Gossypium spp., 190
Grape, muscadine, 14
Grapes, 13
Grass, arrow-, 10, 42–43, 95
Grass, bear, 9, 101–3
Grass, black, 96, 97
Grass, gama, 68–69
Grass, hedgehog-, 47
Grass, highwater, 64
Grass, holy, 52
Grass, lyme, 51
Grass, manatee-, 7
Grass, poverty-, 194
Grass, prairie, 67
Grass, purple sand, 8
Grass, salt hay, 1, 9, 10, 39, 42, 47, 51, 62, 64–66, 96, 127, 129, 130, 135, 212, 233, 250
Grass, salt reed-, 63
Grass, saw-, 11, 99–100
Grass, southern sweet, 9, 53–54
Grass, sweet, 51–52
Grass, sword-, 77
Grass, Terrell, 49
Grass, vanilla, 52
Grass, widgeon-, 7
Grass family, 42, 44–71
Grass-leaved golden aster, 9
Gray goldenrod, 3
Green-fly orchid, 110–12
Groundsel tree, 9, 11, 252–54, 259
Groundsel tree, narrow-leaved, 254
Gum, black, 9, 11, 13, 14, 110
Gum, sweet, 110

Haemodoraceae, 107
Hairgrass, 8
Hairgrass, purple, 53
Halodule wrightii, 4
Halophila engelmanii, 7
Heath-aster, 248
Heather, beach, 8, 9, 194–95
Heather, golden, 8
Heath family, 205–10
Heavenly bamboo, 14
Hedgehog-grass, 47
Hedge-nettle, 224
Hempweed, climbing, 12
Hercules' Club, 14
Heterotheca mariana, 258
Hevea spp., 174
Hibiscus moscheutos, 10, 188–90
Hibiscus palustris, 189
Hibiscus rosa-sinensis, 189
Hibiscus syriacus, 189
Hierochloe odorata, 51–52
Highbush blueberry, 11, 13, 207–9
Hightide bush, 9, 47, 96, 258–60
Highwater-grass, 64
Hippocastanaceae, 186
Hog-plum, 160
Hogweed, 177
Holly, American, 9, 14, 117, 183–85
Holly, myrtle-leaf, 185
Holly, yaupon, 14, 185
Holly family, 183
Holy grass, 52
Honckenya peploides, 4, 139–41, 195
Honey-ball, 236
Honeycup, 12
Honeysuckle, bella, 238
Honeysuckle, bush, 13
Honeysuckle, coral, 236–38
Honeysuckle, Japanese, 14, 238
Honeysuckle, Morrow, 238
Honeysuckle, swamp, 205

Honeysuckle, Tartarian, 238
Honeysuckle, trumpet, 236
Honeysuckle family, 236
Hops, 225
Horned pondweed, 7
Horned poppy, 149–59
Horse-chestnut, 187
Horse-chestnut family, 186–87
Horsetail, field, 26
Horsetail family, 25
Hudsonia ericoides, 8
Hudsonia tomentosa, 8, 194–95
Humulus lupulus, 225
Hydrocotyle bonariensis, 8, 203–4

Ilex cassine, 185
Ilex decidua, 185
Ilex glabra, 13, 185
Ilex myrtifolia, 185
Ilex opaca, 9, 117, 183–85
Ilex verticillata, 9, 185
Ilex vomitoria, 14, 185
Impatiens capensis, 237
Incurvariidae, 103
Indigo, false, 10, 11, 166–67
Indigo-bush, 166
Inkberry, 13, 185
Ipomoea batatas, 221
Ipomoea brasiliensis, 223
Ipomoea imperati, 220–21
Ipomoea pes-caprae, 222–23
Ipomoea stolonifera, 221
Iridaceae, 108
Iris family, 108
Iris prismatica, 11, 108–10
Iris tridentata, 15, 109
Iris versicolor, 109
Iris virginica, 109
Iva frutescens, 9, 47, 96, 258–60
Iva imbricata, 8, 260
Ivy, poison, 9, 13, 14, 18, 178–79, 180
Ixora, 235

Jack-in-the-pulpit, 40, 88, 89, 90, 91, 92
Japanese honeysuckle, 14, 238
Jewelweed, 237
Jointweed, sand, 9, 121–22
Jointweed, slender, 122
Juncaceae, 96–100
Juncaginaceae, 42
Juncus ambiguus, 98
Juncus bufonius, 98
Juncus gerardii, 10, 42, 47, 96–98, 128
Juncus roemerianaus, 10, 54, 97, 98–100
Juncus spp., 9
Juneberry, 156
Juniperus virginiana, 8, 38–40

Knotweed, 121
Kochia scoparia, 123
Kosteletzkya virginica, 11, 190–92
Kudzu, 14, 15

Lachnanthes caroliana, 107–8
Lachnanthes tinctoria, 108
Lamiaceae, 223
Lathyrus japonicus, 8, 169–71
Lathyrus latifolius, 170
Lathyrus maritimus, 171
Laurelcherry, Carolina, 14, 163
Leadwort family, 212
Leafy bulrush, 79
Leatherleaf, 12
Leatherwood, 181
Lechea maritima, 9, 195–96
Lentibulariaceae, 229–32
Leymus arenarius, 51
Leymus mollis, 51
Liatris borealis, 261
Liatris elegans, 262
Liatris gracilis, 262
Liatris graminifolia, 262
Liatris scariosa, 260–62
Liatris spicata, 262
Liatris squarrosa, 262
Liatris squarrulosa, 262
Liatris tenuifolia, 262
Ligustrum spp., 13
Liliaceae, 103–6
Lilies, 15
Lilium spp., 15

Lily, atamasco, 105–6
Lily, swamp, 112
Lily, white water-, 145–47
Lily, yellow pond-, 114
Lily family, 103–6, 108
Lily-of-the-valley, wild, 105
Limonium carolinianum, 36, 62, 135, 212–14, 233, 250
Limonium nashii, 214
Limosella aquatica, 228
Limosella australis, 4, 227–28
Limosella subulata, 228
Little bluestem, 15, 59–60
Little floating-heart, 216–18
Little snowball, 236
Live oak, 14, 29, 106, 110, 117, 118–21
Lizard's tail, 112–13
Lizard's tail family, 112
Lobelia cardinalis, 237
Loblolly bay, 12, 192–93
Loblolly pine, 32, 193
Long-leaf pine, 15, 30–31, 54, 118
Lonicera × *bella*, 13, 238
Lonicera japonica, 14, 238
Lonicera morrowii, 13, 238
Lonicera sempervirens, 236–38
Lonicera tatarica, 238
Lophiola aurea, 108
Lyme grass, 51
Lyonia lucida, 13

Madder, 235
Madder family, 234, 235
Magnolia, southern, 110, 147
Magnoliaceae, 147
Magnolia family, 147
Magnolia grandiflora, 147
Magnolia virginiana, 13, 147–48
Maianthemum canadense, 104
Maianthemum racemosum, 104
Maianthemum stellatum, 103–5
Maize, 69
Mallow, marsh, 191
Mallow, seashore, 11, 12, 190–92
Mallow, swamp rose-, 188–89, 190
Mallow family, 188–92
Malvaceae, 188–92
Manatee-grass, 7
Manihot spp., 174
Maple, red, 9, 11
Marsh elder, 258
Marsh elder, dune, 260
Marsh fern, 12, 27–28, 109
Marsh fern family, 27
Marsh mallow, 191
Marsh rosemary, 212
Mayflower, Canada, 104–5
Meadow fern, 28
Melaleuca quinquenervia, 254
Melia azedarach, 14
Menyanthaceae, 216
Mikania scandens, 12
Milkweed, blunt-leaved, 220
Milkweed, few-flowered, 220
Milkweed, long-leaf, 220
Milkweed, pedicillate, 220
Milkweed, purple, 220
Milkweed, red, 220
Milkweed, smoothseed, 220
Milkweed, swamp, 220
Milkweed family, 218
Milkweeds, 15
Mint family, 223
Morning-glory, beach, 220–21
Morning-glory, fiddle-leaf, 220–21
Morning-glory, goat-foot, 222–23
Morning-glory family, 220–23
Morrow honeysuckle, 238
Moss, ball, 94
Moss, Spanish, 29, 92–94, 119
Moss, sphagnum, 12
Mud-rush, 97
Mudwort, Atlantic, 4, 227–28
Mudwort, northern, 228
Mugwort, 244
Muhlenbergia capillaris, 9, 53–54
Muhlenbergia filipes, 54
Mullein, common, 15
Mulleins, 227
Multiflora rose, 13, 14, 165
Mustard family, 150
Myricaceae, 113
Myrica cerifera, 14, 114

Myrica gale, 12
Myrica heterophylla, 13, 115
Myrica pensylvanica, 3, 113–16, 164, 178
Myrtle, sea, 254
Myrtle, wax-, 114–15

Najas, 7
Naked lady, 106
Nandina domestica, 14
Needlerush, 10, 11, 54, 97, 98–100
Nettle, bull-, 175
Nettle, hedge-, 224
Nettle, stinging, 176
Never-wet, 90
New England aster, 246
New England blazing-star, 261
New York aster, 245–46
New York fern, 28
Northern arrowwood, 13, 239–40
Northern bayberry, 3, 8, 13, 14, 113–16, 178
Northern blazing star, 260–62
Northern mudwort, 228
Nuphar lutea, 12, 144–45, 217
Nutsedge, 73
Nymphaea alba, 146
Nymphaeaceae, 144–47
Nymphaea odorata, 12, 145–47, 217
Nymphoides aquatica, 218
Nymphoides cordata, 216–18
Nymphoides peltata, 218
Nyssa aquatica, 11
Nyssa sylvatica, 9

Oak, bear, 116
Oak, black, 8, 120
Oak, dwarf chestnut, 116–18
Oak, dwarf Chinquapin, 116
Oak, English, 120
Oak, live, 14, 29, 106, 110, 117, 118–21
Oak, myrtle, 118
Oak, poison, 18, 178–79, 180
Oak, sand live, 117
Oak, sand post, 118
Oak, scrub. *See* Bear oak
Oak, turkey, 118
Oak, white, 120
Oaks, 13, 14
October-flower, 121
Oenothera biennis, 202
Oenothera drummondii, 9, 203
Oenothera fruticosa, 203
Oenothera humifusa, 9, 203
Oenothera laciniata, 203
Oenothera speciosa, 15, 201–3
Okra, 190
Olney three-square, 76
Onagraceae, 201
Opuntia compressa, 200
Opuntia drummondii, 200
Opuntia humifusa, 9, 199–201
Opuntia monacantha, 201
Opuntia pusilla, 200
Opuntia spp., 9, 200
Opuntia vulgaris, 201
Orach, 10, 11, 124–25
Orach, seabeach, 8, 122–24
Orchid, green-fly, 110–12
Orchidaceae, 110
Orchid family, 110
Orchids, 12, 13, 15
Oriental poppy, 149
Orontium aquaticum, 12, 89
Ox-eye, sea, 10, 11, 255–56

Painted buckeye, 187
Palm, cabbage, 10, 11, 54, 83–85
Palmetto, blue-stem, 82–83
Palmetto, dwarf, 82
Palmetto, saw, 14, 15, 82, 85–86
Palm family, 82–86
Panax quinquefolius, 214
Panicum amarulum, 56
Panicum amarum, 8, 56
Panicum virgatum, 8, 9, 54–56
Papaveraceae, 149
Papaver orientale, 149
Paperbark tea tree, 254
Papyrus, 73
Parategeticula, 103
Parsley family, 203
Parthenocissus quinquefolia, 9

Partridge pea, 168–69
Pasture rose, 165
Paulownia tomentosa, 14
Pea, beach, 8, 169–71
Pea, everlasting, 170
Pea, partridge, 168–69
Peltandra sagittifolia, 92
Peltandra virginica, 11, 90–92
Pennywort, beach, 8, 9, 203–4
Penstemon spp., 225
Persea borbonia, 12
Peruvian bark, 148
Phragmites, 56–59
Phragmites australis, 10, 47, 54, 56–59, 224, 262
Phragmites communis, 59
Pickerelweed, 11, 94–95
Pie marker, 190
Pinaceae, 30–34
Pin-ball, 236
Pine, eastern white, 30, 31–32
Pine, loblolly, 32, 193
Pine, long-leaf, 15, 30–31, 54, 118
Pine, pitch, 8, 13, 14, 33–35, 116
Pine, pocosin, 34
Pine, pond, 12, 34–35
Pine, sand, 35
Pine, scrub, 35
Pine, short-leaf, 32
Pine, slash, 32
Pine, southern yellow, 31
Pine, Virginia, 35
Pine, white, 30, 31–32
Pine, wild, 94
Pine, yellow, 32
Pineapple, 93
Pine family, 30–34
Pink, perennial saltmarsh, 216
Pink, saltmarsh, 10
Pink, sea, 214, 261
Pink, small saltmarsh, 9, 214–16
Pink family, 139–43
Pink sundew, 154
Pinus clausa, 35
Pinus echinata, 32
Pinus elliottii, 32
Pinus palustris, 15, 30–32, 54, 118
Pinus rigida, 8, 33–35
Pinus serotina, 12, 34
Pinus strobus, 31
Pinus taeda, 32, 193
Pinus virginiana, 35
Pinweed, beach, 9, 195–96
Pitcher-plants, 12, 13, 229
Pitch pine, 8, 13, 14, 33–35, 116
Pityopsis, 258
Pityopsis graminifolia, 9
Plantaginaceae, 232
Plantago maritima, 6, 232–34
Plantain, seaside, 6, 232–34
Plantain family, 232
Platanthera spp., 15
Pleopeltis polypodioides, 29–30
Pleurisy-root, 218
Pluchea camphorata, 263
Pluchea foetida, 263
Pluchea longifolia, 264
Pluchea odorata, 10, 262–64
Pluchea purpurascens, 263
Pluchea rosea, 264
Plum, beach, 9, 158–61
Plum, flatwood, 160
Plum, hog, 160
Plumbaginaceae, 212
Plum curculio, 159
Plymouth gentian, 216
Poaceae, 44–71
Pocosin pine, 34
Pogonia ophioglossoides, 3
Poinsettia, 173
Poison ivy, 9, 13, 14, 18, 178–79, 180
Poison oak, 18, 179, 180
Poison sumac, 13, 18, 180–81
Polygonaceae, 121
Polygonella, fringed, 122
Polygonella americana, 121
Polygonella articulata, 9, 121–22
Polygonella fimbriata, 122
Polygonella gracilis, 122
Polygonella polygama, 121
Polypodiaceae, 29
Polypodium polypodioides, 30
Polypody fern family, 29
Pond cypress, 15, 37

Pond-lily, yellow, 144
Pond pine, 12, 34–35
Pondweed, 7
Pondweed, horned, 7
Pontederiaceae, 94
Pontederia cordata, 11, 94–95
Poor man's weather-glass, 211
Poppy, horned, 149–50
Poppy, oriental, 149
Poppy, sea, 149
Poppy family, 149
Populus tremuloides, 8
Porcelain vine, 13
Possum-haw, 185
Potamogeton spp., 7
Potentilla anserina, 158
Poverty-grass, 194
Prickly pear, eastern, 199–201
Prickly pear cactus, 9, 201
Primrose, evening-, 9, 15, 201–3
Primrose family, 211
Primrose-leaved violet, 197
Primulaceae, 211
Princess tree, 14
Privet, 13, 14
Prunus caroliniana, 14, 163
Prunus maritima, 9, 158–61
Prunus serotina, 9, 161–63
Prunus umbellata, 160
Prunus virginiana, 163
Pteridium aquilinum, 26
Pueraria lobata, 14
Purple bladderwort, 229–30
Purple flag, 15, 109
Purple gerardia, 225–27
Purple hairgrass, 53
Purple milkweed, 220
Purple sand grass, 8
Purple-stemmed aster, 246–47
Purslane, sea, 6, 8, 9, 11, 138–39

Quaking aspen, 8
Quercus alba, 120
Quercus geminata, 117
Quercus ilicifolia, 116
Quercus laevis, 118
Quercus margarettiae, 118
Quercus myrtifolia, 118
Quercus prinoides, 116–18
Quercus robur, 120
Quercus spp., 13
Quercus velutina, 9, 120
Quercus virginiana, 14, 29, 106, 117, 118–21

Railroad-vine, 222–23
Red bay, 12, 14
Red buckeye, 186–87, 237
Red cedar, 8, 13, 14, 38–40, 110
Red maple, 9, 11
Red milkweed, 220
Redroot, 107–8
Reed, common, 10, 54, 56–59, 224, 262
Reed, tall, 47, 56. *See also* Reed, common
Reed-grass, salt, 63
Resurrection fern, 29–30
Rhamnus spp., 13
Rhododendron atlanticum, 206
Rhododendron canescens, 207
Rhododendron serrulatum, 206
Rhododendron spp., 11
Rhododendron viscosum, 13, 205–7
Rhus, 179
Rhus copallinum, 181
Rhus glabra, 181
Rhus hirta, 181
Rhynchospora colorata, 15, 75–76
Rhynchospora latifolia, 75
Ricinus communis, 174
River bulrush, 12, 81
Rocket, sea, 4, 6, 8, 132, 150–52
Rocket, yellow, 152
Rockrose family, 194–96
Rockweed, 7
Rosa carolina, 165
Rosaceae, 155–65
Rosa multiflora, 13, 165
Rosa palustris, 165
Rosa rugosa, 9, 163–65
Rosa virginiana, 165
Rose, China, 189
Rose, hedge, 165

Rose, multiflora, 13, 14, 165
Rose, pasture, 165
Rose, rugose, 163
Rose, salt-spray, 9, 13, 163–65
Rose, swamp, 165
Rose, Virginia, 165
Rose family, 155–65
Rose-mallow, swamp, 10, 188–89, 190
Rose-of-Sharon, 189
Rose pogonia, 3
Rubiaceae, 234, 235
Ruppia maritima, 7
Rush, black, 10, 42, 47, 96–97, 98, 99, 128
Rush, chairmaker's, 76–78
Rush, mud-, 97
Rush, scouring, 25–26
Rush, toad-, 98
Rush, twig-, 100
Rushes, 9, 11
Rush family, 96–100
Russian thistle, 132–33
Rye, wild, 49–51

Sabal minor, 82–83
Sabal palmetto, 10, 54, 83–85
Sabatia dodecandra, 216
Sabatia kennedyana, 216
Sabatia spp., 10
Sabatia stellaris, 9, 214–16, 261
Sagittaria spp., 90, 91
Salicornia bigelovii, 128–29
Salicornia europaea, 131
Salicornia maritima, 131
Salicornia spp., 10, 123, 133
Salicornia virginica, 62, 128, 129–31, 133, 134
Salsola, 123, 135
Salsola kali, 4, 131–33
Salsola tragus, 132
Salt-cedar, 10
Saltgrass, 10, 42, 47–49, 65, 128, 135, 250
Salt hay grass, 1, 9, 10, 39, 42, 47, 51, 62, 64–66, 96, 127, 129, 130, 135, 212, 233, 250
Saltmarsh aster, annual, 10, 11, 247–49
Saltmarsh aster, perennial, 10, 247, 249–51
Saltmarsh bulrush, 80–81
Saltmarsh fleabane, 10, 11, 262–64
Saltmarsh pink, 9, 10, 214–16
Saltmarsh sand spurrey, 10, 11, 141–43
Salt reed-grass, 63
Salt-spray rose, 9, 13, 163–65
Saltwater cordgrass, 61
Saltwort, 10, 11, 135
Saltwort, common, 4, 6, 8, 131–33
Saltwort family, 135
Sandbur, coastal, 47
Sandbur, common, 8, 46
Sandbur, dune, 8, 46–47
Sandbur, long-spined. *See* Sandbur, common
Sand jointweed, 9, 121–22
Sand live oak, 117
Sand pine, 35
Sand post oak, 118
Sandspur, 46
Sand spurrey, common, 143
Sand spurrey, saltmarsh, 10, 11, 141–43
Sandwort, seabeach, 139, 195
Sapindaceae, 187
Sapium sebiferum, 14
Sarcocornia fruticosa, 133, 134
Sarcocornia perennis, 9, 133–35
Sarcocornia spp., 10, 128, 135
Sarracenia spp., 12, 229
Sarvisberry, 156
Sassafras, 9, 13, 14
Sassafras albidum, 9
Saururaceae, 112
Saururus cernuus, 112–13
Saw-grass, 11, 99–100
Saw palmetto, 14, 15, 82, 85–86
Scarlet pimpernel, 6, 211–12, 233
Schizachyrium scoparium, 15, 59–60
Schizachyrium stoloniferum, 60
Schizachyrium tenerum, 60

Scirpus americanus, 10, 76–78
Scirpus fluviatilis, 12, 81
Scirpus maritimus, 80
Scirpus olneyi, 78
Scirpus pungens, 10, 78
Scirpus robustus, 10, 79–81
Scirpus spp., 11, 78
Scouring rush, 25–26
Scrophulariaceae, 225–28
Scrub oak, 118. *See also* Bear oak
Scrub pine, 35
Seabeach orach, 8, 122–24
Seabeach sandwort, 139, 195
Sea blite, low, 137
Sea blite, tall, 10, 11, 135–38
Sea burdock, 266
Sea chickweed, 4, 6, 139–41
Sea daisy, 255
Seagrass, Englemann's, 7
Sea lavender, 6, 10, 62, 135, 212–14, 233, 250
Sea myrtle, 252
Sea oats, 8, 9, 54, 56, 70–71
Sea ox-eye, 10, 11, 255–56
Sea pink, 214, 261
Sea poppy, 149
Sea purslane, 6, 8, 9, 11, 138–39
Sea rocket, 4, 6, 8, 132, 150–52
Seashore mallow, 11, 12, 190–92
Seaside arrow-grass, 10, 42–44, 96
Seaside evening-primrose, 9, 203
Seaside gerardia, 96, 225–27
Seaside goldenrod, 8, 264–66
Seaside panicum, 8, 9, 56
Seaside plantain, 6, 232–34
Seaside spurge, 8, 173–74, 195
Sea spurrey, greater, 143
Sedge, awl-, 71–73
Sedge, umbrella-, 73–75
Sedge, white-topped, 15, 75–76
Sedge family, 71–81, 100
Sedges, 11, 12, 71–73
Senna obtusifolia, 169
Sensitive plant, wild, 169
Serenoa repens, 14, 82, 85–86
Serviceberry, coastal plain, 155
Serviceberry, eastern, 155–56
Sesuvium maritimum, 138
Sesuvium portulacastrum, 138–39
Sesuvium spp., 6
Shadbush, 9, 13, 155–56
Shaggy golden aster, 256–58
Shoalgrass, 4, 7
Short-leaf pine, 32
Showy evening-primrose, 15, 201–3
Sicklepod, 169
Silkgrass, 102
Silver-leaf croton, 6, 8, 9
Silverweed, 156–58
Skunk cabbage, 40, 88, 89, 90, 91
Slash pine, 32
Slipper-flower, 225
Sloughgrass, 67
Smilacina racemosa, 105
Smilacina stellata, 104
Smilax laurifolia, 12
Smilax spp., 13
Smooth cordgrass, 10, 47, 61–63, 64, 98, 130, 233
Snapdragon, 225, 227
Snow-on-the-mountain, 173
Soapberry family, 187
Solidago nemoralis, 3
Solidago sempervirens, 8, 264–66
Solidago spp., 8
Solomon's plume, 104
Solomon's-seal, false, 104
Solomon's-seal, starry false, 103–5
Southern arrow-grass, 11, 43
Southern arrowwood, 13, 240
Southern bayberry, 14, 114–15
Southern blue flag, 109
Southern cattail, 40–41
Southern magnolia, 110, 147
Southern red cedar, 39
Southern seaside spurge, 174
Southern sweet grass, 9, 53–54
Southernwood, 244
Southern yellow pine, 31
Spanish bayonet, 9, 101–2
Spanish moss, 29, 92–94, 119
Sparkleberry, 14
Spartina alterniflora, 10, 47, 61–63, 64, 98, 99, 130, 233

Spartina cynosuroides, 10, 63–64, 67
Spartina patens, 1, 39, 42, 47, 51, 62, 64–66, 96, 99, 127, 129, 135, 212, 233, 250
Spartina pectinata, 10, 63, 67
Spartina spp., 10, 54
Spatterdock, 12, 144–45, 217
Spearscale, 122, 124
Spergularia diandra, 143
Spergularia marina, 143
Spergularia maritima, 143
Spergularia media, 143
Spergularia rubra, 143
Spergularia salina, 10, 141–43
Sphagnum spp., 12
Spikegrass, 47
Spinach, 123
Spinacia oleracea, 123
Spiranthes spp., 15
Splitbeard, 60
Sporolobus virginicus, 49
Spurge, seaside, 8, 173–74, 195
Spurge, southern seaside, 174
Spurge family, 173–77
Spurrey, common sand, 143
Spurrey, greater sea, 143
Spurrey, saltmarsh sand, 10, 11, 141–43
Stachys palustris, 224
Starry false Solomon's-seal, 103–5
Stinging nettle, 176
Stinkweed, 262, 263
Strawberry, 156
Strophostyles helvula, 171–72
Strophostyles spp., 9
Strophostyles umbellata, 172
Suaeda, 123
Suaeda linearis, 10, 135–38
Suaeda maritima, 137
Suaeda richii, 137
Sumac, poison, 13, 18, 179, 180–81
Sumac, shining, 181
Sumac, smooth, 181
Sumac, staghorn, 181
Summer cypress, 123
Sundew, pink, 154
Sundew, round-leaved, 154
Sundew, short-leaved, 154
Sundew, spatulate-leaved, 154
Sundew, thread-leaved, 153–54
Sundew family, 153
Sundews, 12, 229
Sundrops, 203
Supplejack, 11
Swamp aster, 247
Swamp azalea, 13, 205–7
Swamp candleberry, 13, 115
Swamp honeysuckle, 205
Swamp lily, 112
Swamp milkweed, 220
Swamp rose, 165
Swamp rose-mallow, 10, 188–89, 190
Sweet bay, 13, 15, 147–48
Sweet calamus, 87
Sweetflag, 11, 87–88
Sweetflag family, 87
Sweet gale, 12
Sweet grass, 51–52
Sweet grass, southern, 9, 53–54
Sweet gum, 110
Sweet pepperbush, 11
Sweet potato, 221
Sweetrush, 73
Swiss chard, 123
Switchgrass, 8, 9, 54–56
Swordgrass, 77
Symplocarpus foetidus, 40, 88, 89, 91

Tall reed, 47, 56. *See also* Reed, common
Tall sea blite, 10, 11, 135–38
Tall wormwood, 196, 241–42
Tamarix spp., 10
Tarragon, 244
Tartarian honeysuckle, 238
Taxodiaceae, 35
Taxodium ascendens, 15, 37
Taxodium distichum, 11, 35–37
Tea family, 192
Tegeticula, 103
Teucrium botrys, 224

Teucrium canadense, 223–25
Thalassia testudina, 7
Theaceae, 192
Thelypteridaceae, 27
Thelypteris noveboracensis, 28
Thelypteris palustris, 12, 27–28, 109
Thelypteris simulata, 28
Three-square, common, 10, 78
Three-square, Olney, 76
Tillandsia bartramii, 94
Tillandsia recurvata, 94
Tillandsia usneoides, 29, 92–94
Ti-ti, black, 12, 181–83
Ti-ti tree, 182
Toad-rush, 98
Toxicodendron pubescens, 179, 180
Toxicodendron radicans, 9, 178–79, 180
Toxicodendron spp., 18
Toxicodendron vernix, 13, 179, 180–81
Tread-softly, 9, 175–76
Triglochin maritimum, 10, 42–44, 96
Triglochin palustre, 44
Triglochin striatum, 11, 43
Triplasis purpurea, 8
Tripsacum dactyloides, 68–69
Trumpet creeper, 237
Trumpet honeysuckle, 236
Tuckahoe, 90, 92
Tumbleweed, 132–33
Tupelo, 11
Turkeyfoot, 59
Turkey oak, 118
Turtlegrass, 7
Turtlehead, 227
Twig-rush, 100
Typha angustifolia, 10, 40–42, 109
Typhaceae, 40
Typha domingensis, 40
Typha latifolia, 10, 40
Typha spp., 11

Umbrella-sedge, beach, 73–75
Uniola paniculata, 8, 54, 56, 70
Urtica dioica, 175
Utricularia inflata, 231
Utricularia purpurea, 229–30
Utricularia radiata, 230–32
Utricularia spp., 12

Vaccinium arboreum, 14
Vaccinium corymbosum, 11, 207–9
Vaccinium macrocarpon, 209–11
Vaccinium oxycoccos, 209
Vaccinium spp., 12
Vanilla grass, 52
Velvet leaf, 190
Venus fly-trap, 229
Verbascum spp., 227
Verbascum thapsus, 15
Viburnum dentatum, 13, 238–40
Viburnum recognitum, 239
Violaceae, 197
Viola lanceolata, 197–99
Viola primulifolia, 197–98
Violet, lance-leaved, 197–99
Violet, primrose-leaved, 197
Violet family, 197
Virginia chain-fern, 12
Virginia creeper, 9, 13
Virginia pine, 35
Virginia rose, 165
Vitis rotundifolia, 14
Vitis spp., 13

Wand aster, 246
Water-dragon, 112
Water hemp, 10
Water hyacinth, 94–95
Water hyacinth family, 94
Water-lily, European, 146
Water-lily, white, 12, 145–47, 217
Water-lily family, 144–47
Water millet, 11
Water-nymph, 7
Water-shield, 217
Wax-myrtle, 114–15
White arum, 92
White cedar, Atlantic, 11
White oak, 120

White pine, 30, 31–32
White-topped sedge, 15, 75–76
White water-lily, 12, 145–47, 217
Widgeon-grass, 7
Wild azalea, 207
Wild bean, 9, 171–72
Wild black cherry, 9, 13, 14, 161–63
Wild calla, 12
Wild columbine, 237
Wild lily-of-the-valley, 105
Wild pine, 94
Wild rice, 12
Wild rye, 49–51
Wild sensitive plant, 169
Winterberry, 9, 11, 185
Wiregrass, 59
Wood sage, 223
Woodwardia virginica, 12
Wormwood, 244
Wormwood, beach, 243
Wormwood, tall, 196, 241–42

Xanthium echinatum, 267
Xanthium italicum, 267
Xanthium pensylvanicum, 267
Xanthium strumarium, 8, 266–67

Yaupon, 14, 185
Yellow floating-heart, 218
Yellow nutsedge, 73
Yellow pine, 31, 32
Yellow pond-lily, 144
Yellow rocket, 152
Yucca, mound-lily, 102
Yucca aloifolia, 102
Yucca filamentosa, 101–3
Yucca flaccida, 102
Yucca gloriosa, 102
Yucca spp., 9

Zanichellia palustris, 7
Zanthoxylum clava-herculis, 14
Zea mays, 69
Zenobia puverulenta, 12
Zephranthes atamasca, 105–6
Zizania aquatica, 12
Zizaniopsis milacea, 11
Zostera marina, 4